118,000,000,000

5,000,000,000

+ 8,000,000,000
_____
8,000,000,000

McGRAW-HILL'S OUR NATION, OUR WORLD

MEETING PEOPLE

School, Self, Families, Neighborhood, and Our Country

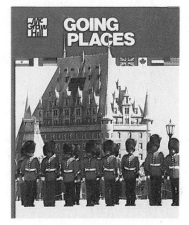

GOING PLACES

People in Groups, Filling Needs in Communities and on Farms

COMMUNITIES

Geography and History of Cities in the United States, Canada, and Mexico

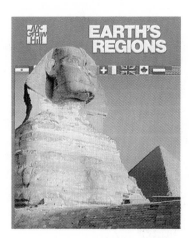

EARTH'S REGIONS

Geography and Ways of Living on Five Continents, Studying the 50 States

UNITED STATES:
Our Nation and Neighbors

Chronological History and Regional Geography of the United States, Our North American Neighbors

THE WORLD

World History, Ancient Civilizations, Important Nations Today

CONSULTANTS

Editor in Chief:	Martha O'Neill
Editor:	Martha Alderson
Editing and Styling:	Robert Towns
Design Supervision:	James Darby, William Dippel, E. Rohne Rudder, Virginia Copeland
Art Editors:	Sydne Silverstein Matus, Alexa Barre
Photo Editor:	Alan Forman
Photo Research:	Ellen Horan
Production Supervision:	Tom Goodwin
Editorial Assistants:	Frieda Amiri, Mindy Mutterperl
Art and Design by:	Function Thru Form, Inc.
Cover Design by:	Alan Forman
Cover Photograph:	The Sphinx, Egypt

EARTH'S REGIONS

BY Alma Graham,
Cleo Cherryholmes,
Gary Manson, Anna Ochoa

SCHOOL DIVISION, McGRAW-HILL BOOK COMPANY

New York   St. Louis   San Francisco   Dallas   Oklahoma City   Atlanta

3

ISBN   0-07-039814-3

6 7 8 9 10 KGP KGP 96 95 94 93 92 91 90 89 88

CONTENTS

1775

1777

1777

1795

1818   1818

1820

1846

8

1851

 1861

1890

 1908

1912

 1959

COMPLETE MAP AND GLOBE COURSE

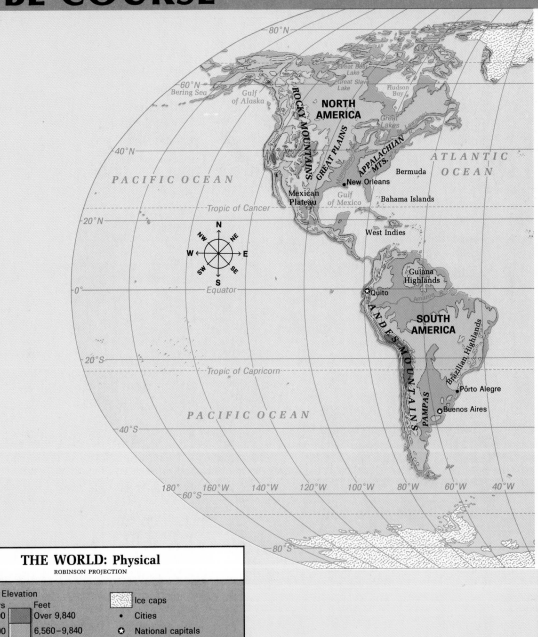

THE WORLD: Physical

ROBINSON PROJECTION

Elevation

Meters	Feet
Over 3,000	Over 9,840
2,000–3,000	6,560–9,840
1,000–2,000	3,281–6,560
200–1,000	656–3,280
0–200	0–656
Below sea level	Below sea level

Ice caps
Cities
National capitals

0   1000   2000 Miles
0   1000   2000 Kilometers

ARCTIC OCEAN

80°N

Barents
Sea

Arctic Circle

EUROPE

Moscow

London

European Plain

North
Sea

ALPS

Black Sea

Plateau of
Asia Minor

ATLAS MTS.

Mediterranean
Sea

Alexandria

Cairo

S a h a r a

AFRICA

Ethiopian
Highlands

Zaire

Lake
Victoria

Lake
Tanganyika

Lake
Nyasa

ATLANTIC
OCEAN

Madagascar

Kalahari
Desert

Prime Meridian

URAL MTS.

Ob R.

Volga

Aral

60°N

ASIA

ALTAI MTS.

Gobi Desert

Huang

Plateau of
Tibet

HIMALAYAS

Ganges

Dacca

Persian
Gulf

Arabian
Sea

Deccan
Plateau

Bay
of
Bengal

Red Sea

Nile

Lake
Baykal

Bering
Sea

40°N

Sea
of Japan

Tokyo

PACIFIC
OCEAN

East
China
Sea

20°N

South
China
Sea

0°

INDIAN OCEAN

New
Guinea

Coral
Sea

Western
Plateau

AUSTRALIA

20°S

Great Barrier Reef

GREAT DIVIDING RANGE

North
Island

South
Island

40°S

20°W   0°   20°E   40°E   60°E   80°E   100°E   120°E   140°E   160°E   180°

60°S

Antarctic Circle

ANTARCTICA

80°S

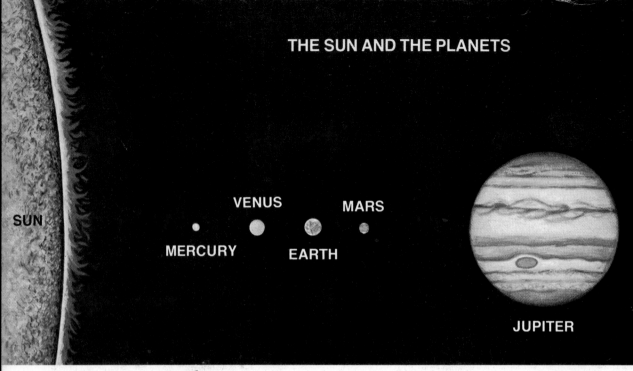

THE SUN AND THE PLANETS

SUN

MERCURY

VENUS

EARTH

MARS

JUPITER

1 EARTH AND MAPS

Lesson 1: Planet Earth

Earth is our home. It is the home of all human beings. It has air we can breathe. It has water for us to drink. It has plants and animals that we can eat. It has solid ground to stand on. Earth is not too hot or too cold for us. It has everything we need to live.

We are on Earth. But we can see things that are not on Earth. Early in the morning, we can see the sun come up. All day, the sun seems to move across the sky. Late in the day, we can see the sun go down. But the sun is not really moving around us. We are the ones who are moving. Every morning, we turn toward the sun. Every night, we turn away from it. Every year, we go around it. Earth is our spaceship. All of us in

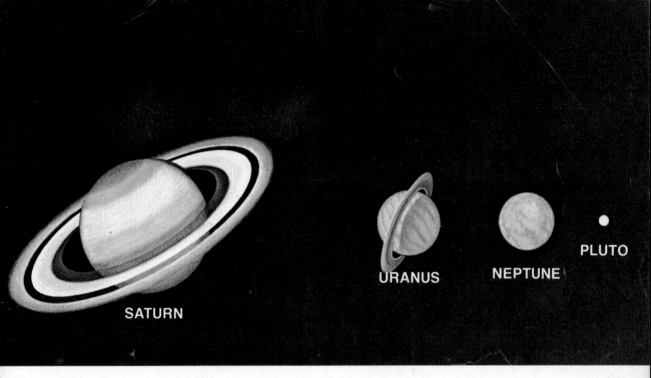

SATURN

URANUS

NEPTUNE

PLUTO

the ship are riding around the sun.

At night, we can often see the moon and stars. From Earth, stars look like little points of light. But stars are really very big. They look small because they are so far away. From Earth, stars may seem cold. But stars are really very hot. A **star** is a great mass of burning gas. It gives off light and heat. Our **sun** is a star. And all the other stars in the sky are also suns.

Our sun is much closer to Earth than the other stars are. That is why it looks so much bigger and brighter than they do. The heat of the sun keeps Earth warm. Suppose Earth were farther away from the sun. It would be much colder here. Suppose Earth were closer to the sun. It would be much hotter all year long.

The sun is a star. Earth is a planet. A **planet** is a world that moves around a star. Nine planets move around our sun. The planets get their light and heat from the sun. A planet that is close to the sun is hot. A planet that is far from the sun is cold.

Look at the picture on pages 14 and 15. Which two planets are closest to the sun? Which two planets are farthest away? The picture shows how big the planets are, compared with the sun.

Earth is the third planet from the sun. It is a small, warm planet. Jupiter and Saturn are giant planets compared to Earth. They are also much colder.

Some of the planets have moons. A **moon** goes around a planet just as a planet goes around a star. Earth has only one moon. Some planets have more. Mercury and Venus do not have any moons.

The sun, planets, and moons make up our **solar system.** *Solar* (SOH lur) means "of the sun." A *system* is a group of parts that work together as a whole. The solar system is the sun and its family of planets and moons. We do not know if any other stars have solar systems. But there are billions of stars. Some of these stars might have planets moving around them. Do you suppose they do?

REVIEW

WATCH YOUR WORDS

1. Earth is a ___.
   star moon planet
2. A ___ gives off light and heat.
   planet star moon
3. A ___ moves around a star.
   solar planet sun
4. ___ means "of the sun."
   System Lunar Solar
5. A ___ moves around a planet.
   star sun moon

CHECK YOUR FACTS

Look at the Picture

6. How many planets are in the solar system?

7. Which planet is closest to the sun?
8. What two planets are closest to Earth?

Look at the Lesson

9. What makes Earth a good planet to live on? Name three things. Can you name more?
10. A planet that is far away from the sun is (hot/cold).

SHARPEN YOUR THINKING

Do you think there could be life on other worlds? What would a new world have to be like for us to live there?

Lesson 2: Time and the Seasons

FIND THE WORDS

revolve   orbit
axis   North Pole
South Pole   rotate
tilted   season

The Moving Earth

Have you ever heard someone say, "Time flies"? Time doesn't fly. We do. Time tells us how long the trip takes. Our spaceship Earth moves in two ways. It rides around the sun. And it spins in a circle. A year is the time it takes Earth to go around the sun. A day is the time it takes Earth to spin around in a circle.

We say that Earth **revolves** (rih VOLVZ) around the sun. That means Earth moves in a special path. You know that an airplane has a flight path to follow. Earth's flight path around the sun is called an **orbit** (OR bit). Earth takes 365 days to revolve around the sun. That is why our year is 365 days long.

Earth moves in its orbit around the sun the way a toy train moves around a track. But Earth also moves in another way. As it goes around the sun, Earth spins like a top. Each day, Earth turns slowly around an axis (AK sis).

Take a little, round cherry tomato. Stick a toothpick through

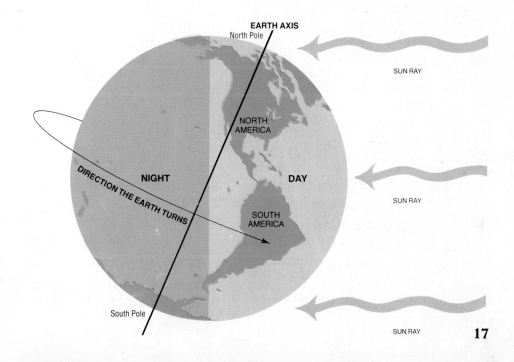

EARTH AXIS
North Pole

SUN RAY

NORTH
AMERICA

NIGHT

DIRECTION THE EARTH TURNS

DAY

SUN RAY

SOUTH
AMERICA

South Pole

SUN RAY

17

the middle, from top to bottom. Then hold the toothpick still. Turn the tomato from left to right. The tomato turns around the toothpick the way Earth turns around its axis.

Earth's **axis** is an imaginary line through the center of Earth. It goes from the North Pole to the South Pole. The **North Pole** is as far north as you can go on Earth. The **South Pole** is as far south as you can go.

To spin around an axis is to **rotate.** Earth takes 24 hours to spin around once on its axis. That is why our day is 24 hours long. *Day* also means the part of the 24 hours when we have sunlight.

You turned the tomato from left to right. Earth turns on its axis from west to east. In the morning, we see the sun come up in the east. That means our part of Earth is turning toward the sun. In the evening, we see the sun go down in the west. That means our part of Earth is turning away from the sun. The sun seems to move because Earth is rotating.

As Earth spins on its axis, only one side faces the sun at a time. The side facing the sun has day. The side turned away from the sun has night. When morning comes to New York, it is still dark in California. When it is late afternoon in California, it is already night in New York.

The Sun and the Seasons

Day and night are not always the same length. The reason for that is Earth's axis. Our axis is not straight up and down. It is **tilted.** That means it slants, or leans. The Earth itself is tilted. Look at your classroom globe. The North Pole is not at the very top. The globe is tilted, just like the Earth.

In many parts of Earth, there are four **seasons.** These seasons are spring, summer, fall, and winter. Usually, the weather changes with the seasons. That happens because the axis of Earth is tilted. It also happens because Earth moves around the sun.

Look at the picture on the next page. On June 22, the North Pole is tilted toward the sun. The northern half of Earth gets a lot of light and heat. Day is longer than night. The weather is warm or hot. It is summer in the United States.

On June 22, the South Pole is tilted away from the sun. The southern half of Earth gets less of the sun's light and heat. Night is longer than day. The weather is cool or cold. It is winter in Argentina.

Now look at December 22 in the picture. Since June, Earth has revolved halfway around the sun. So the North Pole is tilted away from the sun. It is winter in the

THE SEASONS

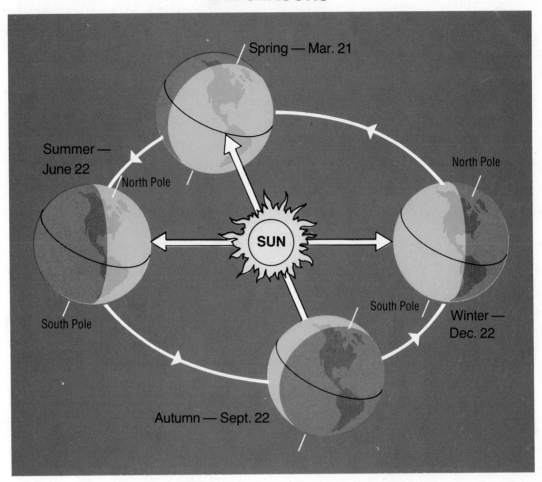

Spring — Mar. 21

Summer — June 22

North Pole

South Pole

North Pole

SUN

South Pole

Winter — Dec. 22

Autumn — Sept. 22

United States. But the South Pole is tilted toward the sun. People in Australia may be swimming at the beach. But it may be snowing in St. Louis, Missouri.

The middle part of Earth is never tilted away from the sun. The rays of the sun always come straight down on it. The middle part of Earth gets a lot of light and heat all year. Suppose you lived in Rio de Janeiro (REE oh dih juh NAIR oh), Brazil. The weather would be warm in spring, summer, fall, and winter.

Near the North Pole, the sun's rays hit Earth at a slant. This makes the weather cold all year. But summer at the North Pole is very different from winter. In the summer, it is light all day and all night. In the winter, it is dark all night and all day. This is true at the South Pole, too. But the South Pole's summer comes in December instead of June.

Now, let's leave the North Pole. Let's travel part way toward the middle of Earth. Suppose you lived in Richmond, Virginia. The weather there changes from season to season. It gets cool in the fall.

Near the North Pole in summer, the sun shines even at midnight. This happens because the North Pole is tilted toward the sun. The North Pole is the place farthest north on Earth.

It is cold in the winter. It gets warm in the spring. It is hot in the summer.

REVIEW

WATCH YOUR WORDS

1. Earth____around the sun.
   rotates revolves tilts

2. Earth's flight path around the sun is its____.
   axis season orbit

3. To spin around an axis is to____.
   revolve tilt rotate

4. An imaginary line from the North Pole to the South Pole is Earth's ____ .
   tilt axis season

5. Something that slants is____.
   rotated seasoned tilted.

CHECK YOUR FACTS

6. Which way does Earth turn on its axis?

7. How long does it take Earth to rotate once?

8. How long does it take Earth to revolve around the sun?

9. What is strange about summer at the North Pole?

10. In the United States, why is June warmer than December?

SHARPEN YOUR THINKING

Suppose Earth were not tilted on its axis. How would life be different? Name three ways.

Lesson 3: Earth and the Globe

FIND THE WORDS

globe   continent   ocean
equator   hemisphere

It would be fun to travel around the Earth. We could drive across the United States, from California to Virginia. We could fly across the Atlantic Ocean to Portugal and Spain. We could travel through Greece and Turkey all the way to the Soviet Union. From there, we could keep heading east to China and Japan. At last, we could sail across the Pacific Ocean. It would bring us back to California. We would have circled the Earth. And there would still be many more places to see!

Few people can travel all over the Earth. Most of us learn about our world in other ways. One way to learn about Earth is to use a globe.

A **globe** is a model of Earth. It is round like Earth. But it is much, much smaller. A globe can tell you many things about Earth. Globes use different colors to help you tell land from water. Earth has seven large masses of land, called **continents** (KON tuh nunts). North America and South America are two continents. They are linked by a narrow strip of land.

Europe and Asia look like one continent on a globe. Actually, they are separated by mountains. The other continents are Africa, Australia, and Antarctica (ANT AHRK tuh kuh). Find the seven continents on a globe.

A globe also shows where the four **oceans** are. Oceans are the largest bodies of water on Earth. Seven-tenths of the whole surface of Earth is covered by water. The United States lies between the Atlantic Ocean and the Pacific Ocean. The Indian Ocean lies between Africa and Australia. The Arctic Ocean is at the top of the globe.

A globe is round like Earth. Its shape makes it the best model of Earth.

ARCTIC OCEAN

NORTH POLE

UNION OF
SOVIET SOCIALIST REPUBLICS

EUROPE

SPAIN

TURKEY

ASIA

PORTUGAL   GREECE

CHINA

EGYPT

JAPAN

INDIA

BURKINA FASO

PACIFIC
OCEAN

AFRICA

EQUATOR

ATLANTIC
OCEAN

INDIAN OCEAN

AUSTRALIA

SOUTH
AFRICA

ANTARCTICA

SOUTH
POLE

EASTERN HEMISPHERE

WESTERN HEMISPHERE

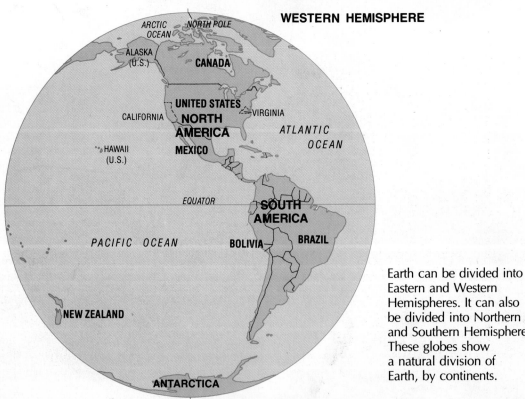

ARCTIC
OCEAN

NORTH POLE

ALASKA
(U.S.)

CANADA

UNITED STATES

CALIFORNIA

NORTH
AMERICA

VIRGINIA

ATLANTIC
OCEAN

HAWAII
(U.S.)

MEXICO

EQUATOR

SOUTH
AMERICA

PACIFIC OCEAN

BOLIVIA

BRAZIL

NEW ZEALAND

Earth can be divided into
Eastern and Western
Hemispheres. It can also
be divided into Northern
and Southern Hemispheres.
These globes show
a natural division of
Earth, by continents.

ANTARCTICA

SOUTH POLE

The North Pole is in the Arctic Ocean. You know that Earth's axis runs from the North Pole to the South Pole. Another important line on the globe is the **equator** (ih KWAY tur). Like the axis, the equator is an imaginary line. It is halfway between the North Pole and the South Pole. The equator circles Earth around the middle, like an invisible belt. It divides Earth into two equal parts.

Pretend that the globe is a ball of clay. The ball has a line around its middle. Suppose you cut the ball in two along the line. Each half of the ball is called a **hemisphere** (HEM uh SFIR). *Hemi-* means "half" and *sphere* means "ball."

Half of the globe is above the equator. The North Pole is in that half. So the top half of the globe is called the *Northern Hemisphere.* The United States is in the Northern Hemisphere.

Half of the globe is below the equator. The South Pole is in that half. So the bottom half of the globe is called the *Southern Hemisphere.* Argentina is in the Southern Hemisphere.

You can cut the globe in half another way. You can divide the western half from the eastern half. North America and South America are in the western half. This half of the globe is called the *Western Hemisphere.* Europe, Asia, Africa, and Australia are in the eastern

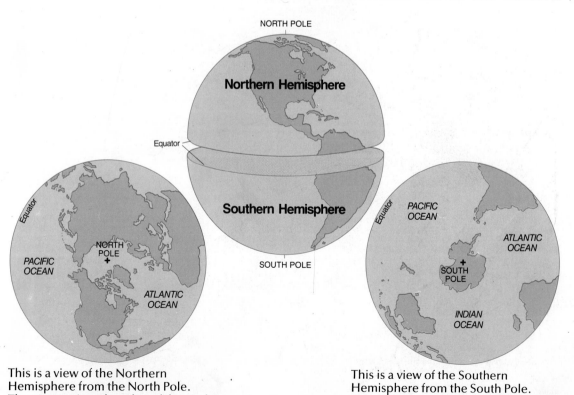

This is a view of the Northern Hemisphere from the North Pole. The equator is at the edge of the circle.

This is a view of the Southern Hemisphere from the South Pole. The equator is at the edge of the circle.

Fun Facts

In North America, people can see penguins only in a zoo. Penguins live near the South Pole. Many of them live in Antarctica.

Penguins are birds, but they cannot fly. They are fine swimmers, though. On land, they waddle about on two feet. To go faster, they slide over the ice on their bellies.

half. That half of the globe is called the *Eastern Hemisphere*. The continent of Antarctica is in the Western Hemisphere and the Eastern Hemisphere. What other hemisphere is Antarctica in?

Dividing the globe into hemispheres helps us find places on Earth. Look at the globes on page 22. Find Mexico and Bolivia. Find South Africa and India. Each nation is in two hemispheres.

REVIEW

WATCH YOUR WORDS

1. A round model of Earth is a____.
   circle   map   globe

2. North America is one of seven ____.
   oceans   continents   hemispheres

3. The Atlantic and the Pacific are ____.
   oceans   hemispheres   continents

4. The ____ is an imaginary line around the middle of Earth.
   axis   globe   equator

5. Half of a globe is a(n)____.
   hemisphere   continent   ocean

CHECK YOUR FACTS
Look at the Globe

6. Find the state of Alaska. What two hemispheres is it in?

7. Find the continent of Australia. What two hemispheres is it in?

Look at the Lesson

8. What is the equator? What is the Northern Hemisphere?

9. What continents are in the Western Hemisphere?

10. What continents are in the Eastern Hemisphere?

SHARPEN YOUR THINKING

Long ago, people thought the Earth was flat. Can you prove that Earth is round? How?

Lesson 4:   Maps of Earth

FIND THE WORDS

map   key   symbol   nation
boundary   natural boundary
political boundary

Globes are round like Earth. This makes a globe the best model of our round planet. But we can also learn a lot about our world from maps. A **map** is a flat drawing of places on Earth. One map may show the whole Earth. Another map may show a single continent. A third map may show only a few city blocks. But all maps are useful. They help us find where places are. People have used maps for a long time. The oldest map in the world is almost 5,000 years old!

It is hard to show the round Earth on a flat map. All the parts won't fit. So a mapmaker has to change their shape. Look at the drawing on this page. It shows what happens when you peel off the surface of a globe. It is like peeling an orange. The peel can be flattened out. But it no longer looks like the orange.

Look at this flat map. Then look at the map of the world on pages 60 and 61. The person who drew that map of Earth took a lot of the water out. This changed the size and shape of the oceans. But it made the shape of the land areas more nearly right.

Now look at the map on page 26. There, the mapmaker added land and water to the map. Look at the continents on the two maps. Then look at a globe. Which map looks most like the globe?

When you look at maps, remember this: The shape of the land is not always exactly right.

Suppose you flattened out a globe. This is how it would look. Mapmakers sometimes add land and water to fill in the gaps.

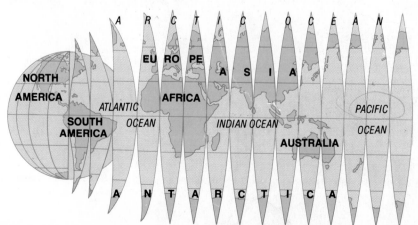

MERCATOR PROJECTION

The mapmaker added land and water to this map. The areas near the poles seem much larger than they really are.

But maps are handy. It is easy to carry them around.

Most maps have a **key.** A key can tell you what the colors on the map mean. It can show you what the symbols (SIM bulz) on the map stand for. A **symbol** is a mark or picture used in place of words. Look at the map on pages 70 and 71. Find the key. Look at the symbols in the key. Then find each symbol on the map.

Maps of Earth do not show only continents and oceans. They can also show nations. A **nation** is a land where people live under one government. The continent of North America has three large nations. They are Canada, the United States, and Mexico.

The shape of a nation is outlined by boundaries. A **boundary** is a line that divides one place from another. Some boundaries

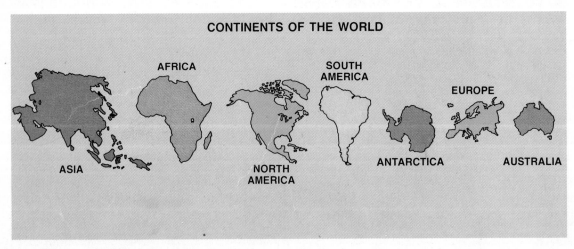

CONTINENTS OF THE WORLD

ASIA

AFRICA

NORTH AMERICA

SOUTH AMERICA

ANTARCTICA

EUROPE

AUSTRALIA

This chart shows the seven continents in order of size.

are natural boundaries. The Atlantic Ocean and Pacific Ocean are **natural boundaries** of the United States.

Other boundaries are called political (puh LIT uh kul) boundaries. **Political boundaries** divide one nation or state from another. The lines that separate Canada from the United States are political boundaries. Mexico is separated from Texas by a river, the Rio Grande. This is a natural boundary. But it is also a political boundary. It divides part of the United States from Mexico.

The map on pages 312 and 313 shows most of the nations in the world. Each nation on the map is a different color from the ones around it. The colors help you tell the nations apart. That is all the colors mean on this map. The map key tells you what the symbols mean. How does the map show boundaries between nations?

The map of nations tells us many things about the continents. Europe is a small continent. But it is divided into many nations. Africa has many nations, too. But North America has only three large nations. And Australia is a continent with only one nation— Australia! One continent has no nations at all. That is Antarctica. Almost all of Antarctica is covered by ice. Antarctica is popular with penguins. But would it be a good place for people?

REVIEW

WATCH YOUR WORDS

1. A flat drawing of places on Earth is a ___ .
   globe   map   boundary
2. A ___ shows what a map's symbols mean.
   globe   boundary   key
3. A line that divides one place from another is a ___ .
   boundary   symbol   nation
4. Canada is separated from the United States by a ___ boundary.
   natural   political
5. The United States is separated from Europe by a ___ boundary.
   political   natural

CHECK YOUR FACTS
Look at the Chart
6. Which two continents are largest?
7. Which two continents are smallest?

Look at the Lesson
8. What does a map key tell you?
9. What is a nation?
10. Which continent has no nations?

SHARPEN YOUR THINKING
Why might a large nation be better off than a small one?

CHAPTER REVIEW

WATCH YOUR WORDS

1. Earth is a ___. It is part of the ___.
   star   solar system   planet   moon

2. Earth takes 365 days to ___ around the sun.
   tilt   revolve   rotate

3. Earth rotates around an imaginary line, the ___.
   equator   North Pole   axis

4. A round model of Earth is a ___. Half of a ___ is a ___. (*Hint:* Use one word twice.)
   map   hemisphere   planet   globe

5. A line that divides one nation from another is a ___.
   natural boundary   hemisphere
   political boundary

CHECK YOUR FACTS

6. Why is Earth a good planet for people to live on?

7. Which way does Earth turn on its axis? How long does it take Earth to rotate once?

8. Why do we have summer in the United States in June instead of January?

9. What is a continent? How many continents are there on Earth? Can you name them?

10. What and where is the equator? What are the seasons like there? Why?

11. How far north can you go on Earth? How far south can you go?

12. On December 22, what season is it in Argentina? Why?

13. What is the difference between a map and a globe?

14. How many hemispheres are there?

15. Draw and label three map symbols.

APPLY YOUR SKILLS

USE YOUR MAP SKILLS

16. Draw a globe.
    a. Show the North Pole, the South Pole, the axis, and the equator.
    b. Show which way the Earth turns.
    c. Label the Northern Hemisphere and the Southern Hemisphere.

17. Draw the sun. Show where Earth is on June 22. Then show where Earth is on December 22. Put in Earth's axis, the poles, and the equator.

18. Draw an imaginary continent. Put oceans around it. Then divide it into three nations. Name the nations anything you like. Include a key.

SHARPEN YOUR THINKING

19. Suppose you were on a planet in another solar system. What would our sun look like from there?

20. The planet Venus rotates from east to west. Suppose you could see the sunrise on Venus. Where would you see it? Where would the sunset be?

21. Venus takes 225 days to revolve around the sun. How long is a year on Venus? Is a Venus year longer or shorter than an Earth year?

22. Why does a mapmaker change the shape of Earth's land and water?

23. When are a natural boundary and a political boundary the same?

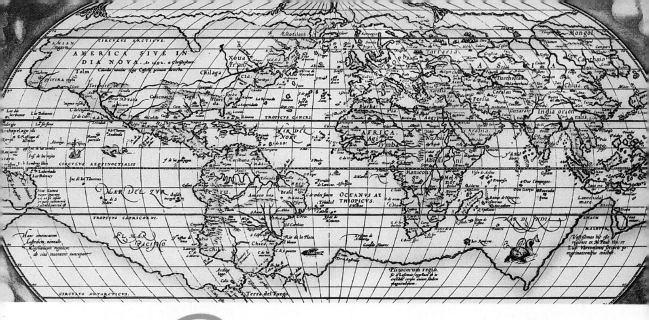

CHAPTER 2

ALL ABOUT MAPS

Lesson 1: How Far? . . . Distance

FIND THE WORDS

scale   distance
customary system   metric system
centimeter   kilometer

Maps can show places of many different sizes. Some maps show the whole world. Other maps show a state or a city. Maps can show places no larger than your school. In fact, you could draw a map of your room.

Look at the maps of Chestnut County and one small section of that county. Each map covers the same amount of space on the page. But one map shows a much larger place than the other map. Which map shows the larger place? What do the symbols in the map key stand for?

Each map has a **scale.** You can use the scale to find how much land the map covers. Look at the map of Chestnut County on page 30. One centimeter stands for 100 kilometers (62 miles). The map of Chestnut County is 7 centimeters (about 3 inches) wide. So Chestnut County is 700 kilometers (430 miles) wide.

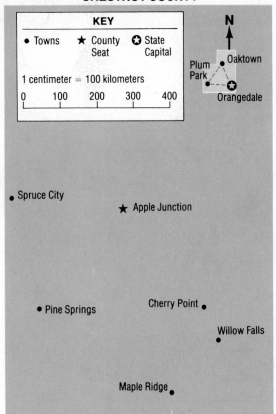

CHESTNUT COUNTY

KEY

| • Towns | ★ County Seat | ✪ State Capital |

1 centimeter = 100 kilometers

0   100   200   300   400

N

Plum Park • Oaktown

Orangedale

• Spruce City

★ Apple Junction

• Pine Springs

Cherry Point •

Willow Falls

Maple Ridge •

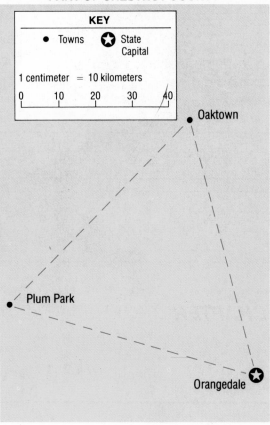

PART OF CHESTNUT COUNTY

KEY

| • Towns | ✪ State Capital |

1 centimeter = 10 kilometers

0   10   20   30   40

• Oaktown

• Plum Park

Orangedale ✪

Now look at the map of Part of Chestnut County. This map is also about 7 centimeters across. But on it, 1 centimeter stands for 10 kilometers (6⅕ miles). So this section is really 10 times smaller than Chestnut County. It is 70 kilometers (about 43 miles) wide.

A map scale tells you something else, too. You can find how far one place on the map is from another place. How far one place is from another is the **distance** between the two. Look again at the

map of Chestnut County. How far is it from Pine Springs to Willow Falls? On the map, those towns are 5 centimeters apart. Each centimeter stands for 100 kilometers. So, on Earth, those towns are 500 kilometers (310 miles) apart.

Find Plum Park on the map of the section of Chestnut County. Plum Park is 7 centimeters from Orangedale. On that map, each centimeter stands for 10 kilometers. How far is Plum Park from Orangedale? Which city is the state capital?

The Metric System

There are two major systems of measurement. One is the **customary system.** It uses inches, feet, yards, and miles to measure distances. The other is the **metric system** (MEH trik). It uses centimeters, meters, and kilometers to tell "how far." Most of the world uses the metric system. In this book, we use both systems.

We count by 10s. So does the metric system. The word *meter* means "measure." *Centi-* means 1/100. A cent is 1/100 of a dollar. A **centimeter** (SEN tuh MEE tur) is 1/100 of a meter. *Kilo-* means 1,000.

A **kilometer** (KIL uh MEE tur *or* ki LOM uh tur) is 1,000 meters.

Map scales in this book use centimeters and kilometers. They also show distances in miles.

1 centimeter = 2/5 inch
1 kilometer = 3/5 mile
5 centimeters = 2 inches
5 kilometers = 3 miles

Learn to "think metric." Then, you can figure out "how far" away a place is anywhere in the world.

REVIEW

WATCH YOUR WORDS

1. A ____ shows how much land a map covers.
   meter   centimeter   scale

2. The ____ system of measurement uses centimeters and kilometers.
   metric   solar   customary

3. A ____ is equal to 3/5 mile.
   meter   centimeter   kilometer

4. How far one place is from another is the ____ between them.
   time   rate   distance

5. A ____ is equal to 2/5 inch.
   meter   kilometer   centimeter

CHECK YOUR FACTS
Look at the Maps

6. How far is Plum Park from Apple Junction? How many centimeters? How many kilometers?

7. Is Cherry Point closer to Maple Ridge or to Pine Springs?

8. How far is Cherry Point from Willow Falls?

9. How far is Orangedale from Cherry Point?

10. How far is Plum Park from (a) Spruce City? (b) Oaktown?

TRY SOMETHING NEW

Figure out how tall you are in centimeters.

Lesson 2: Which Way? . . . Direction

Maps tell us about distance. They help us answer the question "How far?" Maps also tell us about direction. They help us find out "Which way?"

There are four **cardinal directions** on Earth. The word *cardinal* means "most important." The four most important directions are north, south, east, and west. They are abbreviated N, S, E, W.

Look at the map of North America on page 33. *North* is printed at the top of the map. *South* is printed at the bottom. *East* is on the right. *West* is on the left.

But directions are more than words printed on a map. Directions apply to the planet Earth as well. *North* really means "toward the North Pole." *South* means "toward the South Pole."

Find Canada and Mexico on the map. Canada is closer to the North Pole than Mexico is. So Canada is north of Mexico. That means Mexico is south of Canada.

You know that Earth rotates from west to east. In the morning, we see the sun "rise" in the east. We are turning east, toward the sun. So east is "toward the sunrise." In the evening, we see the sun "set" in the west. We are turning away from the sun. So west is "toward the sunset." When you face toward the North Pole, the sunrise is on your right. The sunset is on your left. When we draw maps and globes, we usually face north. That means that north is usually at the top. So east is right, west is left, and south is at the bottom.

Find Cuba and Haiti (HAY tee) on the map. Which way would you travel to go from Cuba to Haiti? Would you travel east or west? Which way would you go to get from Haiti to Cuba?

Most maps do not print directions around the edges. Instead, some maps use a **compass.** A compass has arrows that point north, south, east, and west. On a compass, the cardinal directions are abbreviated: N, S, E, W. Some maps use only a single arrow, marked N, for north. If you know where north is, you can find south, east, and west.

NATIONS OF NORTH AMERICA

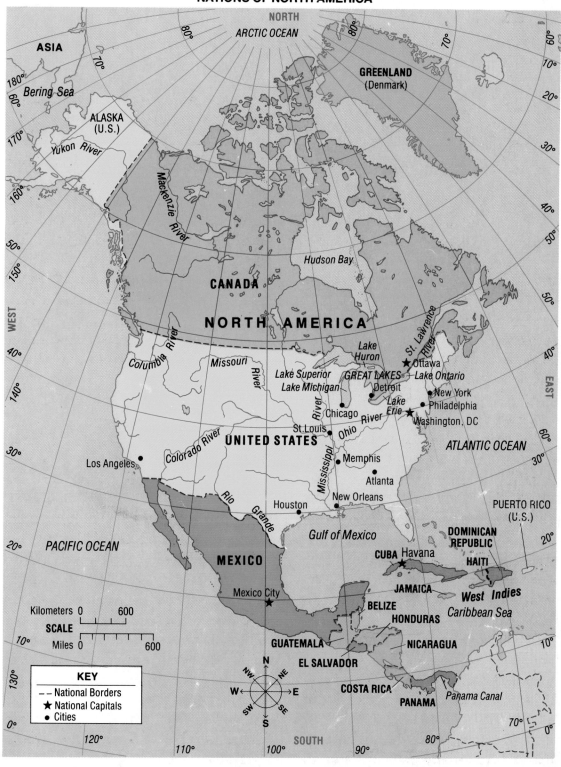

ASIA

ARCTIC OCEAN

NORTH

GREENLAND
(Denmark)

Bering Sea

ALASKA
(U.S.)

Yukon River

Mackenzie River

Hudson Bay

CANADA

NORTH AMERICA

WEST

Columbia River

Missouri River

Lake Superior
Lake Michigan

Lake Huron

GREAT LAKES

St. Lawrence River

★ Ottawa

Lake Ontario

Detroit

• New York

Chicago

Lake Erie

• Philadelphia

River

Ohio River

★ Washington, DC

St. Louis

UNITED STATES

ATLANTIC OCEAN

Colorado River

Los Angeles

• Memphis

Mississippi

• Atlanta

Rio Grande

Houston

New Orleans

PUERTO RICO
(U.S.)

Gulf of Mexico

DOMINICAN
REPUBLIC

PACIFIC OCEAN

MEXICO

CUBA Havana

HAITI

★

Mexico City

★

JAMAICA

West Indies

BELIZE

Caribbean Sea

HONDURAS

SCALE

Kilometers 0   600

GUATEMALA

NICARAGUA

Miles 0   600

EL SALVADOR

N
NW   NE
W   E
SW   SE
S

COSTA RICA

PANAMA

Panama Canal

SOUTH

KEY
- - National Borders
★ National Capitals
• Cities

Intermediate Directions

The four cardinal directions help you find places on Earth. Try adding these directions together.

Look at the map of North America again. Mexico is south of Alaska. It is also east of Alaska. So we can say that Mexico is southeast of Alaska. Alaska is north and west of Mexico. So Alaska is northwest of Mexico.

Find Washington, DC, on the map. Mexico is south of Washington. It is west of Washington, too. So Mexico is southwest of Washington, DC. Washington is north and east of Mexico. So we can say that Washington, DC, is northeast of Mexico.

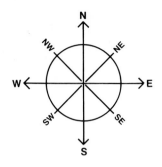

Northeast, northwest, southeast, and southwest are called the **intermediate directions.** These directions are often written NE, NW, SE, SW. Find them on the compass on this page.

Find the Bering Sea on the map of North America. It is in the far north. It is west of Alaska. Here, northwest North America almost touches Asia!

REVIEW

WATCH YOUR WORDS

1. North, south, east, and west are the ___.
   compass   cardinal directions
   metric system

2. Northeast and southwest are ___ .
   cardinal directions   scales
   intermediate directions

3. A ___ on a map has arrows that point N, S, E, W.
   scale   key   compass

CHECK YOUR FACTS
Look at the Lesson

4. What does *north* really mean?

5. When you face north, where is south? Where is east? Where is west?

Look at the Maps (pages 33 and 30)

6. Mexico is ___ of Cuba. Cuba is ___ of Canada.
   north   south   east   west

7. Apple Junction is ___ of Pine Springs. Maple Ridge is ___ of Willow Falls.
   northeast   northwest   southeast   southwest

Lesson 3: Where and What? . . . Location

FIND THE WORD
grid

Maps tell you "which way" and "how far." They can also show you "where." Finding places on a map is easy if you use a grid. A map **grid** is made up of lines on the map. Some lines run north and south (up and down). Other lines run east and west (right and left). Together, the grid lines form squares, or boxes, on the map.

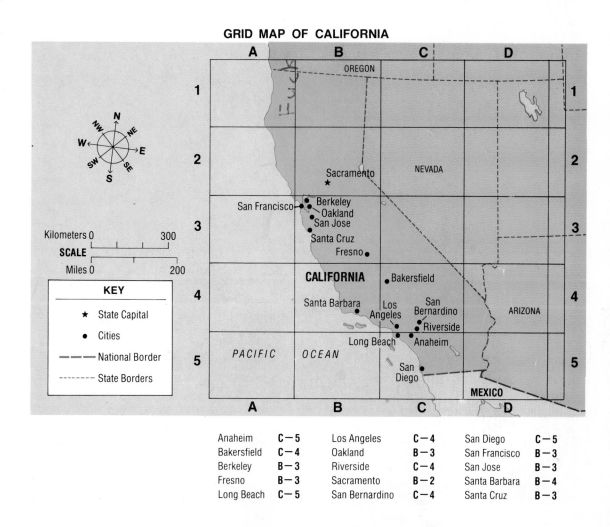

GRID MAP OF CALIFORNIA

Anaheim	C — 5	Los Angeles	C — 4	San Diego	C — 5
Bakersfield	C — 4	Oakland	B — 3	San Francisco	B — 3
Berkeley	B — 3	Riverside	C — 4	San Jose	B — 3
Fresno	B — 3	Sacramento	B — 2	Santa Barbara	B — 4
Long Beach	C — 5	San Bernardino	C — 4	Santa Cruz	B — 3

On many maps, each square has a number and a letter. Look at the map on page 35. It shows some cities in California. Below the map is a list of those cities. Next to each place name are a letter and a number. The letter and the number are clues. They mark a square on the grid. The city is in that square.

Suppose you wanted to find Santa Barbara. Santa Barbara's place on the grid is B-4. Letters are at the top and bottom of the map. Find B. Numbers are at the sides of the map. Find 4. Santa Barbara is in square B-4.

You just used the grid to *find* "where." You can also use it to *tell* "where." Suppose you have a map with a grid but with no list of cities. You want to help a friend find San Diego (dee A goh). First, look at the square San Diego is in. Find the letter of the square. It is C. Find the number of the square. It is 5. You can say that San Diego is in square C-5. Then your friend will be able to find it.

Remember the map key? Look at the symbols in the key. Find those symbols on the map of California. What is the capital of the state of California?

REVIEW

WATCH YOUR WORDS

1. Lines on a map that form squares make up a ____ .
   key   compass   grid
2. The symbol for a state capital on a map is in the ____ .
   grid   key   cardinal directions
3. To measure distances on a map, you use the ____ .
   compass   grid   scale

CHECK YOUR FACTS

Look at the Map

Cover up the list of cities. Then answer questions 4 and 5.

4. Find Los Angeles on the map. What square is it in?
5. Where in California are most of the cities? East or west?
6. Draw four symbols from the map key. Tell what they stand for.

Lesson 4: Latitude and Longitude

FIND THE WORDS

lines of latitude
lines of longitude
degrees   parallels
meridians   prime meridian

One special kind of grid can help you find any place on Earth. You can see this grid on your classroom globe. It is made up of two sets of lines.

Look at the globes below. The globe on the left has lines that run right and left. The globe in the middle has lines that run up and down. Now look at the globe on the right. When you put the lines together, they form a grid. This grid helps you find places.

The lines that go across the globe are called **lines of latitude** (LAT uh TOOD). Lines of latitude show how far north or south you are.

The lines that go up and down are called **lines of longitude** (LON juh TOOD). Lines of longitude show how far east or west you are.

More about Latitude

Remember that the globe is round, like a circle. A circle is divided into 360 parts, or **degrees.** The distance from the North Pole to the South Pole is half a circle. Half a circle is 180 degrees.

Lines of latitude always start in the middle of the globe. The starting place is the equator. So

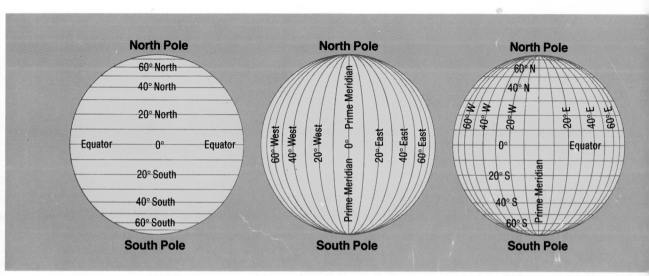

Quito is the capital of Ecuador in South America. It lies on the equator (0° latitude). The land is very high, though. So the weather is not as hot as you might think. To find out why, see "Fun Facts" on page 56.

The prime meridian of Earth passes through Greenwich, England (0° longitude). The old Royal Observatory building there has a split in it. That split shows where longitude starts. There, a telescope points up at the sky.

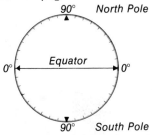

starting place is the equator. So the latitude of the equator is zero degrees. It is 90 degrees from the equator to the North Pole. It is also 90 degrees from the equator to the South Pole.

We can say this another way. We measure distance from the equator in degrees of latitude. We write 90 degrees as 90°. The North Pole is 90° north of the equator. So the North Pole is at 90° north

latitude. The South Pole is 90° south of the equator. So the South Pole is at 90° south latitude.

Quito, Ecuador (KEE toh EK wuh DOR), is on the equator. So Quito is at 0° latitude. Every place between the equator and the poles has a number between 0 and 90°. New Orleans, in the United States, is at 30° north latitude.

Lines of latitude have another name. They are called **parallels.** When lines are parallel, they are an equal distance apart at every point. They never cross one another. Lines of latitude run in the same direction as the equator.

They are parallel to the equator. So we call them parallels.

More about Longitude

Lines of longitude run from the North Pole to the South Pole. But there is no natural starting point for longitude. So, in 1884, 25 nations agreed on a starting point. They said that longitude would begin in Greenwich, England. Greenwich (GREN ich) is near London. England's old Royal Observatory is there.

Lines of longitude have another name. They are called **meridians** (muh RID ee unz). *Meridian* means "midday." When the sun crosses a meridian, it is noon there.

The line of longitude at Greenwich is the **prime meridian.** *Prime* means "first." The longitude of the prime meridian is zero degrees (0°).

Remember, LONgitude starts at LONdon. New Orleans, Louisiana, is 90 degrees west of London. New Orleans is at 90° west longitude. Dacca, Bangladesh, is 90 degrees east of London. Dacca is at 90° east longitude.

The farthest you can go from Greenwich is half a circle, or 180° The line for 180° longitude goes through the Aleutian (uh LOO shun) Islands. They are part of Alaska. Can you find them on your globe? At the 180° line, east meets west.

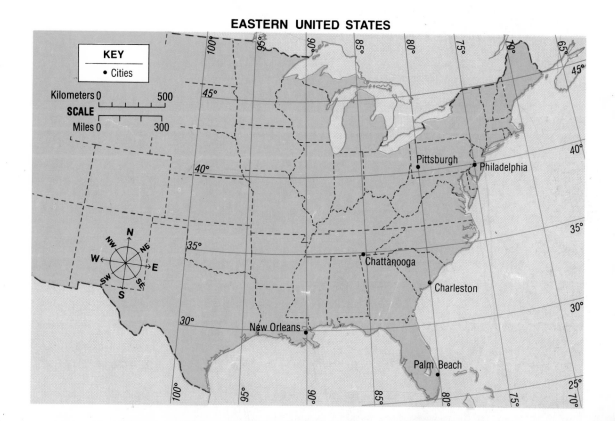

EASTERN UNITED STATES

Finding Places

Look at the map on page 39. It is a map showing part of the United States. The map has a grid. Lines of latitude run crosswise. They measure distance north and south of the equator. (*Remember:* lATitude starts at the equATor.) The degrees of the lines are marked on the sides of the map.

Lines of longitude run up and down. They measure distance east and west of the prime meridian. (*Remember:* LONgitude—LONdon.) The degrees of the lines are marked at the top and bottom of the map.

With latitude and longitude, you can find any place on Earth. Find New Orleans again. It is on the 30° line running crosswise. It is north of the equator. So New Orleans is at 30° north latitude.

Now find the longitude of New Orleans. It is on the 90° line running up and down. It is west of the prime meridian. New Orleans is at 90° west longitude.

Now try finding places another way. Use latitude and longitude as an address on Earth. The address is 40° north latitude, 75° west longitude. What is the city?

REVIEW

WATCH YOUR WORDS

1. Lines that measure distance north or south of the equator are ___ .
   lines of longitude   lines of latitude   degrees

2. Greenwich, England, is the location of the ___ .
   lines of latitude   prime meridian   parallels

3. Lines that measure distance east or west of London are ___ .
   lines of longitude   lines of latitude   parallels

4. A circle is divided into 360 ___ .
   parallels   degrees   meridians

5. Lines of latitude are also called ___ .
   meridians   parallels   degrees

CHECK YOUR FACTS

Look at the Lesson

6. What is the starting place for lines of latitude? Where do lines of longitude start?

7. How far north of the equator can you go?

8. How far west of the prime meridian can you go?

Look at the Map

9. Find Charleston, South Carolina, and Pittsburgh, Pennsylvania. What line of longitude are they on? Are they west or east of the prime meridian?

10. Find Chattanooga, Tennessee. What line of latitude is it on? Is it north or south of the equator? What line of longitude is it on? Is it west or east of the prime meridian? Now, state the location of Chattanooga.

Lesson 5: How High? . . . Elevation

FIND THE WORDS

meter
elevation   sea level
political map   physical map
physical-political map

Another question maps can answer about places is "How high?" To measure how tall a person is, you start at the floor. Then you measure to the top of the person's head. You can measure height in meters and centimeters. Or you can measure in feet and inches. Someone who is 3 feet, 3 inches tall is about 1 **meter** high.

    1 meter = 3.28 feet
    1 mile   = 5,280 feet = 1,609 meters

The height of land is the land's **elevation** (EL uh VAY shun). To measure land's elevation, you start at **sea level.** Sea level is the surface of the ocean.

Suppose you are wading on a beach. The beach slopes up from the ocean. Where the beach meets the ocean is sea level. Now suppose there is no beach. A mountain goes all the way down to the sea. To measure the mountain, you start at sea level. Then you count the number of meters or feet from the ocean to the mountaintop. Now you know how high the mountain is. Its height above sea level is its elevation.

Suppose someone asks you, "What is the elevation of Sea Peak?" You could say, "Sea Peak is 4,300 meters high." Or you could say, "Sea Peak is 14,100 feet above sea level." Both answers

Fun Facts

Have you ever heard of Pikes Peak? It is a famous mountain in Colorado. Pikes Peak has exactly the same elevation as Sea Peak. It is 4,300 meters (14,100 feet) above sea level. You can ride a train from the bottom of Pikes Peak to the top. But if you do, you will not go up 14,100 feet. You will go up only 7,530 feet. How can that be so?

The reason is that the ground below Pikes Peak is high ground. It is 6,570 feet above sea level. At the foot of the mountain, you are already over a mile high!

would be right. They are different ways of saying the same thing.

Now suppose you ask a mapmaker, "What is the elevation of Sea Peak?" The mapmaker will make a map. The map won't *tell* you "4,300 meters." But it can *show* you that Sea Peak is over 4,000 meters high.

How can a flat map show where mountains are? How can it tell you whether land is high or low?

A map shows elevation in two ways. One way is to use different colors for different heights. Look at the drawing below. All land that is over 4,000 meters high is colored brown. That is the highest land on the map. Mapmakers can use any colors they like to show the elevation of land. The key to an elevation map will say what the colors mean.

Many elevation maps show height by using colors. This one shows height by using lines and shading. Mountains look wrinkled on this map.

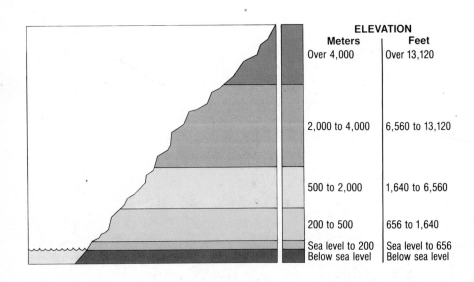

ELEVATION	
Meters	**Feet**
Over 4,000	Over 13,120
2,000 to 4,000	6,560 to 13,120
500 to 2,000	1,640 to 6,560
200 to 500	656 to 1,640
Sea level to 200	Sea level to 656
Below sea level	Below sea level

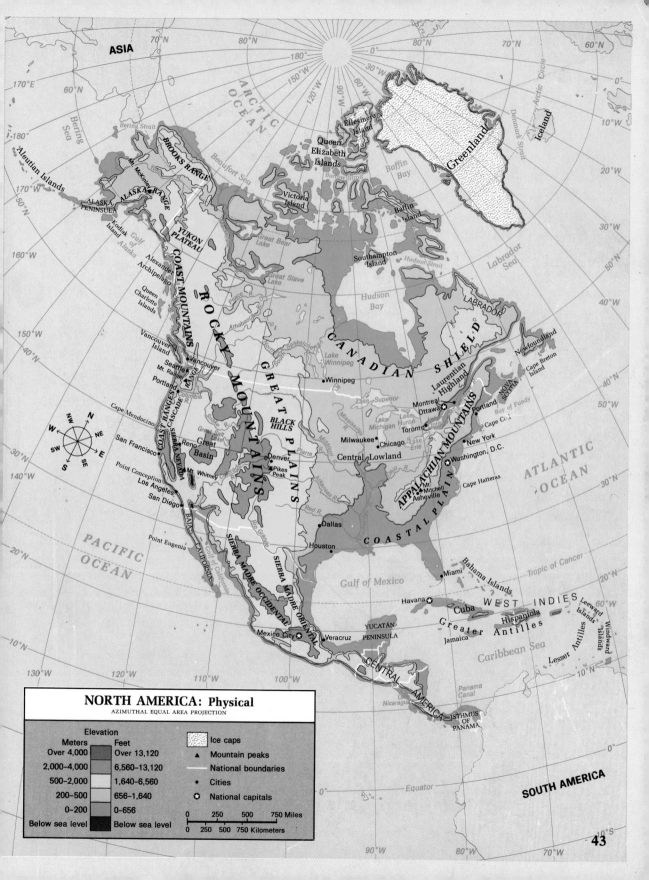

NORTH AMERICA: Physical

AZIMUTHAL EQUAL AREA PROJECTION

Elevation

Meters	Feet
Over 4,000	Over 13,120
2,000–4,000	6,560–13,120
500–2,000	1,640–6,560
200–500	656–1,640
0–200	0–656
Below sea level	Below sea level

Ice caps
▲ Mountain peaks
— National boundaries
• Cities
✪ National capitals

0   250   500   750 Miles
0 250 500 750 Kilometers

ASIA

ARCTIC OCEAN

Bering Strait
Bering Sea
Aleutian Islands
ALASKA PENINSULA
Mt. McKinley
ALASKA RANGE
BROOKS RANGE
Kodiak Island
Gulf of Alaska
Alexander Archipelago
Queen Charlotte Islands
YUKON PLATEAU
COAST MOUNTAINS
Vancouver Island
Vancouver
Seattle
Mt. Rainier
Portland
Cape Mendocino
San Francisco
Point Conception
Los Angeles
San Diego
Point Eugenia
COAST RANGES
CASCADE RANGE
SIERRA NEVADA
Reno
Mt. Whitney
Great Basin
Great Salt Lake
Denver
Pikes Peak
BLACK HILLS
ROCKY MOUNTAINS
GREAT PLAINS
BAJA CALIFORNIA
Gulf of California
SIERRA MADRE OCCIDENTAL
SIERRA MADRE ORIENTAL
Mexico City
Veracruz
YUCATÁN PENINSULA
CENTRAL AMERICA
Panama Canal
Nicaragua
ISTHMUS OF PANAMA

PACIFIC OCEAN

Beaufort Sea
Great Bear Lake
Great Slave Lake
Victoria Island
Queen Elizabeth Islands
Ellesmere Island
Banks Strait
Hudson Strait
Southampton Island
Hudson Bay
Baffin Bay
Baffin Island
CANADIAN SHIELD
LABRADOR
Lake Winnipeg
Winnipeg
Lake Superior
Lake Michigan
Lake Huron
Lake Erie
Lake Ontario
Milwaukee
Chicago
Central Lowland
Dallas
Houston
Gulf of Mexico
Miami
Havana
Cuba
Jamaica
Hispaniola
Greater Antilles
WEST INDIES
Leeward Islands
Windward Islands
Lesser Antilles
Caribbean Sea
COASTAL PLAIN
APPALACHIAN MOUNTAINS
Mt. Mitchell
Asheville
Cape Hatteras
Washington, D.C.
New York
Portland
Cape Cod
Bay of Fundy
NOVA SCOTIA
Cape Breton Island
Newfoundland
Laurentian Highland
Montreal
Ottawa
Toronto
Bahama Islands
Tropic of Cancer

ATLANTIC OCEAN

Greenland
Denmark Strait
Iceland
Arctic Circle
Labrador Sea

Equator

SOUTH AMERICA

43

Mapmakers have another way to show elevation. An artist can show mountains by using lines and shading. Look at the drawing at the top of page 42. Areas with mountains look creased and wrinkled on the map.

Now look at the elevation map on page 43. How can you tell the elevation of Mexico City? First, look at the color of the land around Mexico City. Then look at what that color means in the map key. Is the land around Mexico City high or low? Next, look at Denver, Colorado. Do you know why Denver is called the "Mile-High City"?

Physical and Political Maps

In Chapter 1, you learned about political boundaries. You used a map that showed most of the nations of the world. A map that shows political boundaries is called a **political map.** A map showing the 50 states of the United States is a political map. So is a map showing the three large nations of North America.

A map that shows the shape of land is called a **physical map.** An elevation map is a physical map.

Sometimes a map shows both political boundaries and physical features. Such a map is called a **physical-political map.**

REVIEW

WATCH YOUR WORDS

1. You measure the height of a mountain by starting at ____.
   ground level   the prime meridian   sea level

2. The height of a mountain is its ____.
   longitude   latitude   elevation

3. A map that shows the boundaries of the 50 states is a ____.
   physical map   political map   scale map

4. A map that shows the shape of land is a ____.
   political map   climate map   physical map

5. A map that shows elevation and political boundaries is a ____.
   political map   physical map   physical-political map

CHECK YOUR FACTS

Look at the Lesson

6. How does a flat map show elevation? Name two ways.

7. Why doesn't the railroad at Pikes Peak go up 14,100 feet?

Look at the Maps

8. What color is Miami, Florida, on the elevation map? What does this color stand for?

9. What color is Asheville, North Carolina, on the map? What does this color stand for?

10. Where are most of the mountains in North America?

CHAPTER REVIEW

WATCH YOUR WORDS

1. A ___ tells you how far one place on a map is from another.
   key   compass   scale

2. A ___ has arrows that point toward the ___.
   scale   cardinal directions   key   compass

3. A pattern of squares on a map is a ___.
   key   grid   scale

4. ___ , or ___ , measure distance north and south of the equator. ___ , or ___ , measure distance east and west of Greenwich, England.
   Lines of longitude   parallels   meridians   Lines of latitude

5. The starting point for latitude is the ___. The starting point for longitude is the ___.
   North Pole   prime meridian
   South Pole   equator

6. Latitude and longitude are measured in ___.
   centimeters   meters   degrees

7. A map showing the boundaries of the 50 states is a ___.
   physical map   political map   elevation map

8. A ___ map shows how high land is.
   political   climate   physical

9. The height of land is its ___.
   sea level   elevation   longitude

10. Five ___ are equal to three miles.
    meters   centimeters   kilometers

CHECK YOUR FACTS

11. What are the two major systems of measurement?

12. List the cardinal directions and the intermediate directions.

13. What line is at 0° longitude? What line is at 0° latitude?

14. How do you measure the elevation of a mountain?

15. How can a mapmaker show high land?

APPLY YOUR SKILLS

USE YOUR MAPS

16. Look at the map on page 30. How far is Pine Springs from Spruce City?

17. Look at the direction map on page 33. Fill in the cardinal directions:
    Ottawa is _a_ of Washington, DC.
    The Columbia River is _b_ of Ottawa.
    The Rio Grande is _c_ of Canada.
    Puerto Rico is _d_ of Mexico.

18. Look at the grid map on page 35. What square is Sacramento in? What square has the most cities?

19. Look at the elevation map on page 43. Is the highest land in the east or west?

20. Look at the latitude and longitude map on page 39. What is the latitude and longitude of Philadelphia?

SHARPEN YOUR THINKING

21. How can two maps the same size show places of different sizes?

22. How far west can you go on Earth?

23. Suppose you have two maps of California. One map tells you that Santa Cruz (KROOZ) is in square B-3. The other map shows Santa Cruz at 37° north latitude and 122° west longitude. Which map would a sailor use?

24. Why don't we just measure all mountains from the bottom to the top?

25. Suppose you were lost in the woods. How could you find east and west? How could you find north?

3 ALL ABOUT EARTH

Lesson 1: Landforms of Earth

FIND THE WORDS

landform   mountain
mountain range   hill   valley
plateau   plain

No two people on Earth are exactly alike. No two places are exactly the same, either. Some places are hot, while others are cold. Some places have water, while others are dry. Some places have trees, while others have only sand. Even when places look alike, their plants and animals may be different.

The shape of the land also helps to make places different. The many shapes of land on Earth are called **landforms.** Earth has four main landforms. They are mountains, hills, plateaus, and plains.

The highest form of land on Earth is a **mountain.** It is much higher than the land around it. It goes up sharply and often has a jagged top. The bottom of a mountain is called the foot. The top is called the peak, or summit.

Mountains are usually found in groups. A group of mountains is called a **mountain range.** There are many different ranges in the Rocky Mountains. These mountains are in the western United States. Find the Rocky Mountains on the map on page 43. Then find the Appalachian Mountains in the eastern United States.

Now look at the map on pages 48 and 49. Where are the mountains in South America? Can you find the mountains that separate Europe and Asia?

A **hill** also rises higher than the land around it. But hills are not as high or as steep as mountains. A hill often has rounded sides and a rounded top. The low land between a group of hills or mountains is called a **valley.**

It is not easy to live in the hills or on a mountain. It is hard to travel up and down. It takes more time and work to get where you are going. It is also hard to build

A river carved the Grand Canyon out of a plateau. You can see the plateau at the back of the picture. (36° N latitude, 112° W longitude)

a road up a mountain. And it is hard to carry up the things you need to build a house.

Like a mountain, a **plateau** (pla TOH) rises above the land around it. But a plateau is usually flat on top. From the air, it looks like a table. So a plateau is sometimes called a *tableland.* Some plateaus are small. Others are very big. Look at the map of Earth on pages 48 and 49. Find the huge plateau in western China. It is in a region known as Tibet (ti BET). This plateau is the largest area of high land on Earth.

A **plain** is a big, open area of level land. Sometimes the land is as flat as a floor in every direction. Most times, the land is slightly "rolling." That doesn't mean the land moves. Rolling land has gentle little hills but no high ones. Usually, there are no big hills on the plains.

Hills are not as high or as steep as mountains. These hills are in Virginia.

80°N

Great Bear
Lake
60°N
Bering Sea
Great Slave
Lake
Hudson
Bay
Gulf
of Alaska

ROCKY MOUNTAINS

**NORTH
AMERICA**

Great
Lakes

St. Lawrence

ATLANTIC

40°N

GREAT PLAINS

*APPALACHIAN
MTS.*

OCEAN

PACIFIC OCEAN

Bermuda

New Orleans

Mexican
Plateau

Gulf
of Mexico

Bahama Islands

Tropic of Cancer

20°N

West Indies

N

NW   NE

W   E

SW   SE

S

Guiana
Highlands

Amazon

0°

Equator

Quito

ANDES MOUNTAINS

**SOUTH
AMERICA**

Brazilian Highlands

20°S

Tropic of Capricorn

Pôrto Alegre

PAMPAS

Buenos Aires

PACIFIC OCEAN

40°S

180°   160°W   140°W   120°W   100°W   80°W   60°W   40°W

60°S

80°S

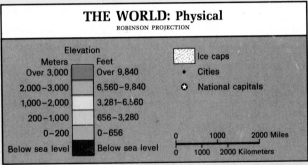

THE WORLD: Physical
ROBINSON PROJECTION

Elevation

Meters	Feet
Over 3,000	Over 9,840
2,000–3,000	6,560–9,840
1,000–2,000	3,281–6,560
200–1,000	656–3,280
0–200	0–656
Below sea level	Below sea level

Ice caps

• Cities

✪ National capitals

0   1000   2000 Miles

0   1000   2000 Kilometers

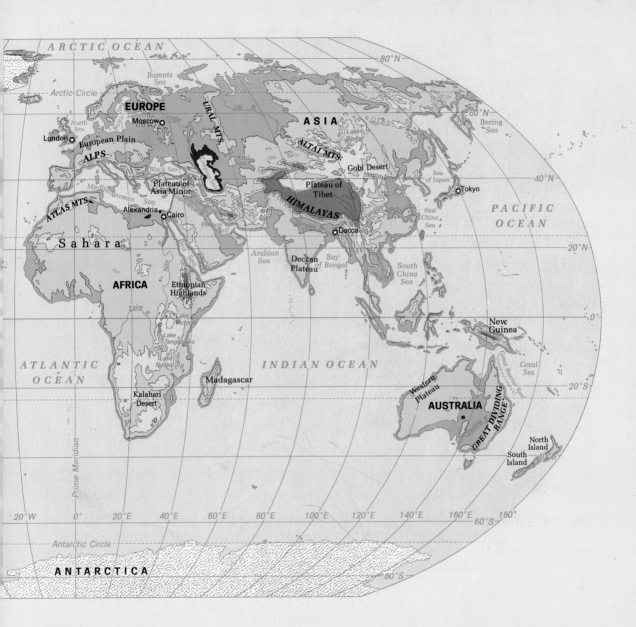

ARCTIC OCEAN

80°N

Barents
Sea

Arctic Circle

EUROPE

URAL MTS.

Ob R.

60°N

Bering
Sea

Moscow

Volga

ASIA

London

North
Sea

European Plain

Baltic Sea

ALTAI MTS.

ALPS

Aral
Sea

Gobi Desert

Sea
of Japan

40°N

Black Sea

Huang

Tokyo

Plateau of
Asia Minor

Plateau of
Tibet

PACIFIC
OCEAN

ATLAS MTS.

Mediterranean
Sea

HIMALAYAS

Yangtze

Alexandria

Cairo

Persian
Gulf

Ganges

Dacca

East
China
Sea

Sahara

Red Sea

Euphrates

Tigris

Nile

Arabian
Sea

Deccan
Plateau

Bay
of
Bengal

20°N

AFRICA

South
China
Sea

Ethiopian
Highlands

Zaire

Lake
Victoria

New
Guinea

0°

ATLANTIC
OCEAN

Lake
Tanganyika

INDIAN OCEAN

Coral
Sea

Lake
Nyasa

Great Barrier Reef

Madagascar

Western
Plateau

20°S

Kalahari
Desert

AUSTRALIA

GREAT DIVIDING RANGE

Darling

North
Island

Prime Meridian

South
Island

20°W

0°

20°E

40°E

60°E

80°E

100°E

120°E

140°E

160°E

180°

60°S

Antarctic Circle

ANTARCTICA

80°S

49

Many crops are grown on the plains. Here, hay is being gathered in.

Often, plains are lowlands. But the land on top of a plateau can also be a plain. Look at the map on page 43. Find the Great Plains in the middle of the United States. Some places in the Great Plains are as high as mountains. For example, Dodge City, Kansas, is 761 meters (2,496 feet) high.

There are many large plains on Earth. Look at the map on pages 48 and 49. Plains are medium green or light green. Find the plain that goes across the middle of Europe. Moscow is on this plain.

Plains are the places on Earth where most people live. Land in the mountains is often rocky. But much of the land in the plains has rich soil. This land is good for growing food. It is also easier for people to farm flat land than hilly land. It is easier to build roads and houses where the land is level. And it is easier to travel from place to place.

What is the land like where you live? How high is it? What shape is it? What kind of land do you like best?

Lesson 2: Weather and Climate

FIND THE WORDS

atmosphere   climate
tropical climate
mid-latitude climate
high-latitude climate
tropical rain forest
savanna   tundra
Arctic Circle   Antarctic Circle

"What is the weather going to be tomorrow?" That is something everyone wants to know. Will it be a fair day with sunny skies? We think of that as "good" weather. Will it be rainy or stormy? Then we say that "bad" weather is on the way. "Good" weather doesn't bother us. "Bad" weather can make us uncomfortable or spoil our plans. The weather report can tell us what the weather will be like. But what *is* the weather?

We live at the bottom of a thick layer of air. This air surrounds Earth. We call it Earth's **atmosphere** (AT muh SFIR). When we talk about the weather, we are really talking about the atmosphere.

What do you say when someone asks about tomorrow's weather? In summer, you might say, "It's going to be warm and rainy." In winter, you might say, "It's going to be cold, windy, and clear." In both cases, you are really talking about the atmosphere. How hot or cold is the air? How wet or dry is it? Is the air still or moving?

The climate is more than just the weather. People won't ask you what the climate will be tomorrow. But someone might ask what winters are like where you live. Suppose you live in northern Vermont. You might say, "We have cold winters and a lot of snow." Suppose you live in southern Florida. You might say, "We have mild winters. It doesn't get cold enough to snow."

The average weather over a long period of time is the **climate.** Knowing the climate won't tell you exactly what tomorrow's weather will be. But it will tell you what to expect from season to season. In winter, you won't expect snow in southern Florida. But you will expect snow in northern Vermont.

There are many different climates on Earth. Among them are hot climates and cold climates, wet climates and dry climates. We can divide Earth's climates into three groups. There are **tropical climates** near the equator. There are **mid-latitude climates** between the equator and the poles. There

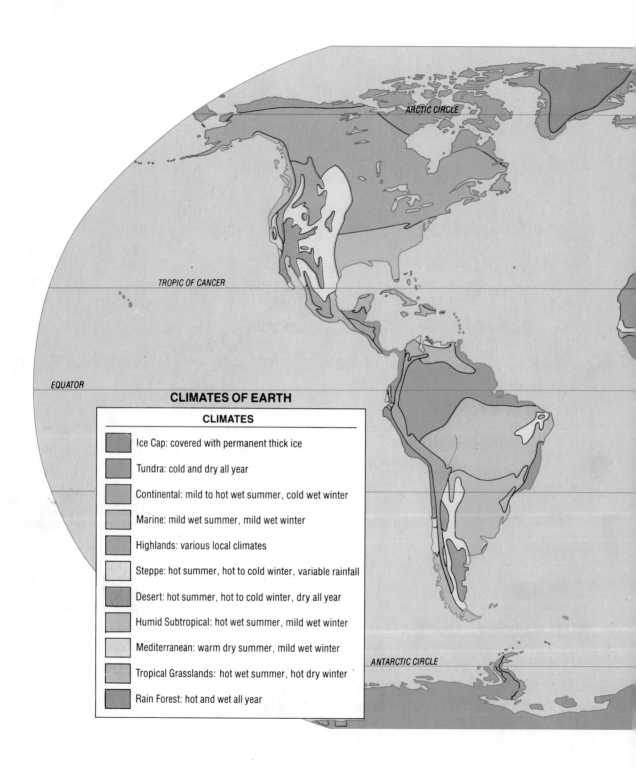

CLIMATES OF EARTH

CLIMATES

Ice Cap: covered with permanent thick ice

Tundra: cold and dry all year

Continental: mild to hot wet summer, cold wet winter

Marine: mild wet summer, mild wet winter

Highlands: various local climates

Steppe: hot summer, hot to cold winter, variable rainfall

Desert: hot summer, hot to cold winter, dry all year

Humid Subtropical: hot wet summer, mild wet winter

Mediterranean: warm dry summer, mild wet winter

Tropical Grasslands: hot wet summer, hot dry winter

Rain Forest: hot and wet all year

ARCTIC CIRCLE

TROPIC OF CANCER

EQUATOR

ANTARCTIC CIRCLE

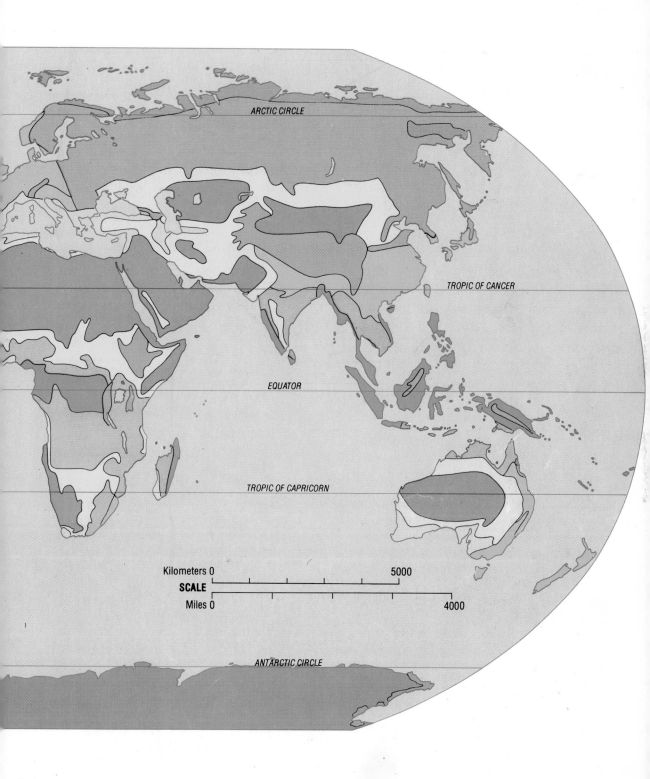

ARCTIC CIRCLE

TROPIC OF CANCER

EQUATOR

TROPIC OF CAPRICORN

Kilometers 0   5000
SCALE
Miles 0   4000

ANTARCTIC CIRCLE

are **high-latitude climates** near the poles. You will learn more about these climates as you read.

Tropical Climates

Near the equator, the weather is hot almost all year. The parts of Earth closest to the equator are called the *tropics* (TROP iks). So the climates found along the equator are known as tropical (TROP uh kul) climates.

A good deal of rain falls in the tropics. This heavy rain makes thick forests grow. These forests are called **tropical rain forests.** In an area with less rain, grass grows. An area like that is called a tropical grassland, or **savanna** (suh VAN uh). In areas where little or no rain falls, there are *deserts*. Few plants can grow in the desert.

Look at the climate map of Earth on pages 52 and 53. Find the tropical desert in northern Africa. Then find the tropical grasslands and rain forests.

Mid-latitude Climates

In mid-latitude climates, the weather changes a lot from season to season. Most of the United

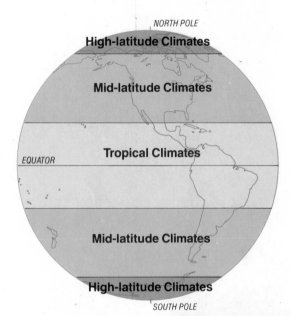

Tropical climates are found between 23° north latitude and 23° south latitude. A tropical grassland is called a savanna.

States is located in this climate zone. Find your part of the United States on the climate map. There are seven kinds of mid-latitude climates on the map, including highlands and deserts. What climate area do you live in?

High-latitude Climates

High-latitude climates can be found near the North Pole and the South Pole. There, the weather is almost always cool or cold. The summers are short. The winters are very long.

The area of Earth closest to the North Pole is called the *Arctic*. In the Arctic, parts of the land and ocean are covered with ice and snow all year. Find the Arctic ice cap on the climate map.

South of the Arctic are cold, treeless plains called the **tundra** (TUN druh). Here the soil beneath the surface stays frozen all year. Thus plants with deep roots cannot grow on the tundra. Only the surface layer of soil thaws in the short, cool spring and summer. Then flowering plants and mosses grow.

Look at the globe on page 54. Find the line of latitude that is about 66° north of the equator. This is called the **Arctic Circle.** The Arctic and the tundra are north of the Arctic Circle.

Just south of the Arctic Circle is an area with a *subarctic climate*. This area has long, cold winters and short, cool summers. It is mostly covered with forests.

The area closest to the South Pole is called the *Antarctic*. Find the line of latitude that is about 66° south of the equator. This is called the **Antarctic Circle.**

Heavy rains fall in the tropics. The rains cause thick forests to grow. They are called tropical rain forests.

The cold, treeless tundra region is near the Arctic Circle. Only the surface soil ever thaws.

No matter what a climate area is like, the mountains are usually different. The higher you go above sea level, the thinner the air becomes. This thin air holds less heat and wetness than heavier air does. So, as you go up a mountain, the weather gets cooler and cooler. Did you ever drive to the top of a high mountain? You can go through subarctic and tundra regions when you do. Even in the tropics, the tops of high mountains are cold. Very high mountains in the tropics may be covered with snow all year round.

The Antarctic area includes the continent of Antarctica and the oceans around it. Antarctica is covered by thousands of feet of ice and snow. Penguins, whales, and fish live in the Antarctic. Some scientists live there, too. The weather is almost always cold.

People like to live in climates where they are comfortable. Because of this, most people live in certain parts of Earth. Few people live in the Arctic. Not many people live in the mountains or deserts. In fact, large areas of Earth have few people or none at all.

REVIEW

WATCH YOUR WORDS

1. Belém (buh LEM), Brazil, is near the equator. It has a___climate.
   mid-latitude   high-latitude
   tropical

2. Detroit, Michigan, is in the area between the equator and the North Pole. It has a___climate.
   tropical   mid-latitude
   high-latitude

3. Nome, Alaska, is just south of the Arctic Circle. It has a___climate.
   high-latitude   tropical
   mid-latitude

4. Another name for a tropical grass-land is a___.
   rain forest   savanna   tundra

5. In the bare___, the ground is frozen most of the year.
   desert   savanna   tundra

CHECK YOUR FACTS

6. What is the difference between climate and weather?

7. What do we call the line of latitude 66° north of the equator? What do we call the line of latitude 66° south of the equator?

8. What is the climate like in the Arctic and the Antarctic?

9. What is a subarctic climate like?

SHARPEN YOUR THINKING

Look at the climate map. See if you can guess which parts of Earth have the most people.

Lesson 3: Resources of Earth

People can live on almost any part of Earth's land. But most people prefer places where the land and climate make living easier. People also like to live near the resources they need.

A **resource** is anything people use to help them live. Resources that are found on Earth are called **natural resources.** You use natural resources all the time. This book is made from resources. The paper and ink come from trees and other plants. The house you live in is made from resources. It may be built of wood, stone, clay, or metal. Your food and water are resources. The clothes you wear are made out of resources.

As you can see, there are many kinds of resources. But all natural resources can be put into one of two groups. One group is living resources. The other group is nonliving resources.

Living resources are plants and animals. Some living resources grow by themselves. But often, people have to grow or raise these resources. Because the resources are alive, people can use some and grow more. But suppose people use all of a living resource. For example, suppose hunters kill all the seals in the sea. If we use up a resource, we run out of it.

Let's look for a minute at a few of our living resources.

Plants are very important to people. Plants such as cotton and flax are used to make cloth. We also get oils, dyes, rubber, and medicines from plants. From trees we get wood for houses and paper for books. We also get fruit. Apples, oranges, grapefruit, pears, and peaches grow on trees. Some other fruits grow on smaller plants.

We eat many other parts of plants besides their fruit. We eat seeds, such as peas, beans, and corn. We eat stems, such as celery. We eat leaves, such as lettuce. We eat roots, such as carrots and beets. We even eat flowers, such as broccoli and cauliflower!

Many of our most important foods come from grasses. Bread and spaghetti are made from wheat. Breakfast cereals are made from wheat, oats, and rice. Wheat, oats, and rice are all grasses with seeds we can eat. Most of the people on Earth eat one or more of these grass crops.

Cotton grows in the southern United States. We use the fluffy part of this plant to make cloth. First, the cotton seeds are separated from the fibers. Then, the fibers are spun into thread and the thread is woven into cloth. The cotton seeds contain oil. Cottonseed oil is used in cooking.

Some foods are made from grasses. Wheat is a grass with seeds we can eat. The seeds, called grain, are ground into flour. Flour is used to make dough, which is baked into bread. The United States grows much of the world's supply of wheat. It grows more cotton than any other nation on Earth.

Most people also use animals for food. From these animals we get meat, eggs, and milk. We also get leather for shoes and coats. We get wool for sweaters. We get feathers for pillows. We even get some medicines, such as cod-liver oil. And these are only a few of our living resources.

Nonliving resources are land, water, and minerals. Coal and oil are minerals. People burn coal and oil as fuel. Metals are also min-erals. Iron, aluminum, and copper are metals. People use them to make tools, buildings, cars, and many other things. They use gold and silver for money and jewelry.

Two of our most important nonliving resources are land and water. People need good land to grow food. Nothing useful grows unless the soil is fertile (FUR tul). **Fertile soil** contains the minerals that plants need to be healthy. Sometimes the land needs extra minerals. Then people add them to the soil. These added minerals are called *fertilizer*.

But land is useless without water. Water is an important resource. People cannot live long without it. That is why few people live in deserts. There is no water in the desert, and few plants grow there.

People, animals, and plants drink water. But people use water in many other ways as well. We use water to wash, to cook, and to put out fires. People also use water for transportation. Sometimes, it is easier to travel over water than over land. So a river or seaport is a very valuable resource. What are some of the ways in which you use water?

Most nonliving resources cannot be replaced. When they are used up, there will be no more. When we use wood, we can plant more trees. But when we use fuel oil, we cannot replace it. When rain or snow falls, we get more water. But suppose it doesn't rain for a long time. Then we may not have as much water as we need. We may have a water shortage.

Many people are concerned about our resources. They say we must use resources carefully. They say we must not waste them. They believe we should learn to use them over and over again.

REVIEW

WATCH YOUR WORDS

1. Plants and animals are ____ .
   nonliving resources
   living resources
2. Land, water, and minerals are ____ .
   nonliving resources
   living resources
3. Plants grow well in ____ .
   mountains   deserts   fertile soil

CHECK YOUR FACTS

4. What is a resource?
5. Name three living resources.
6. Name three nonliving resources.
7. What parts of plants do we eat as food?
8. Why is water an important natural resource?

TRY SOMETHING NEW

Play "Twenty Questions" in a new way. Choose a place at home or at school. It can be indoors or outdoors. List the things you see there. Then say whether each thing is animal, vegetable, or mineral.

SHARPEN YOUR THINKING

Suppose your community did not have enough water. What would you do? Think of a plan. Then tell the class about it.

Lesson 4: People and Earth

FIND THE WORDS

population map   population
desert   oasis

"I can't find you. Where on Earth have you gone?" Have you ever heard anyone say that?

People have gone all over Earth. People could live almost anywhere on this planet of ours. But they don't. Most people live in only a few places. They live on only a small part of Earth's land.

Where on Earth are all the people? Look at the map below. It shows where most of the world's people live. This map is called a **population map.** The **population** (POP yuh LAY shun) of a place is the number of people who live there.

You can see that many people live in India and China. Many also live in the western part of Europe. And many live in the eastern part of North and South America. Why do people live crowded together

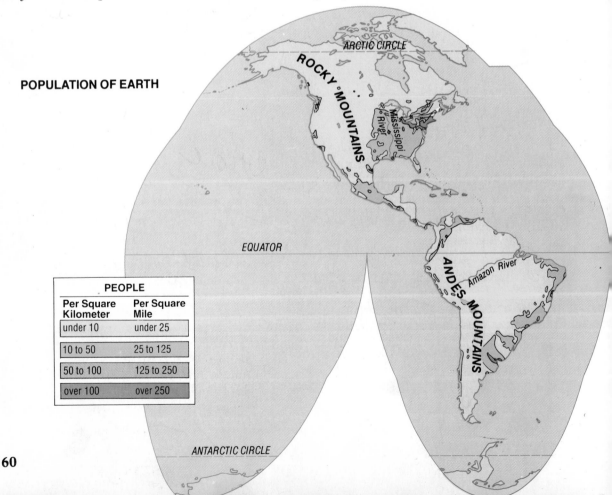

POPULATION OF EARTH

PEOPLE	
Per Square Kilometer	Per Square Mile
under 10	under 25
10 to 50	25 to 125
50 to 100	125 to 250
over 100	over 250

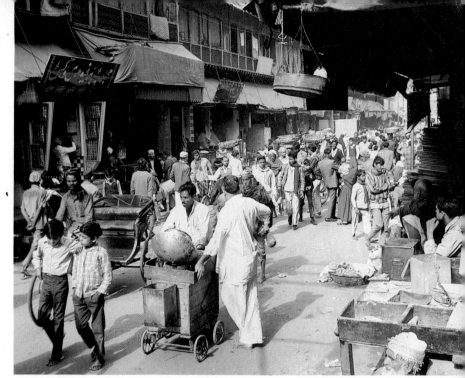

India is one of the most crowded nations on Earth. It lies between 8° and 36° north latitude.

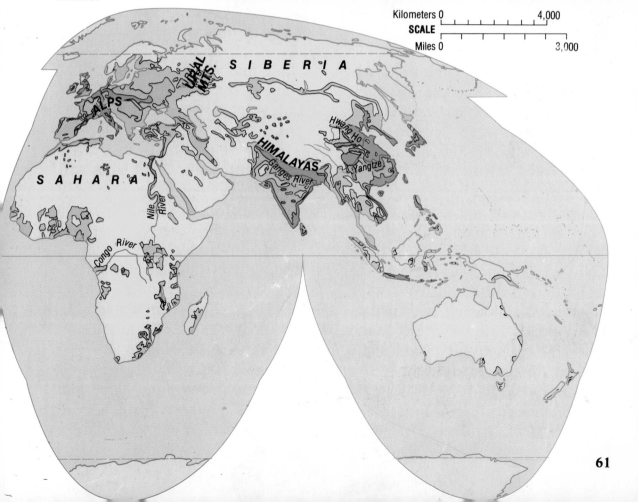

Kilometers 0   4,000
SCALE
Miles 0   3,000

SIBERIA

URAL MTS.

ALPS

HIMALAYAS

Hwang Ho

Yangtze

Ganges River

SAHARA

Nile River

Congo River

The desert is very dry. Without water, few plants can grow there. The cactus grows in the desert, though. This plant can store water in its thick stems. The giant cactus, shown here, is the largest cactus that grows in the United States.

on Earth? Why don't they spread out more, instead?

The lands around the poles are too cold for most people. Find the lands near the Antarctic Circle on the population map. No one lives on the continent of Antarctica. But a few scientists stay there to study the weather. Now find the lands near the Arctic Circle. Only a few people live in the Arctic. Those few who live there cannot farm and grow food. The ground is frozen. Instead, they must live by hunting and fishing. The animals and fish they catch are not enough to feed many people. So not many people live in the Arctic. In recent years, oil was found in the Arctic. Many workers went there to drill for it.

Food for them came from other lands.

Now find Africa on the population map. The largest desert in the world is in the north of Africa. It is the Sahara. A **desert** is a very dry place. Parts of it are often covered with sand. Few plants will grow there. Food grows only where there is water. So food does not grow in the desert.

A place in a desert where there is water is called an **oasis** (oh A sis). But an oasis can grow only a little food. This food is not enough to feed many people. So not many people live in the desert.

There is not much fertile land in the mountains, either. And the land in the mountains is not level. It is very hard to grow crops on hilly land. So not many people live in the mountains. Some people who do live there raise animals. They may keep sheep or goats. And mountain areas have other natural resources. Mountain people may work in mines to take minerals out of the Earth. Or they may cut down trees in the forests to get wood. These are some ways they can make a living.

Look at the population map again. Find the Andes Mountains in South America. You can see that few people live in these high mountains.

Next, find the Amazon River on the map. It is in South America. This river runs through the largest rain forest on Earth. Not many people live in the Amazon rain forest. Tropical rain forests are not good places for people. The heavy rains wash the minerals from the soil. So it is hard for people to grow food.

Now you can see why certain places cannot support many people. Some places are too cold. Some are too dry. Some are too wet. Some are too rocky and uneven.

Most people live where the land is level. They live where the climate is comfortable. They live where the soil is good for growing food. They live where there are natural resources for them to use.

Maps can tell you a lot about what places are like. They can also answer the question: "Where on Earth are all the people?"

REVIEW

WATCH YOUR WORDS

1. The people who live in a place are the _____.
   culture population resources

2. A place in a desert where there is water is a(n) _____.
   landform rain forest oasis

CHECK YOUR FACTS

Look at the Lesson

3. How do people get their food in the Arctic?

4. What is the largest desert on Earth? Where is it?

5. What is the largest rain forest? Where is it?

6. Name three ways mountain people can make a living.

7. What kind of land is good for people to live on? Name three things this land should have.

Look at the Maps

8. Compare the population map with the physical map. What landforms do most people live on?

9. Compare the population map with the climate map. What climate areas do most people live in?

Lesson 5: Ways of Living

People live in different places. They do things in different ways. But they are alike in at least one way. They all have the same basic needs.

All people need certain things to stay alive and well. They need air, water, and food. They need protection from the weather. They need to feel safe. And they need to feel good about themselves.

We do not think much about the air around our Earth. But we cannot live without it. We need air to breathe.

Some people in Mongolia live in felt-covered tents called yurts. Mongolia is north of China.

We also must have water to drink. People get water from rivers, lakes, and springs. In dry places, people dig deep holes in the ground to find water. In cold places, people melt ice. Sometimes, people build dams across rivers to hold back water. Or they dig ponds to catch water when it rains. In these ways, people can store water for future use.

People everywhere need food. All people eat plants. Most people also eat fish, birds, and certain other animals. But people prepare their food in many different ways.

People everywhere wear some form of clothes. In cold climates, people wear heavy clothes to keep warm. In hot climates, people wear less clothing. Clothes protect people from sun and cold, wind and rain.

People everywhere need places to live in. Some people build their homes of wood or stone. Others build homes of grass or clay. People may even build homes of ice and snow. Or they may live in caves or tents. People's homes may look very different. But they all serve the same purposes. A home protects people from the weather. It is a place where people can rest. Home is a place where people can feel safe.

People also need other people. People help each other. They protect each other. They share the work that has to be done. They have fun together. And they care about each other.

People everywhere live in groups. Most people live in families. A group of families may live together in a community. The community may be a village, a town, or a city.

To understand a group of people, we have to study their culture. **Culture** is the way of living shared by the people in a group. People in a culture share behavior, beliefs, language, and artifacts.

Behavior is anything people do. Smiling is a form of behavior. Shaking hands is behavior. Cooking is behavior.

People in the same culture behave like one another. Most of them do the same sorts of things. And they do things in the same ways. They prepare their food in much the same way. They raise their children in the same way. They act like one another when they work or play.

Sharing behavior does not mean that everyone acts exactly alike. People in a culture do not do exactly the same things. But they have the same ways of doing things. They are more alike than different.

A **belief** is anything people think

In warm lands, like Africa, people may live in grass huts.

is true or right. People in a culture believe certain things. They behave the way they do because of their beliefs.

People in a culture also share a **language.** The words in their language have special meanings for them. Other people cannot understand those meanings unless they learn the language. Some cultures have special words. The Innuit (IN yoo it), or Eskimos, have many different words for *snow*. Each word describes a different kind of snow. Other people on Earth live where it never snows. Some languages do not have even one word for *snow*.

People of different cultures make different artifacts. An **artifact** (AHR tuh FAKT) is any object that people make. A cup, a blanket,

In dry lands, people dig holes in the ground to find water. They use jars or buckets to draw water out of these wells.

and a necklace are artifacts. A plow and a wagon are artifacts.

Artifacts tell us something about the people who made them. They show what the people of a culture can do. People who make blankets can weave. People who make wagons know how to use wheels. People who make bronze tools know how to use metals.

In this book, you will be studying Earth's regions. A **region** is an area with the same kind of landforms or climate. You will learn about your own country and other continents. And you will see how people live in different regions of the Earth.

REVIEW

WATCH YOUR WORDS

1. A way of living that a group of people share is their____.
   behavior   belief   culture

2. ____are objects that people make.
   Artifacts   Beliefs   Languages

3. What people do is their____.
   belief   behavior   culture

4. ____ are things people think are true or right.
   Artifacts   Cultures   Beliefs

5. A(n)____has the same kind of landforms or climate.
   artifact   region   culture

CHECK YOUR FACTS

6. Name five things that all people need.

7. Tell three ways by which people get water.

8. Why do people live together in groups?

9. Why do people have homes?

10. Here is a list of ten things. Which of them are artifacts? Which are natural resources?
    clothes   corn   dishes   gold
    coins   oil   ships   water
    weapons   wool

SHARPEN YOUR THINKING

Suppose you found a spear point and an arrowhead in a cave. What could you guess about the people who made them?

CHAPTER REVIEW

WATCH YOUR WORDS

1. A mountain, hill, plateau, or plain is a ___.
   climate   landform   resource

2. Another name for a tableland is a ___.
   mountain   plain   plateau

3. A flat or slightly rolling grassland is a ___.
   plain   plateau   hill

4. A tropical grassland is a ___.
   plateau   savanna   tundra

5. Treeless land where the soil under the surface stays frozen is ___.
   desert   savanna   tundra

6. Treeless land that is too dry for most plants is ___.
   tundra   desert   savanna

7. A place at sea level close to the equator has a ___ climate.
   mid-latitude   tropical   high-latitude

8. Cotton, coal, oil, and rubber are ___.
   artifacts   resources   minerals

9. People who share language, behavior, and beliefs make up a ___.
   culture   continent   region

10. Tools, pots, and arrows are ___.
    natural resources   artifacts
    nonliving resources

CHECK YOUR FACTS

11. What are the four main landforms of Earth?

12. How are the weather and the atmosphere alike? How do the weather and the climate differ?

13. What are the three main kinds of climates? Where do you find each?

14. Name four things that people in a culture share.

15. What is a region?

APPLY YOUR SKILLS

USE YOUR MAPS

16. Look at the physical map on pages 48 and 49. Name mountains in Europe and North America.

17. Look at the climate map on pages 52 and 53. Where are the deserts in the United States?

18. Look at the population map on pages 60 and 61. Which three continents have the most people?

19. Compare the physical map and the population map. On what kind of land do most people live? How high is that land?

20. Compare the climate map and the population map. In what climate areas do most people live?

SHARPEN YOUR THINKING

21. What kind of land do most people like best? Describe the landform, the climate, the soil, and the resources.

22. Think of all the ways we use water. List all the uses you can think of. Now, suppose there was a water shortage. List ways to save water.

23. What did you bring to school with you today? Look in your pocket, wallet, or purse. Look in your bookbag or notebook. Which of these things are artifacts? What resources were they made from? What do they tell about your culture?

24. Suppose you were all alone on an island. Suppose there were no other people to do things for you. What would you have to do for yourself?

25. When would you be cold even if you were close to the equator?

UNIT REVIEW

WATCH YOUR WORDS

Use the words below to complete the unit summary. Use each term only once.

axis
cardinal directions
climate
compass
continents
elevation
equator

globe
grid
key
lines of latitude
lines of longitude
map
Northern Hemisphere

North Pole
oceans
physical maps
planet
political boundaries
political maps
prime meridian

revolves
rotates
scale
seasons
Southern Hemisphere
South Pole
tilt

Earth is a __1__. Earth __2__ around its __3__ once every 24 hours. Every 365 days, Earth __4__ around the sun. The __5__ of Earth's axis causes the __6__ to change.

A round model of Earth is a __7__. The __8__ is an imaginary line that circles Earth in the middle. It is midway between the __9__ and the __10__. It divides Earth into the __11__ and the __12__. The __13__ measure distance north and south of the equator.

The __14__ is an imaginary line that runs north and south through Greenwich, England. The __15__ measure distance east and west of Greenwich.

A flat drawing of Earth is a __16__. A map __17__ tells what the symbols on the map mean. The map __18__ tells how much distance the map covers. The __19__ has arrows that point in the __20__, which are north, south, east, and west. A map __21__ forms a pattern of squares on the map. Some maps show the __22__ between nations. These maps are called __23__. Other maps show the height, or __24__, of land. These maps are called __25__. Earth has seven __26__ and four __27__. Most people live in those parts of Earth where the __28__ makes them comfortable.

CHECK YOUR FACTS

1. What is the solar system?

2. What is Earth's orbit? Why is our year 365 days long?

3. What is Earth's axis?

4. Why is it summer in the Southern Hemisphere when it is winter in the Northern Hemisphere?

5. What is a globe? What is a map?

6. Name four things you can find on a map or globe.

7. What is the equator? What is the Arctic Circle? What is the Antarctic Circle?

8. What is a hemisphere?

9. Why is it hard to show the Earth on a flat map?

10. What is a key on a map? What is a map symbol?

11. What can you do with a map scale?

12. What are the cardinal directions?

13. What is a grid?

14. What are the lines of latitude and longitude? How can you use them?

15. What is the elevation of land?

16. What is a political map? What is a physical map?

17. Name three different ways that mapmakers can use colors on maps.

18. Name the four main landforms of Earth.

19. Name the three main kinds of climates.

20. Name two living resources. Then name four nonliving resources.

SKILL DEVELOPMENT

USE YOUR MAP SKILLS

Use this globe to answer questions **1** and **2**.

1. Identify the following if A is the North Pole.
   a. line *EF*   **b.** line *GH*
   c. line *AB*   **d.** line *CD*
   e. the area between *CD* and point *A*

2. Draw a globe.
   a. Label the North Pole, the South Pole, the equator, the Arctic Circle, and the Antarctic Circle.
   b. Give the latitude of each.
   c. Label the three main climate zones.
   d. Color the climate zone where you live.

3. On a separate sheet of paper, draw an outline of an imaginary place. It could be a continent, a country, or an island. Then put these things on the map:
   a. a distance scale
   b. political boundaries
   c. cities
   d. a compass
   e. rivers and oceans
   f. labels for places on the map
   g. lines of latitude and longitude, with degrees to show where your place is located
   h. symbols that show where cities, roads, lakes, and mountains are

Make your map as fancy as you wish. You can use colors to show anything you like—elevation, climate zones, states, or countries. Use your map to show others what your place is like. Include a key that tells what the symbols and colors mean.

USE YOUR MAPS

4. Look at the map on page 33. List three nations in North America.

5. Look at the map on pages 70 and 71. Give the latitude and longitude of Denver, Colorado.

6. Look at the map on page 30. Measure the distance between Plum Park and Orangedale.

7. Look at the map on pages 48 and 49. What is the elevation of the Himalayas? The Appalachian Mountains?

8. Look at the map on pages 52 and 53. What climates can you find in North America? List them.

SHARPEN YOUR THINKING

9. Suppose Earth was not tilted on its axis. How would life be different on Earth?

10. You are at the North Pole. Your friend is at the South Pole. How far apart are you? Draw a globe with lines of latitude to show how far.

11. You are at 180° west longitude. Your friend is at 180° east longitude. How far apart are you? Draw a map with lines of longitude to show how far.

12. Suppose all the land on Earth was a fertile plain. Suppose the climate everywhere was mild and pleasant. Suppose every place had plenty of living and nonliving resources. Would the population map change? How?

13. Where in the tropics would you find snow? Why?

KNOW YOUR COMMUNITY

14. Get a map of your local community. Tell where you live by giving your latitude and longitude. Describe the climate.

NORTH AMERICA AND
THE UNITED STATES

CANADA

125°W   120°W   115°W   110°W   105°W   100°W

130°W

50°N

45°N

Olympia ★ • Seattle
WASHINGTON

Columbia R.

• Portland
★ Salem

OREGON

★ Boise
IDAHO

Missouri   R.

Helena ★ MONTANA

• Billings

WYOMING

Casper •

NORTH DAKOTA

Bismarck ★

SOUTH DAKOTA
Pierre ★

40°N

NEVADA

San Francisco • ★ Sacramento
Carson City •

35°N

CALIFORNIA

Great
Salt Lake

Salt Lake City ★

UTAH

Cheyenne ★

Denver ★

COLORADO

Pueblo •

NEBRASKA

Omaha •
Lincoln ★

Topeka ★

KANSAS

• Wichita

125°W

Las
Vegas •

Colorado

• Los Angeles

• San Diego

30°N

PACIFIC   OCEAN

ARIZONA

★ Phoenix

Tucson •

Albuquerque • ★ Santa Fe

NEW MEXICO

Tulsa •
Oklahoma City ★

OKLAHOMA

Fort Worth • • Dallas

TEXAS

120°W   115°W

180

170°E   180   170°W   160°W   150°W

ASIA

160°E

Gulf of
California

110°W

170°W

160°W

70°W

140°W

105°W

Austin ★

San Antonio •

Houston •

MEXICO

Arctic Circle

65°N

Rio   Grande

60°N

25°N

0   250   500 Miles

0   250   500 Kilometers

ALASKA

• Fairbanks

• Anchorage

Bering   Sea

170°E

Gulf of Alaska

• Juneau

130°W

55°N

180°   170°W   160°W   150°W   140°W   100°W

CANADA

Lake Superior

MINNESOTA
Duluth

St. Paul
Minneapolis

WISCONSIN
Madison
Milwaukee

Lake Michigan

MICHIGAN
Lansing
Detroit

Lake Huron

IOWA
Des Moines

Chicago
Gary
Toledo
Cleveland

Lake Erie

ILLINOIS
INDIANA
OHIO
Columbus

Springfield
Indianapolis

Kansas City
St. Louis

Jefferson City

MISSOURI

WEST VIRGINIA
Charleston

KENTUCKY
Frankfort
Louisville

Nashville

ARKANSAS

Little Rock

Memphis

TENNESSEE

Lake Ontario
Buffalo

Albany

VERMONT
Montpelier

MAINE
Augusta

NEW HAMPSHIRE
Concord

Boston
MASSACHUSETTS
Providence
RHODE ISLAND
CONNECTICUT
Hartford

NEW YORK

New York

PENNSYLVANIA
Harrisburg
Philadelphia
Trenton
NEW JERSEY

MARYLAND
Dover
DELAWARE
Washington
Annapolis
DISTRICT OF COLUMBIA

Richmond

VIRGINIA

Raleigh

Charlotte
NORTH CAROLINA

Columbia

SOUTH CAROLINA

Atlanta
Charleston

ALABAMA
GEORGIA

Jackson
Montgomery

MISSISSIPPI

LOUISIANA
Baton Rouge
New Orleans

Mobile

Galveston

Tallahassee
Jacksonville

FLORIDA
Tampa

Gulf of Mexico

Miami

ATLANTIC OCEAN

UNITED STATES OF AMERICA: Political
ALBERS EQUAL AREA PROJECTION

National boundaries
State boundaries
• Cities
★ State capitals
✪ National capitals

| 0 | 100 | 200 | 300 Miles |
| 0 | 100 | 200 | 300 Kilometers |

N
NW NE
W E
SW SE
S

Tropic of Cancer

| 0 | 100 Miles |
| 0 | 100 Kilometers |

Honolulu

HAWAII

95°W 90°W 85°W 80°W 75°W 70°W 65°W 60°W 50°N

45°N
60°W
40°N
65°W
35°N
30°N
25°N
20°N

160°W 155°W

85°W 80°W 75°W 70°W

CHAPTER 1 NORTH AMERICA AND ITS PEOPLE

Lesson 1: Land and Climate

FIND THE WORDS

gulf   coast   isthmus
canal   lock   sierra
foothills   prairie   lake

Most of the United States is on the continent of North America. North America is the third-largest continent on Earth. Only Asia and Africa are larger. Europe is much smaller than North America.

Look at North America on a globe. Part of the continent is north of the Arctic Circle. Some islands are less than 10° from the North Pole. Another part of the continent touches South America. The nation of Panama is less than 10° from the equator. So North America covers a lot of the Northern Hemisphere.

Now look at the physical map of North America on page 73. The

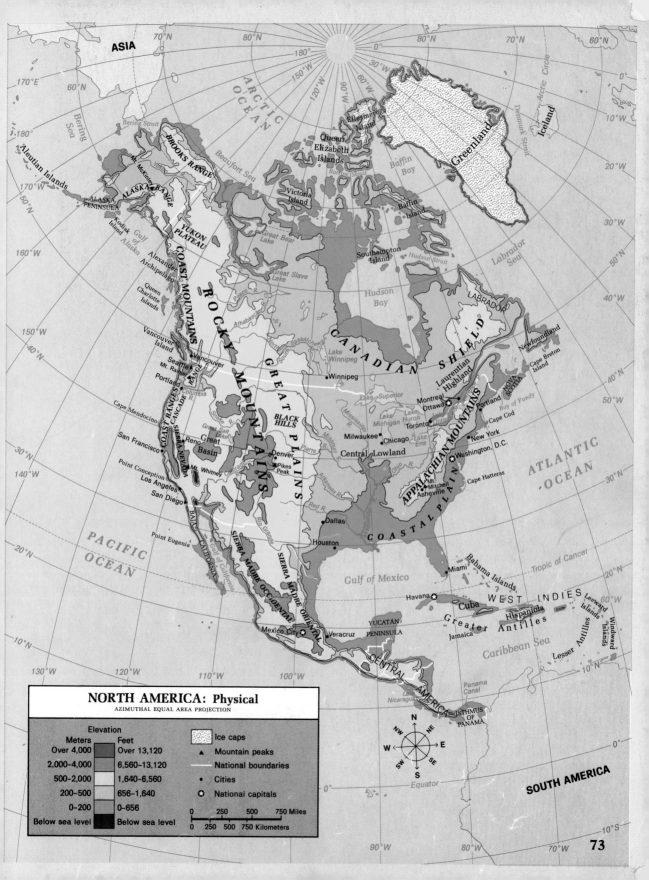

NORTH AMERICA: Physical

AZIMUTHAL EQUAL AREA PROJECTION

Elevation

Meters	Feet
Over 4,000	Over 13,120
2,000–4,000	6,560–13,120
500–2,000	1,640–6,560
200–500	656–1,640
0–200	0–656
Below sea level	Below sea level

- Ice caps
- ▲ Mountain peaks
- National boundaries
- • Cities
- ✪ National capitals

0 250 500 750 Miles
0 250 500 750 Kilometers

ASIA

SOUTH AMERICA

ARCTIC OCEAN

Bering Sea
Bering Strait
Aleutian Islands
ALASKA PENINSULA
Kodiak Island
Gulf of Alaska
ALASKA RANGE
Mt. McKinley
BROOKS RANGE
Beaufort Sea
Queen Elizabeth Islands
Ellesmere Island
Greenland
Iceland
Denmark Strait
Arctic Circle

Victoria Island
Great Bear Lake
Southampton Island
Baffin Island
Baffin Bay
Hudson Strait
Labrador Sea
Newfoundland

YUKON PLATEAU
Great Slave Lake
Peace R.
Athabasca R.
Hudson Bay
LABRADOR
Cape Breton Island

Queen Charlotte Islands
Alexander Archipelago
COAST MOUNTAINS
ROCKY MOUNTAINS
Saskatchewan R.
Lake Winnipeg
CANADIAN SHIELD
Laurentian Highland

Vancouver Island
Vancouver
Seattle
Mt. Rainier
Portland
CASCADE RANGE
COAST RANGES
Columbia R.
Snake R.
North South R.
• Winnipeg
Lake Superior
Lake Michigan
Lake Huron
Montreal
Ottawa ✪
Toronto
Lake Ontario
Lake Erie
NOVA SCOTIA
Portland
Bay of Fundy
Cape Cod
APPALACHIAN MOUNTAINS

Cape Mendocino
San Francisco
Point Conception
Los Angeles
San Diego
Point Eugenia
SIERRA NEVADA
Reno
Great Salt Lake
Great Basin
Mt. Whitney
GREAT PLAINS
BLACK HILLS
Denver •
Pikes Peak
Platte R.
Missouri R.
Mississippi R.
Milwaukee •
• Chicago
Central Lowland
Ohio R.
• New York
Washington, D.C. ✪
Mt. Mitchell
Asheville
Cape Hatteras
ATLANTIC OCEAN

PACIFIC OCEAN

BAJA CALIFORNIA
Gulf of California
SIERRA MADRE OCCIDENTAL
SIERRA MADRE ORIENTAL
Colorado R.
Rio Grande
Arkansas R.
Red R.
• Dallas
• Houston
COASTAL PLAIN
Gulf of Mexico
• Miami
Bahama Islands
Tropic of Cancer

Mexico City ✪
Veracruz
YUCATÁN PENINSULA
Havana ✪
Cuba
Jamaica
Greater Antilles
Hispaniola
WEST INDIES
Leeward Islands
Lesser Antilles
Windward Islands
Caribbean Sea

CENTRAL AMERICA
Lake Nicaragua
Panama Canal
ISTHMUS OF PANAMA

Compass rose: N, NE, E, SE, S, SW, W, NW

Equator

Pacific Ocean is on the west. The Atlantic Ocean is on the east. The Arctic Ocean is to the north. To the south are two smaller parts of the Atlantic Ocean. They are the Gulf of Mexico and the Caribbean (KAR uh BEE un) Sea. A **gulf** is part of an ocean with land curving around it.

The land next to an ocean is called a **coast.** Part of North America is near the Pacific Ocean. That part is called the Pacific Coast or the West Coast. Another part of the continent is near the Atlantic Ocean. That part is called the Atlantic Coast or the East Coast. The land around the Gulf of Mexico is called the Gulf Coast.

Find Panama again. There, a narrow strip of land links North America and South America. That narrow strip of land is called an **isthmus** (ISS muss). The Isthmus of Panama also divides the Pacific Ocean from the Caribbean Sea. In the early 1900s, the United States built the Panama Canal. A **canal** is a waterway that people build across the land. A ship canal connects one body of water with another. Now, ships can sail from the Atlantic to the Pacific. They pass through the Panama Canal.

Fun Facts

Doors are not the only things with locks. Canals have locks, too. A **lock** is part of a canal with gates on either side. It works somewhat like an elevator. First, a ship enters a lock. Then the gates of the lock are closed. Suppose the ship is at sea level. Suppose the next part of the canal is a lake. This lake is above sea level. That means the water in the next part of the canal is higher. So more water is pumped into the lock. The water level in the lock gets higher. The ship rises with the water. Then the gates are opened. The ship can go into the next part of the canal.

Sometimes, the water in the next part of the canal is lower. Then water is drained out of the lock. The water level in the lock gets lower. The ship gets lower, too. Sometimes, a ship goes through two or three locks in a row. In the locks, it is raised or lowered. Then it can sail safely on its way.

Landforms of North America

Do you remember the main landforms of Earth? They are mountains, hills, plateaus, and plains. North America has all these landforms.

Mountains run all the way down the western part of the continent. Find the Rocky Mountains on the map. They are also called the Rockies. This great mountain system stretches from Alaska to New Mexico. The Rockies are the longest, highest mountains in North America. They extend for more than 4,800 kilometers (3,000 miles). The highest mountain in North America is in the Rockies. It is Mount McKinley in Alaska. Mount McKinley is 6,194 meters (20,320 feet) above sea level.

Now find the Appalachian (AP uh LAY chun) Mountains. The Appalachians are the major mountain system in the east. These mountains extend for more than 2,570 kilometers (1,600 miles). The highest mountain in the Appalachians is in North Carolina. It is Mount Mitchell. Mount Mitchell has an elevation of 2,037 meters (6,684 feet). Mount McKinley is three times higher than Mount Mitchell.

South of Alaska, the highest mountain in the United States is Mount Whitney. Mount Whitney is in California. It is in a mountain range called the Sierra (see EHR uh) Nevada. In Spanish, the word *sierra* means "a saw." Pointed mountain peaks look like the teeth of a saw. So a **sierra** is a range of steep mountains. Mount Whitney rises 4,418 meters (14,494 feet) above sea level. It is more than twice as high as Mount Mitchell. The highest mountains in North America are in the west!

Near many mountain ranges are hills. Hills near the bottom of a mountain are called **foothills**. There are many hills and foothills in North America.

North America also has plateaus. Find Mexico City on the physical map on page 73. Mexico City is on the Mexican Plateau. Parts of this plateau are higher than Mount Mitchell. But the land on top of the plateau is flat. Mexico City is 2,380 meters (7,800 feet) above sea level!

North America has several large areas of plains. There are the Great Plains, the Central Lowland, and the coastal plains. The Great Plains are east of the Rocky Mountains. These plains are also a plateau. The western part of the Great Plains is the highest part. This part begins near the foothills of the Rockies. There, the land is 1,830 meters (6,000 feet) above sea level. Gradually, the Great Plains slope downward. The eastern part of the plains is much lower than the western part.

American Indians used to hunt buffaloes on the Great Plains. The buffalo of western North America is called a bison (BY sun).

East of the Great Plains is the Central Lowland. The Central Lowland is very fertile. Many crops are grown there. Large parts of the Central Lowland and Great Plains were once prairies (PREHR eez). A **prairie** is a large area of flat or rolling grassland. It has fertile soil and few trees.

More plains are found along the Atlantic Coast and the Gulf Coast. These are called the coastal plains. In the west, there are coastal ranges of mountains.

Rivers and Lakes of North America

Rivers begin in high lands. They flow from higher lands to lower lands. Find the Mississippi River on the map on page 71. *Mississippi* is an American Indian word. It means "big river." The Mississippi begins in a lake in Minnesota. It flows south to the Gulf of Mexico. Many other rivers flow into the Mississippi.

Another big river in North America is the Missouri. It begins in the Rocky Mountains in western Montana. The Missouri River flows into the Mississippi River. Find the Missouri River on the map on pages 70 and 71. Follow it from western Montana to the Gulf of Mexico. Add on the part where the two rivers flow together. With the lower Mississippi added on, the Missouri is the longest river in North America.

The *Delta Queen* is a famous riverboat. It travels on the lower Mississippi River. The Mississippi flows from 47° north latitude, 94° west longitude to 29° north latitude, 89° west longitude.

The second-longest river in North America flows north, not south. It is the Mackenzie River in Canada. The Mackenzie River begins at Great Slave Lake. It flows northwest into the Arctic Ocean. Another great river in North America is the Rio Grande (REE oh GRAND). *Rio Grande* means "big river" in Spanish. Part of the Rio Grande forms the border between Texas and Mexico. So it divides the United States and Mexico.

The Great Lakes are a famous feature of North America. These five lakes are between the United States and Canada. A **lake** is a body of water surrounded by land. Many lakes have fresh water. The Great Lakes do. They are the largest group of freshwater lakes in the world. Some lakes have salt water, though. Find the Great Salt Lake on the map. It is west of the Great Lakes. This lake is so salty that people floating cannot sink.

Climates of North America

In the south, North America is close to the equator. In the north, it is close to the North Pole. So North America has many different kinds of climates. Tundra and continental climates are found in the far north. There are tropical grasslands and rain forests in the far south. There are highlands in the west. There are deserts in the southwest. You can find North America's many climates on the map below.

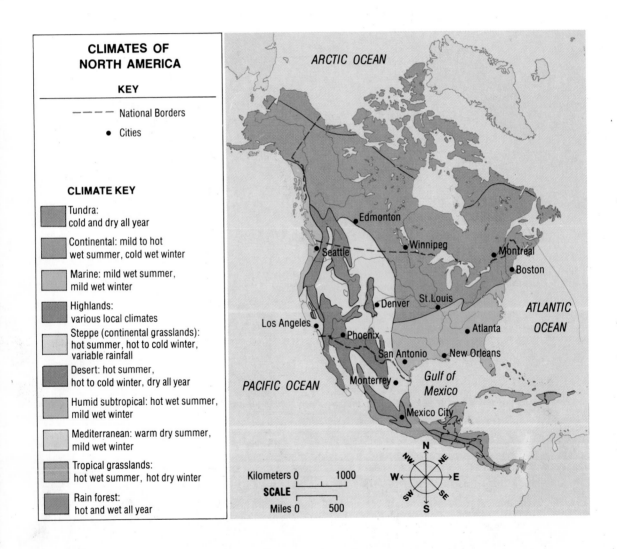

CLIMATES OF NORTH AMERICA

KEY

- - - - - National Borders
• Cities

CLIMATE KEY

Tundra: cold and dry all year

Continental: mild to hot wet summer, cold wet winter

Marine: mild wet summer, mild wet winter

Highlands: various local climates

Steppe (continental grasslands): hot summer, hot to cold winter, variable rainfall

Desert: hot summer, hot to cold winter, dry all year

Humid subtropical: hot wet summer, mild wet winter

Mediterranean: warm dry summer, mild wet winter

Tropical grasslands: hot wet summer, hot dry winter

Rain forest: hot and wet all year

ARCTIC OCEAN

Edmonton

Winnipeg

Seattle

Montreal

Boston

Denver

St. Louis

ATLANTIC OCEAN

Los Angeles

Atlanta

Phoenix

San Antonio

New Orleans

PACIFIC OCEAN

Monterrey

Gulf of Mexico

Mexico City

Kilometers 0 — 1000
SCALE
Miles 0 — 500

Most of the people in North America live in mid-latitude climates. Look at the climate map on page 78. Find the climates from Continental to Mediterranean. These are mid-latitude climates. Most of them have four seasons. Summer is warm or hot. Winter is cool or cold. During spring and fall, the weather changes. Many people enjoy the change of seasons. Others like climates where the weather is much the same all year. Whatever climate people like, they will probably find it in North America!

REVIEW

WATCH YOUR WORDS

1. The land next to an ocean is a
   ___ .
   gulf   canal   coast

2. The part of North America near the Pacific Ocean is called the ___ .
   East Coast   West Coast   Gulf Coast

3. A ___ may have fresh water or salt water.
   lake   sierra   gulf

4. A ___ is part of an ocean.
   canal   gulf   lake

5. A(n) ___ is a waterway built by people.
   gulf   isthmus   canal

6. A ship can be raised or lowered in a ___ .
   lake   lock   gulf

7. A(n) ___ is a narrow strip of land.
   isthmus   prairie   lock

8. A(n) ___ is a range of high, steep mountains.
   prairie   isthmus   sierra

9. ___ are found near the bottom of mountains.
   Sierras   Foothills   Locks

10. ___ are fertile grasslands.
    Locks   Sierras   Prairies

CHECK YOUR FACTS

11. What continents are larger than North America?

12. List North America's three oceans.

13. Where is the Panama Canal? Why is it useful?

14. What are the longest, highest mountains in North America?

15. What is the major mountain system in eastern North America?

16. What is the highest single mountain in North America? Where is it found?

17. List three large areas of plains.

18. Name a river that flows south. Then name one that flows north.

19. What river divides Mexico and the United States?

20. Where are the Great Lakes?

WRITE ABOUT IT

Look at the physical map and the climate map of North America. Suppose you could live anywhere on the continent. What place would you choose? What is the land like there? What is the climate like? Write a paragraph.

Lesson 2: Resources of North America

FIND THE WORDS

dairy   poultry   petroleum
conserve   conservation
preserve   pollution

North America is rich in natural resources. It has a great deal of fertile soil. Corn, wheat, and soybeans grow in most parts of the continent. Oats and barley grow in the west. Potatoes grow in the north. Cotton, rice, peanuts, and sugar cane grow in the south. There are many other crops, too.

North America also has good land for raising cattle and sheep. In the west, cattle are raised for their meat. Around the Great Lakes, they are raised for their milk. Cream, butter, cheese, and ice cream are made from milk. Milk and other foods made from it are called **dairy** products.

Plants and animals are living resources. Look at the map of North America's living resources on page 82. You can see that this continent produces a lot of food. Many different fruits and vegetables grow well in North America. Wheat is used to make bread and cereals. Cattle, hogs, and young sheep provide plenty of meat.

Chickens provide both meat and eggs. Chickens and turkeys are also called **poultry** (POHL tree). Along the coasts and rivers, people catch fish.

North America has resources to clothe its people, too. Cotton grows in the fields. Wool grows on animals. It is cut from sheep. The cotton and wool are used to make cloth and clothing.

North America also has extra resources to sell. Many people on other continents eat food that comes from North America.

North America also has many nonliving resources. The map of nonliving resources on page 83 shows a few of them. There are metals such as iron ore, copper, and lead. These metals are important in manufacturing. North America also has silver and gold. These metals have a high value all over the world.

Many other important minerals are found in North America. Coal and oil are used as fuels. Coal is also used with iron ore to make steel. Coal is like a black rock. Crude oil is a thick, dark liquid. Both coal and crude oil are found under the earth. Sometimes, crude oil is found beneath oceans and seas. Another name for crude oil is **petroleum** (puh TROH lee um). Other kinds of oil come from animals and plants. Whale oil was once used to make candles and fuel for lamps. Corn oil can be used for cooking.

Today, petroleum is one of the most important resources on Earth. It is burned to heat homes and to make electricity. It is also used to make gasoline. Most cars have gasoline engines. They cannot run without petroleum.

There is a lot of petroleum in Mexico. Mexico sells some of this petroleum to other nations. The United States has petroleum in Texas, Oklahoma, Louisiana, California, and Alaska. But the United States does not have enough petroleum to meet its needs. It has to buy the extra petroleum from other nations.

Conserving Resources

There is no limit to the things people want. But there is a limit

Some natural resources can be renewed. Young trees are planted to replace trees that were cut down.

LIVING RESOURCES OF NORTH AMERICA

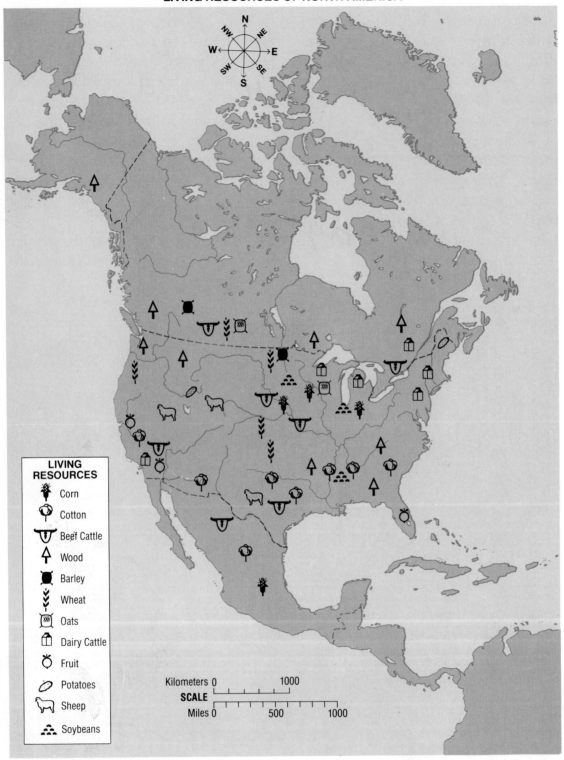

LIVING
RESOURCES

🌽 Corn
🌸 Cotton
🐂 Beef Cattle
↑ Wood
◼ Barley
🌾 Wheat
▣ Oats
🏠 Dairy Cattle
🍑 Fruit
🥔 Potatoes
🐑 Sheep
🔺 Soybeans

Kilometers 0   1000
SCALE
Miles 0   500   1000

NONLIVING RESOURCES OF NORTH AMERICA

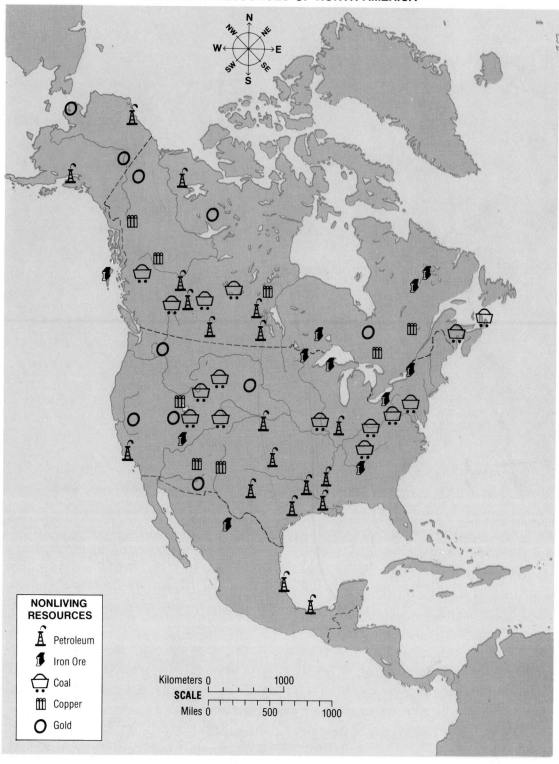

NONLIVING RESOURCES

- Petroleum
- Iron Ore
- Coal
- Copper
- Gold

Kilometers 0 — 1000

SCALE

Miles 0 — 500 — 1000

Elk are in danger of dying out. A game preserve in Grand Teton National Park protects them from hunters. Grand Teton National Park is in Wyoming at 44° north latitude, 110° west longitude.

to the natural resources they have. Some resources can be used and then renewed. Flowing water can be used again and again. It can provide the power to make electricity. Sunlight renews itself every day. It can provide energy to heat homes and make wheels turn. Trees in a forest can be cut down for their wood. Then, more trees can be planted. But it takes many years for a tree to grow. So it is important not to cut too many trees too fast. That could destroy the forests.

Other resources can be used up. They cannot be renewed. They do not replace themselves. When they are used up, they disappear. Coal and petroleum are resources of this kind. It takes millions of years for these minerals to form in the earth! So it is important not to waste them.

To use resources carefully and wisely is to **conserve** them. Wise use of natural resources is called **conservation** (KON sur VAY shun). Resources such as water, forests, soil, and fuels can be conserved.

You conserve a resource when you use some and save some.

Another way to protect resources is to keep them as they are. People **preserve** resources by not letting them be destroyed. For example, some animals are in danger of dying out. Many of these animals are being preserved. No one is allowed to kill any of them. A game preserve is a place where wild animals are protected from hunters. Land in its natural state is preserved in national parks. But many people like to visit the parks. It is hard to protect the land completely. When people use the land, they often change it.

The continent of North America has a great wealth of resources. It has fertile soil, tall trees, and valuable minerals. It also has clean water and fresh air. But sometimes, people make the air and water dirty. Adding something harmful to air or water is called **pollution** (puh LOO shun). Breathing polluted air or drinking polluted water can make people sick.

Through conservation, we can use natural resources wisely. We can protect the air and water from pollution. We can preserve wild animals and natural land. That way, we can help save North America's resources for the future.

REVIEW

WATCH YOUR WORDS

1. Chickens and turkeys are called ———.
   dairy poultry cattle
2. Cheese, milk, and ice cream are ——— products.
   poultry petroleum dairy
3. Gasoline for cars is made from ———.
   petroleum coal copper
4. Wise use of resources is called ———.
   pollution conservation waste
5. Making the air dirty is called ———.
   conservation preservation pollution

CHECK YOUR FACTS

6. List five plants that grow in North America.
7. List three kinds of animals that are raised in North America.
8. How long does it take for coal and petroleum to form in the earth?
9. How do people conserve resources?
10. List two resources that are being preserved.

WRITE ABOUT IT

Suppose North America used up all its coal and petroleum. What might happen then? Write two paragraphs.

Lesson 3: Nations and People of North America

FIND THE WORDS

province   territory   seaway
peninsula   pyramid

Most of the world's continents have many nations. North America has only a few. Three large nations take up most of the continent. They are Canada, the United States, and Mexico. In this lesson, we will study Canada and Mexico. The next chapter will be about the United States.

Look at the political map of North America on page 87. Find Canada, the United States, and Mexico. Which of these nations has the most land? If you said the United States, you are wrong.

Canada

Canada is the largest nation in North America. In fact, Canada is the second-largest nation in the world. Only the Soviet Union has more land than Canada. But Canada does not have many people. Fewer than 25 million people live there. The United States has less land than Canada. But it has more than nine times as many people.

The nation of Canada has 10 provinces. A **province** in Canada is like a state in the United States of America. Canada also has two territories. A **territory** is part of a country that has not yet become a state or province. Find the 10 provinces on the map on page 88. Then find the Yukon Territory and the Northwest Territories. More than one-third of Canada's land is in those two territories. But very few people live there. Winters in those northern regions are very cold. Most of the people of Canada live in the southeast.

Citizens of Canada are called Canadians. Most Canadians live in the provinces of Ontario and Quebec (kwih BEK). Find these two provinces on the map. To the north, these provinces are divided by Hudson Bay. In the south, they border on the United States.

The Great Lakes form most of the southern boundary of Ontario. The United States and Canada share four of these five lakes. They also share the continent's most famous waterfall, Niagara Falls. Niagara Falls is between Lake Ontario and Lake Erie. One part of the falls is in New York. The other part is in Ontario. The capital of Canada is in Ontario. It is Ottawa. Find Ottawa on the map.

NATIONS OF NORTH AMERICA

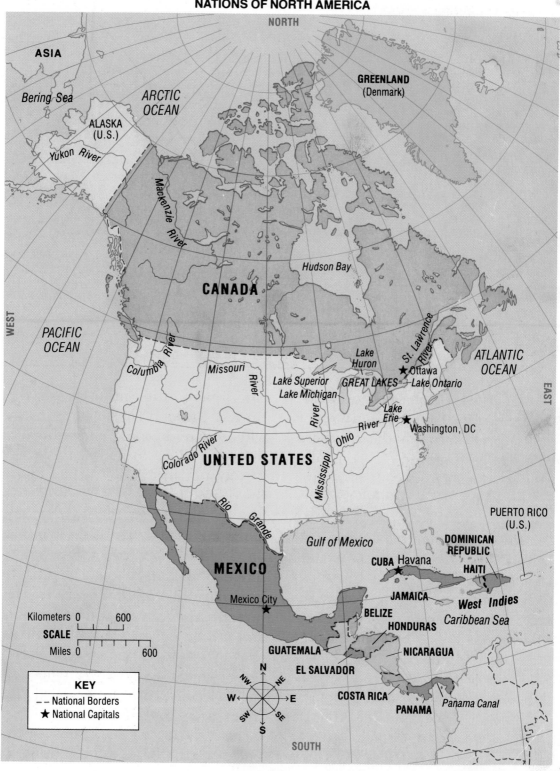

NORTH

ASIA

Bering Sea

ARCTIC OCEAN

GREENLAND
(Denmark)

ALASKA
(U.S.)

Yukon River

Mackenzie River

Hudson Bay

CANADA

WEST

PACIFIC OCEAN

Columbia River

Missouri River

Lake Superior
Lake Michigan

Lake Huron

GREAT LAKES

St. Lawrence River

★ Ottawa
Lake Ontario

ATLANTIC OCEAN

EAST

Lake Erie

Colorado River

UNITED STATES

Ohio River

★ Washington, DC

Mississippi River

Rio Grande

Gulf of Mexico

PUERTO RICO
(U.S.)

DOMINICAN REPUBLIC

MEXICO

CUBA Havana
★

HAITI

Mexico City
★

JAMAICA

West Indies

BELIZE

Caribbean Sea

HONDURAS

GUATEMALA

NICARAGUA

EL SALVADOR

Kilometers 0   600
SCALE
Miles 0   600

N
NW   NE
W   E
SW   SE
S

COSTA RICA

PANAMA

Panama Canal

KEY
- - National Borders
★ National Capitals

SOUTH

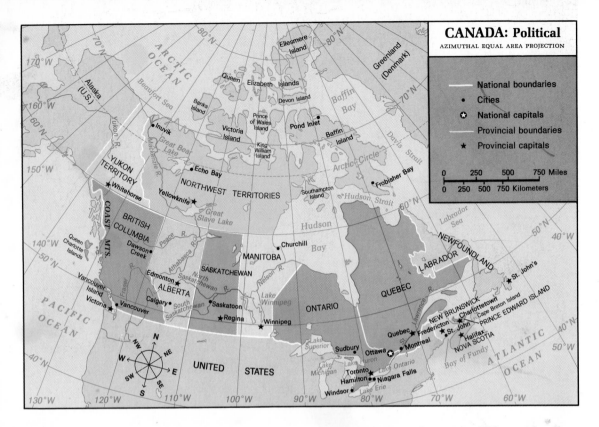

CANADA: Political
AZIMUTHAL EQUAL AREA PROJECTION

— National boundaries
• Cities
⊛ National capitals
— Provincial boundaries
★ Provincial capitals

0   250   500   750 Miles
0   250 500 750 Kilometers

The province of Quebec is east of Ontario. The St. Lawrence River flows through the southern part of this province. There is also a city named Quebec. It is on the St. Lawrence River. Find the city of Quebec on the map.

Do you remember what you learned about the Panama Canal? Canals have also been built between the United States and Canada. These canals link the St. Lawrence River and the Great Lakes. The canals are part of the St. Lawrence Seaway. This **seaway** is a water route to and from the ocean. Ships sail from the Atlantic Ocean through the river and canals to the lakes. That way, they

can reach the middle of the United States! These ships carry wheat, wood, coal, and iron ore from one place to another.

Canada has many other large rivers besides the St. Lawrence. It has thousands of islands. It has more lakes than any other nation on Earth! There are many other interesting facts about Canada. It is a nation of differences. In the far north, there is almost always ice and snow. In the south, there are great forests. In the west, there are huge cattle ranches. In the east, on Prince Edward Island, there are small farms. Canada's largest cities are in the south. Look at the map of Canada on

Ships use the St. Lawrence Seaway to travel between the Atlantic Ocean and the Great Lakes. The seaway extends from Montreal (about 74° west longitude) to Lake Superior (about 85° west longitude).

page 88. Find the cities of Montreal and Toronto. Then find Vancouver and Winnipeg.

One very important difference in Canada is language. Most Canadians speak English. But more than 7 million Canadians speak French. French is the language of the province of Quebec. The city of Montreal is in Quebec. There, French is spoken by almost everyone. Some people want Quebec to become a separate nation. Others want Quebec to remain a part of Canada. Many people in Canada speak both English and French. They like knowing two languages.

Did you know that some children in Maine go to French schools in Canada? Their families are French Canadians. These families moved south to the United States. But they still speak French as their native language. Every school day, the children cross the border into Canada. They go to a French school in the province of Quebec.

Canada has a wealth of natural resources. It also has many factories and manufactures many goods. Canada sells paper, wood, and minerals to the United States. The United States sells cars, clothes, machines, and other goods to Canada. These two giant nations depend on each other. They are good neighbors.

Mexico City may soon be the largest city on Earth. It lies on the Mexican Plateau, at 19° north latitude, 99° west longitude.

Mexico

The United States has another good neighbor to the south. It is Mexico. Mexico is divided into 31 states and 1 federal district. The full name of the nation is the United Mexican States.

Citizens of Mexico are called Mexicans. Most Mexicans speak Spanish. More than 70 million people live in Mexico today. And the population is growing very fast. When you grow up, Mexico may have more than 125 million people!

Find Mexico on the physical map of North America on page 73. The Gulf of Mexico is on the east. The Pacific Ocean is on the west. Part of Mexico is directly south of California. This part is called Baja (BAH hah) California. The word *baja* means "low" in Spanish. On a map, Baja California looks like a long, narrow finger of land. There is water to the west and east of it. Land almost surrounded by water is called a **peninsula.** Mexico has another peninsula in the southeast. It curves upward like a hook. It is the Yucatán (YOO kuh TAN) Peninsula.

Like Canada, Mexico is a nation of great differences. Much of the north is desert. Much of the south is covered by tropical rain forests. In the east and west are mountains, the Sierra Madres (MAH drays). In the middle of Mexico is the Mexican Plateau. Most of Mexico's people live on the plateau. There, the climate is cool and dry. It is more comfortable than the desert and rain forests.

Mexico City is on the Mexican Plateau. It is the capital of Mexico. It is one of the highest cities on Earth. Soon, it may be the world's largest city! More than 16 million people live in or near it.

Not all Mexicans live in cities. Most live in villages and raise food on farms. Mexican farmers grow a lot of cotton, corn, and squash. They also raise cattle and grow coffee and sugar cane. Many Mexican farmers are poor. Their farms are small. Sometimes the soil is not very good. Often, these farmers use old-fashioned ways of farming.

Other farms in Mexico are large and modern. They have good soil. The owners of these farms use new and better ways of farming. They add minerals to the soil to make it richer. They use special seeds that grow large crops. They hire people to work in their fields. They use large farm machines. Money is needed to use these methods. Poor farmers cannot afford them. In Mexico, there is a great gap between the rich and the poor. They live very different lives.

Some Mexican families have moved north to the United States. These people are called Mexican-Americans. Their children often go to schools where two languages are used. The children speak Spanish as their native language. They are learning English in school.

Mexico buys many goods from other nations. It buys more than it sells. But this may change. In the 1970s, large amounts of petroleum

Many people from other nations visit Mexico. Cancun (kan KOON) is a vacation area on the Caribbean Sea.

were found in Mexico. Now, petroleum is Mexico's most important mineral resource. Mexico is selling petroleum to other nations. This resource promises a better future for the people of Mexico.

Central America

South of Mexico is a region called Central America. Central America is between North America and South America. It is part of the continent of North America. But in climate and culture, it is more like South America.

Look at the political map of North America on page 87. Central America has twice as many nations as the rest of North America! Guatemala (GWAH tuh MAH luh) and Honduras (hon DOO russ) are there. So are Nicaragua (NIK uh RAH gwah) and El Salvador. Costa Rica, Panama, and Belize (buh LEEZ) are in Central America, too. Find these nations on the map.

The West Indies

East of Central America are islands called the West Indies. Some of these islands are also nations. Cuba is the largest of these islands. It is a nation. East of Cuba on another island are two more nations. They are Haiti and the Dominican Republic. East of the Dominican Republic is Puerto Rico (PWEHR toh REE koh). Puerto Rico is part of the United States. Many people from Mexico, Central America, and the West Indies now live in the United States.

The Maya built great pyramids. They put temples on top. This pyramid is called the Castle. It is at Chichén-Itzá (chuh chen ut SAH) at about 21° north latitude, 89° west longitude.

People of North America

We studied the nations of North America from north to south. We can study the people the same way. Experts think the first people came to North America thousands of years ago. At that time, part of the Bering Sea was land. People could walk across from Asia to North America!

The early people who came from Asia are now called American Indians. These people were the first Americans. Some of them stayed in Alaska and Canada. Others settled in the plains and woodlands of the United States. Still others went south to Mexico and Central America. There, they created great cultures long before people from Europe came.

One of the greatest cultures was that of the Maya (MAH yah). The Maya lived on the Yucatán Peninsula. There, they built great **pyramids** (PIR uh midz) with temples on top. A Mayan pyramid was not a tomb. It was a place of worship. The Mayan priests studied the movements of the moon and planets. They were expert at math. They made a calendar as good as the one we use today.

Later, the Aztecs came to power. They built Mexico City on two islands in the middle of a lake. In the lake, they built floating gardens. They grew vegetables and flowers there. Now the lake has been drained and filled in. But you can still visit floating gardens in Mexico City. And in parts of Mexico, you can climb pyramids.

Another group of people from Asia called themselves the Innuit (IN yoo it). *Innuit* means "the people." Others called these people Eskimos. *Eskimo* means "someone who eats raw fish." The Innuit stayed in the far north. They

This Innuit hunter uses a telescope to look for seals. He is in the Arctic region.

learned how to live in a cold climate. They fished for their food. They also hunted seals, whales, and deer. They used the animal skins to make clothes, tents, and canoes. They used whale oil for fuel. They kept strong dogs to pull their sleds across the snow. Sometimes, they even built houses out of blocks of ice. A house like this is called an igloo. Some of the Innuit still follow their old ways. Others have found new jobs. Some

now work in mines or help drill for petroleum. The Innuit are still using the resources of their land.

In the 1500s, people from Europe began to come to North America. People from Spain came to Mexico and Central America. People from France and England settled in Canada. The English, French, and Spanish also settled in the United States. Since that time, people have come to North America from all over the Earth!

REVIEW

WATCH YOUR WORDS

1. Canada is divided into 10____.
   seaways   territories   provinces
2. Canada has two ____ in the far north.
   territories   provinces   states
3. The St. Lawrence River is part of a(n)____.
   peninsula   seaway   isthmus
4. Baja California is a____.
   seaway   province   peninsula
5. The Maya built ____ on the Yucatán Peninsula.
   canals   pyramids   seaways

CHECK YOUR FACTS

6. What nation in North America has the most land?

7. Do most Canadians live in the northwest or the southeast?
8. Where is the St. Lawrence Seaway? What is it?
9. Name two languages spoken in Canada.
10. What language do most Mexicans speak?
11. What is a peninsula?
12. Where do most Mexicans live? Why?
13. What is Mexico's most important mineral resource?
14. Where is Central America?
15. How did the Innuit use natural resources to live?

SHARPEN YOUR THINKING

Why do you think so many people settled in North America?

CHAPTER REVIEW

WATCH YOUR WORDS

1. A waterway was built across the ____ of Panama.
   Gulf   Isthmus   Peninsula

2. Ships can sail from one ocean to another through the Panama ____.
   Sierra   Peninsula   Canal

3. A(n) ____ is part of a canal.
   lock   isthmus   sierra

4. Canals are part of the St. Lawrence ____.
   Isthmus   Seaway   Lake

5. The ____ of Mexico is part of the Atlantic Ocean.
   Lake   Bay   Gulf

6. A ____ is land almost surrounded by water.
   pyramid   peninsula   sierra

7. The grasslands in the middle of North America were called ____.
   foothills   sierras   prairies

8. A(n) ____ is a range of mountains with pointed peaks.
   sierra   isthmus   pyramid

9. You can ____ a resource by using less of it.
   pollute   destroy   conserve

10. You can ____ a resource by keeping it from being destroyed.
    waste   preserve   pollute

CHECK YOUR FACTS

11. Name three of North America's coasts.

12. List three landforms found in North America. Give an example of each.

13. Where are North America's highest mountains?

14. Where are the Great Plains?

15. Name two of North America's longest rivers.

16. How are the Great Lakes like the Great Salt Lake? How do they differ?

17. Name four North American climates.

18. List four living resources and four non-living resources of North America.

19. List two resources that can be renewed and two that cannot.

20. What are the three largest nations of North America?

APPLY YOUR SKILLS

USE YOUR MAP SKILLS

21. Draw or trace an outline map of North America.

22. Label the Rocky Mountains and the Appalachian Mountains.

23. Label the Atlantic Ocean, the Pacific Ocean, the Arctic Ocean, the Bering Sea, the Caribbean Sea, the Gulf of Mexico, and Hudson Bay.

24. Label the three largest nations.

25. Label the capital cities of Canada, the United States, and Mexico.

SHARPEN YOUR THINKING

26. How would ships get from the Atlantic Ocean to the Pacific Ocean without the Panama Canal?

27. How are Canada and Mexico alike? How are they different?

28. Suppose you had been one of the early peoples from Asia. Would you have stayed in Alaska or moved to Mexico? Tell why.

USE YOUR RESEARCH SKILLS

29. Find out more about the Maya, the Aztecs, or the Innuit. Use your library. Write a report. Then make an oral report to the class.

2 A NATION OF STATES

Lesson 1: The United States

FIND THE WORDS

colony	state	legislature
Congress	governor	capital
capitol	federal district	
commonwealth	territory	

The United States is a giant nation. It stretches across the center of North America, from coast to coast. It includes Alaska far in the north. It includes Hawaii far

out in the Pacific Ocean. The United States ranks fourth among the world's nations in land. It also ranks fourth in numbers of people. Look at the chart on page 97. It shows which three nations have more land than the United States. It also shows which three nations have more people.

The United States may not be the largest nation in the world. But it is the world's most powerful nation. Size alone does not make a nation great. More important than size is good government.

From Colonies to States

Today, the United States includes 50 states. But the nation began as 13 colonies. A **colony** is an area of land that a foreign country rules. It is also the group of people who settle in such a place.

Great Britain started its first successful colony in North America in 1607. By 1776, there were 13 colonies along the East Coast.

Then, on July 4, 1776, these colonies changed the world. People from the 13 colonies signed the Declaration of Independence. In this paper, the colonies said they were free and independent states. A **state** has its own government. It is not ruled by another country.

The 13 states joined together to form the United States. They set up a new form of government. The states agreed that each state would send representatives to Congress. A group of representatives that meets to make laws is a **legislature** (LEJ iss LAY chur). **Congress** is the legislature of the United States.

The people of each state vote for President. They elect members of Congress. They also elect a governor and a state legislature. A **governor** is the chief leader of a state. In many ways, a governor is like the President.

Every state has a capital city. A **capital** is the city where the government of a state or a nation meets. A capital city is usually marked on a map with a star.

A **capitol** is a building where a legislature meets. In the capital city of your state, you can see the capitol building. The capital of the United States is Washington, DC. The Capitol is the building in Washington where Congress meets. Look at the picture of the Capitol on page 96.

FIVE LARGE NATIONS

Nation	Area		Number of people
	square miles	square kilometers	
SOVIET UNION	8,600,383	22,274,900	272,500,000
CANADA	3,831,033	9,992,330	25,142,000
UNITED STATES	3,679,201	9,529,081	236,413,000
CHINA	3,630,747	9,403,600	1,034,097,000
INDIA	1,237,061	3,203,975	746,388,000

Other Parts of the Whole

Some parts of the United States are not states. The nation also includes the District of Columbia and the Commonwealth of Puerto Rico. Several territories are also part of the United States.

The District of Columbia is between Maryland and Virginia. It is a **federal district.** That is an area where a national capital is located. The City of Washington is in the District of Columbia. So it is called Washington, DC. The city and the district are exactly the same size. That way, the national capital is not in any state.

The Commonwealth of Puerto Rico (PWEHR toh REE koh) is on islands south of Florida. A **commonwealth** is a place that is governed by its people. Some states are called commonwealths. Puerto Rico is not a state. But it is part of the United States.

A U.S. **territory** is an area governed by the United States. It is not a state, district, or commonwealth. However, 31 of the 50 states were once territories or parts of territories. The United States now has several island territories. Guam is an island territory in the Pacific Ocean.

REVIEW

WATCH YOUR WORDS

1. The city where a state government meets is the ___.
   capitol   Congress   capital
2. The building where a state legislature meets is the ___.
   capital   capitol   colony
3. A ___ is a group that meets to make laws.
   capitol   legislature   state
4. Puerto Rico is a ___.
   territory   state   commonwealth
5. Guam is a ___.
   state   territory   district
6. Washington, DC, is in a ___.
   federal district   state   colony

CHECK YOUR FACTS

7. What is the difference between a colony and a state?
8. How many states were there when the United States began?

USE YOUR CHART

9. What nations are larger than the United States in both land and people?
10. What nation has more land but fewer people? What nation has more people but less land?

SHARPEN YOUR THINKING

Why shouldn't the nation's capital be in one of the states? Give reasons.

Lesson 2: The New England States

Maine New Hampshire Vermont
Massachusetts Rhode Island Connecticut

FIND THE WORDS

bay hardwood softwood

Six states in the northeast are known as New England. They are Maine, New Hampshire, Vermont, Massachusetts, Rhode Island, and Connecticut. Look at the chart on this page. The six states in New England are small in area. Even so, several of these states have many people. Most of the people live in southern New England.

Many live along the Atlantic Coast.

The coast of New England is rocky and uneven. Find Cape Cod on the map on page 101. It is a hook of land that juts into the Atlantic Ocean. There, in a sheltered bay, the Pilgrims landed in 1620. A **bay** is a part of the ocean with land part way around it.

The Pilgrims had sailed from Plymouth, England, to Massachusetts. There, they started the first lasting colony north of Virginia.

THE NEW ENGLAND STATES

State name and nickname		Date state entered union	Area		Number of people	State capital
			square miles	square kilometers		
Maine (Pine Tree State)		1820	33,215	86,027	1,156,000	Augusta
New Hampshire (Granite State)		1788	9,304	24,097	977,000	Concord
Vermont (Green Mountain State)		1791	9,609	24,887	530,000	Montpelier
Massachusetts (Bay State)		1788	8,257	21,386	5,798,000	Boston
Rhode Island (Ocean State)		1790	1,214	3,144	962,000	Providence
Connecticut (Constitution State)		1788	5,009	12,973	3,154,000	Hartford

Another group from England, the Puritans, came next. Soon, some settlers left Massachusetts to start other colonies. By 1790, four New England colonies were states of the United States.

Land and Climate

West of the coast, New England has many highlands and mountains. Several Appalachian Mountain ranges are in New England. In summer, visitors can hike in the Green Mountains of Vermont. They can listen to music in the Berkshire Hills of Massachusetts. They can also visit the White Mountains of New Hampshire. Some of the White Mountains are named for Presidents. The tallest is Mount Washington. There, visitors can ride in a train to the top of the mountain.

New England has a varied climate. In spring and fall, the air is crisp and cool. Winters are cold and snowy. Then, people from many Eastern states come to the mountains to ski. In summer, the weather gets warm or hot. Then, many people go swimming and boating at Cape Cod. New England is also famous for its forests. Fall brings a blaze of color to the

Fun Facts

Many people think Captain John Smith named New England because the coast reminded him of England. Settlers often named their new homes for the places they had left.

What is a Yankee? A Yankee can be a Northerner in general or a New Englander in particular. In other nations, a Yankee can be any citizen of the United States.

Massachusetts was the place where the Pilgrims landed in 1620. The first Thanksgiving was celebrated there.

Maine once held its elections 2 months before the other states did. People believed other states would vote the way Maine had. They said, "As Maine goes, so goes the nation."

New Hampshire is always the first state to choose a candidate for President. Everyone running for President tries to get New Hampshire's votes.

Rhode Island is the smallest state. But it has more people than the largest state, Alaska! Rhode Island was founded by Roger Williams and Anne Hutchinson. Each of them went there to find religious freedom.

Connecticut was the first state to use modern methods of manufacturing. It was the home of Eli Whitney, a famous inventor.

Vermont is famous for its mountains, marble, and maple syrup. The Green Mountains gave the state its name. *Ver mont* means "green mountain" in French.

Sometimes, you could get blown away on top of Mount Washington in New Hampshire. This mountain had one of the highest surface winds ever recorded on Earth. On April 12, 1934, the wind blew there at 372 kilometers (231 miles) per hour!

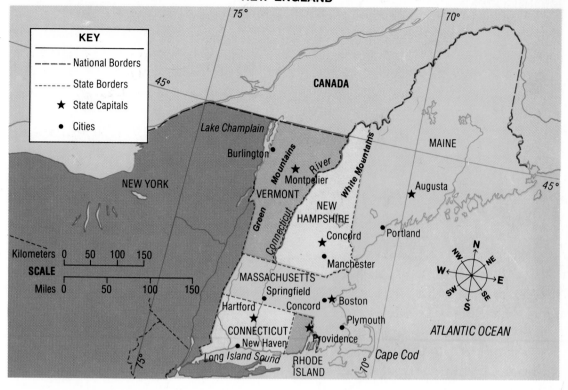

region. The leaves turn brilliant shades of red, yellow, and gold. Many visitors travel to New England to see the autumn leaves.

Resources

For New England, the Atlantic Ocean is a valuable resource. In the past, many of the people made a living by fishing. Some New Englanders hunted whales all over the world. Others caught fish such as cod and mackerel. New England is still famous for its fish and shellfish. Many people like to eat New England clam chowder.

Land in New England is not very good for farming. In most places, the soil is very thin. But New England is a good place for dairy farms. The cows can eat grass on the hillsides. The poor soil can be used to grow hay. People in the cities buy the milk products. Vermont is famous for its cheese.

Some parts of New England are known for special farm products. In Maine, farmers grow potatoes. In Vermont, people make maple syrup from the sap of sugar maple trees. Rhode Island is noted for its chickens, called Rhode Island Reds. In Massachusetts, farmers grow cranberries for cranberry sauce.

Visitors to Plymouth Plantation see what a Pilgrim village was like. The Pilgrims landed at 42° north latitude, 71° west longitude.

The thick forests of northern New England are another living resource. Some of the trees are cut down for their wood. Trees that lose their leaves, such as oaks and maples, are **hardwoods.** Hardwood goes to sawmills. It is cut into boards and used to build things. Trees with cones and needles, such as pines, are **softwoods.** Softwood can be ground up and used to make pulp. Then the wood pulp is used to make paper.

Manufacturing, Business, and Trade

Most people in New England make their living by manufacturing. Once, most factories in the United States were in New England. The mills of New England spun the nation's cotton and woolen cloth. Other New England factories made shoes and boots. New Englanders became famous as traders. Yankee merchants were known all over the world. The nation's fastest sailing ships were built in Mystic, Connecticut.

Today, New England still makes cloth and paper products. But now many cloth and clothing factories have moved to the Southern States. Some new factories have come to take their place. Now machines and plastics are made in New England. So are electrical products. Airplane engines, helicopters, and submarines are built in Connecticut.

Many New Englanders provide services to visitors. They run restaurants, gift shops, and hotels. New England is noted for its schools. It has famous colleges such as Harvard and Yale.

Places to Go

In December 1620, the Pilgrims anchored their ship, the *Mayflower*, near Plymouth Rock. Today, you can still see Plymouth Rock in Plymouth, Massachusetts. You can visit a ship built to look like the *Mayflower*. You can also visit a "living museum" nearby. It is called Plymouth Plantation. The people who work there dress like Pilgrims. You can see what life in a Pilgrim village was like.

Boston is the capital of Massachusetts. In Boston, you can walk along the Freedom Trail. You can see many places that have been important in American history.

REVIEW

WATCH YOUR WORDS

1. A ___ tree loses its leaves in the fall.
   softwood   hardwood   prairie
2. A ___ tree has needles and cones.
   prairie   hardwood   softwood
3. A(n) ___ is part of the ocean partly surrounded by land.
   peninsula   bay   island

CHECK YOUR FACTS

4. List the six states in New England.
5. Where and when did the Pilgrims land?
6. List four farm products of New England.
7. What are two ways in which wood is used?
8. List three modern products made in New England.

USE YOUR CHART

9. Four New England states were among the original 13 states. List them.
10. What was the last New England state to enter the Union?

11. Which New England state has the most land?
12. Which New England state has the most people?
13. Does the state with the least land have the fewest people?

USE YOUR MAP

14. Which New England state is not on the Atlantic Coast?
15. Name the river that forms the border between New Hampshire and Vermont.

USE YOUR MAP SKILLS

16. Your teacher will give you an outline map and a regional fact sheet to fill out. Using the fact sheet, complete the map of the New England States. You will do six maps of state regions in this chapter. At the end, you can tape them together to make a map of the United States.

SHARPEN YOUR THINKING

Why do you suppose the Pilgrims anchored their ship in a bay?

Lesson 3: The Middle Atlantic States

New York   New Jersey   Pennsylvania
Delaware   Maryland   West Virginia

FIND THE WORDS

harbor   natural gas   port

The Middle Atlantic States are south or west of the New England States. Six states and the District of Columbia are in this region. More than 40 million people live in the Middle Atlantic States. That is about 19 out of every 100 people in the United States.

People from northern Europe settled the Middle Atlantic States. Five of the Middle Atlantic States were among the original 13 states. In fact, Delaware was the first state to join the Union.

Land and Climate

Mountains stretch across much of New York, Pennsylvania, and West Virginia. You can see them on the map. Find the Adirondack

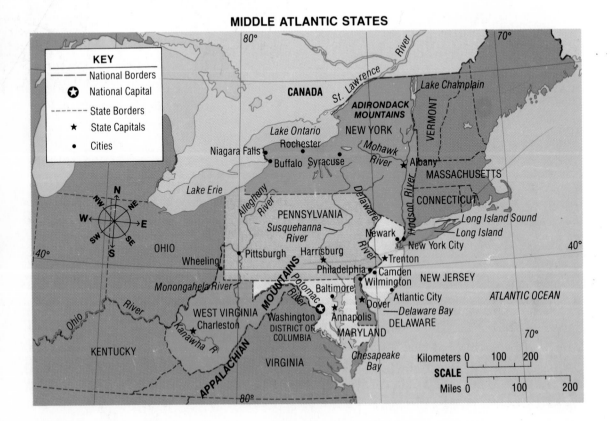

MIDDLE ATLANTIC STATES

KEY
— — National Borders
⊗ National Capital
- - - - - State Borders
★ State Capitals
• Cities

Mountains in New York. There are also mountains in Pennsylvania, Maryland, and West Virginia. These ranges are part of the Appalachian Mountain chain.

Not many people live in the mountains. But millions of people live on the low plain along the coast. There, the land is flat and the climate is favorable. Look at the map again. Trace with your finger from New York City to Washington, DC. Few regions of Earth have as many people as this region. Some of the nation's largest cities are here. Find New York, Philadelphia, Baltimore, and Washington on the map. There are many more cities along the coast. The Middle Atlantic coast has good harbors for ships. A **harbor** is a protected place on a coast where ships can anchor. Other large cities are found near the Great Lakes and near important rivers.

Resources

The Middle Atlantic States have farms as well as cities. There are large poultry farms in Maryland, Delaware, and New Jersey. They supply millions of chickens and eggs. All the Middle Atlantic States have vegetable farms. New York also has dairy farms. Still, the states of the Middle Atlantic region do not raise all the food they need. They buy a lot of their food from other regions.

The Statue of Liberty is in New York harbor at 41° north latitude, 74° west longitude.

Rivers, lakes, and the Atlantic Ocean are natural resources of this region. Pennsylvania and West Virginia have important mineral resources, too. West Virginia supplies much of the nation's coal and natural gas. **Natural gas** is a mixture of gases found in the ground. Like coal, it is used as a fuel. Coal and iron ore are found in Pennsylvania. They are used to make steel. There are many steel mills in Pennsylvania.

THE MIDDLE ATLANTIC STATES

State name and nickname	Date state entered union	Area square miles	Area square kilometers	Number of people	State capital
New York (Empire State)	1788	49,576	128,402	17,735,000	Albany
New Jersey (Garden State)	1787	7,836	20,295	7,515,000	Trenton
Pennsylvania (Keystone State)	1787	45,333	117,412	11,901,000	Harrisburg
Delaware (First State)	1787	2,057	5,328	613,000	Dover
Maryland (Old Line State)	1788	10,577	27,394	4,349,000	Annapolis
West Virginia (Mountain State)	1863	24,181	62,629	1,952,000	Charleston

Fun Facts

The United States has had three capitals. All three have been in the Middle Atlantic region. New York City was the first capital of the United States. In 1789, George Washington was sworn in as President in New York. Philadelphia was the capital from 1790 until 1800. Then Washington, DC, became the capital in 1800.

Pennsylvania was founded by William Penn. The state name means "Penn's woods" in Latin.

New Jersey was the scene of 90 battles in the American Revolution. In one battle, Mary Ludwig Hays carried water to the soldiers. They called her Molly Pitcher. Another woman, Margaret Corbin, fought bravely in a battle in New York.

Delaware is the second-smallest state in the nation. It was named for Baron De la Warr. Until 1792, Delaware had a president, not a governor.

Maryland was a scene of battle in the War of 1812. There, the British attacked a fort in Baltimore. British ships fired bombs at the fort. But they could not get too close. The Americans had sunk ships to block the harbor. When the attack was over, the American flag was still flying. This inspired Francis Scott Key to write our national anthem, "The Star-Spangled Banner."

West Virginia wanted to stay in the Union during the Civil War. So it separated from Virginia and became the 35th state.

Manufacturing and Transportation

Many factories are found in the Middle Atlantic States. New York makes a variety of products, from clothing to cameras. New York, New Jersey, and Pennsylvania make machines and chemicals. West Virginia manufactures glass. Steel is made in Pennsylvania and West Virginia. These are only a few of the many products made in the Middle Atlantic States.

The Middle Atlantic States have many means of transportation. They have long highways, bridges, and tunnels. They have many railroads and airports. They have good river ports and seaports. A **port** is a town on the water where ships can load and unload. Cars, trucks, trains, planes, and ships move people and goods around.

Places to Go

New York is the largest city in the United States. In fact, it is one of the largest cities in the world. At New York, the Hudson River flows into the Atlantic Ocean. The harbor there is a fine place for ships to anchor. Ships and planes from all over the world come to New York. New York also has busy highways and railroads. It is a center of transportation.

Most of the nation's books and magazines are published in New York. Many television programs are made there. New York is world-famous for its Broadway plays. News and ideas from New York go all over the nation.

Every year, millions of people visit New York. They go to see the Statue of Liberty and the Empire State Building. They visit Wall Street, where traders buy and sell shares in the nation's businesses.

Independence Hall is in Philadelphia. The Declaration of Independence was signed there on July 4, 1776. Philadelphia is at 40° north latitude, 75° west longitude.

Philadelphia is another great city in this region. Independence Hall is in Philadelphia. In 1776, the Declaration of Independence was signed in Independence Hall. You can see the room where it was signed. Philadelphia is also the home of the Liberty Bell. The United States Mint was started in Philadelphia. The mint is the place which makes the nation's money. In Philadelphia, you can see how money is made. You can also visit the house where Betsy Ross lived. Some people believe she made the first American flag.

REVIEW

WATCH YOUR WORDS

1. A protected place on a coast where ships can anchor is a(n)____.
   isthmus   harbor   canal
2. A town on the water where ships can unload is a____.
   port   lock   seaway
3. ____ is a mixture of gases found in the ground.
   Coal   Iron ore   Natural gas

CHECK YOUR FACTS

4. List the six states of the Middle Atlantic region.
5. Which was the first state to join the Union?
6. List four large cities in the Middle Atlantic region.
7. Name a mineral resource that is found in both Pennsylvania and West Virginia.
8. Where was the Declaration of Independence signed?

USE YOUR CHART

9. Which Middle Atlantic state has the most people?
10. Which Middle Atlantic state entered the Union last?
11. Find a very small state with more than 5 million people

USE YOUR MAP

12. Which Middle Atlantic states are not on the Atlantic Coast?
13. What river forms the boundary between Pennsylvania and New Jersey?

USE YOUR MAP SKILLS

14. Your teacher will give you an outline map and a regional fact sheet to fill out. Using the fact sheet, complete the map of the Middle Atlantic States.

SHARPEN YOUR THINKING

15. What kinds of transportation does your state have?
16. Why did people build cities on seacoasts and by lakes and rivers?

Lesson 4: The Southern States

**Virginia   North Carolina   South Carolina
Georgia   Florida   Kentucky   Tennessee
Alabama   Mississippi   Arkansas   Louisiana
Oklahoma   Texas**

FIND THE WORDS

**wilderness   barge   delta
swamp   refine**

There are 13 states in the South. The Southern States cover almost a fourth of the land in the United States. They have more than a fourth of the people. Over 70 million people live in the Southern States. That is 30 out of every 100 Americans.

Today, the South is growing faster than most other parts of the nation. Many people and businesses are moving to the Southern States. These states have a mild climate. All 13 states gained population from 1970 to 1980.

THE SOUTH

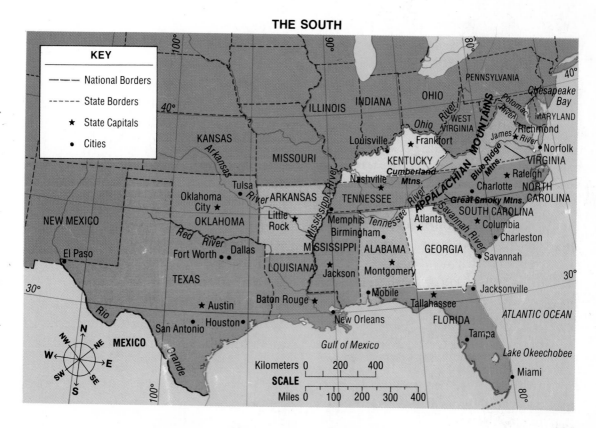

KEY

- - - - National Borders
- - - - State Borders
★ State Capitals
• Cities

History

The South has always been a very important region. The history of the colonies and the nation began there. In 1565, the Spanish built a fort at St. Augustine, Florida. This was the first lasting European settlement in the United States. Later, in 1607, the first lasting English colony began in Jamestown, Virginia.

Virginia, North Carolina, South Carolina, and Georgia were among the original 13 states. All four of these states are on the East Coast. Next, settlers began to move west of the Appalachian Mountains. For a long time, these mountains had blocked the way west. Then, explorers found the Cumberland Gap. It was a natural opening between the mountains. American Indian trails led on into Kentucky. In 1775, Daniel Boone marked and connected these trails. Boone's big trail was called the Wilderness Road. **Wilderness** is wild land where no one lives. The Wilderness Road opened up this mountain region to settlers. Now people could go from Virginia into Kentucky and Tennessee.

Then, in 1803, the United States bought Louisiana from France. Louisiana was a huge region. It stretched from the Mississippi River to the Rocky Mountains. What is now the state of Louisiana was only a small part of it. The Louisiana Purchase doubled the size of the United States. Look at the map on the next page. You can see how much land was added in 1803.

The United States got Florida from Spain. Florida was a territory before it was a state. Texas was an independent nation. Until 1835, Texas was part of Mexico. Then the Texans fought for their independence. For 9 years, Texas was a nation. Then, in 1845, Texas became a state.

The last state in this region to enter the Union was Oklahoma. For many years, Oklahoma was an American Indian territory. In 1907, Oklahoma became a state.

Land and Climate

Most of the land in the Southern States is a low plain. The land is level along the Atlantic and Gulf coasts. In some places, the coastal plain goes inland for hundreds of miles. Many rivers flow through the plain. Much fertile soil is found there.

Appalachian Mountain ranges stretch across many states in the region. Have you heard of the beautiful Blue Ridge Mountains of Virginia? Actually, these mountains go all the way from Georgia to Pennsylvania. The Great Smoky Mountains stretch along the border between North Carolina and Tennessee. Forests grow there.

WHERE WE ARE IN TIME AND PLACE

WESTWARD GROWTH OF THE UNITED STATES

Kilometers 0 — 500
SCALE
Miles 0 — 500

CANADA

NEW HAMPSHIRE 1788
MAINE 1820
VERMONT 1791

WASHINGTON 1889

MONTANA 1889
NORTH DAKOTA 1889
MINNESOTA 1858

MICHIGAN 1837
MASSACHUSETTS 1788
NEW YORK 1788
RHODE ISLAND 1790

OREGON 1859

IDAHO 1890
WYOMING 1890
SOUTH DAKOTA 1889

WISCONSIN 1848
CONNECTICUT 1788

NEBRASKA 1867
IOWA 1846
ILLINOIS 1818
OHIO 1803
PENNSYLVANIA 1787
NEW JERSEY 1787

NEVADA 1864
UTAH 1896
COLORADO 1876
KANSAS 1861
MISSOURI 1821
INDIANA 1816
WEST VIRGINIA 1863
DELAWARE 1787
MARYLAND 1788
Washington, DC

CALIFORNIA 1850
ARIZONA 1912
NEW MEXICO 1912
OKLAHOMA 1907
KENTUCKY 1792
VIRGINIA 1788
NORTH CAROLINA 1789

PACIFIC OCEAN

ARKANSAS 1836
TENNESSEE 1796
SOUTH CAROLINA 1788

TEXAS 1845
ALABAMA 1819
GEORGIA 1788

MEXICO

LOUISIANA 1812
MISSISSIPPI 1817
FLORIDA 1845

ATLANTIC OCEAN

Gulf of Mexico

Alaska: purchased from Russia in 1867

ALASKA 1959

Juneau

Kilometers 0 — 400
Miles 0 — 300

Hawaii: annexed in 1898

HAWAII 1959
Honolulu

Kilometers 0 — 300
Miles 0 — 200

KEY

— — — National Borders
- - - - State Borders
⊛ National Capital

GROWTH OF THE UNITED STATES

- United States in 1783
- Louisiana Purchase (from France), 1803
- Ceded by Britain in 1818
- Florida: treaty with Spain, 1819
- Texas: annexed in 1845
- Oregon: treaty with Britain, 1846
- Ceded by Mexico in 1848
- Gadsden Purchase (from Mexico), 1853

East of these mountain ranges is the Piedmont (PEED mont) Plateau. *Piedmont* means "at the foot of a mountain." Parts of Virginia, the Carolinas, Georgia, and Alabama are on this low plateau. It slopes gently downward from the mountains to the coast. Many rivers flow from the mountains through the Piedmont to the sea.

The Southern States have many important rivers. Look at the map on page 109. Find the James River where the colony of Jamestown was started. Find the Ohio River. It forms Kentucky's northern border. Find the Rio Grande. It forms the boundary between Texas and Mexico.

Now find the Mississippi River. This river is a "road" through the middle of the nation. Long, flat boats called **barges** carry goods up and down the river. Barges can travel by water from the Great Lakes to the Gulf of Mexico.

The soil in the Mississippi River valley is very fertile. The river carries rich black soil full of minerals. It drops the soil before it flows into the Gulf of Mexico. This rich soil forms a very fertile area called a **delta.** Many crops are grown in the rich delta soil. Sometimes, the river overflows before it reaches the ocean. Then it leaves some of the rich soil along its banks.

Forests cover much of the land in the Southern States. Many kinds of pine trees grow in this region. Swamps are also found

Fun Facts

Five Southern states were named for rulers in Europe. Virginia was named for Queen Elizabeth I of England. She was known as the Virgin Queen. North and South Carolina were named for King Charles I of England. King George II of England gave his name to Georgia. Louisiana was named for King Louis XIV of France.

Ponce de León named Florida. Florida means "full of flowers." The names of the other Southern states come from American Indian languages. Mississippi means "big river." Kentucky means "level land, or plain." Arkansas means "downstream from the Kansas River." Oklahoma means "red people." Texas means "allies, or friends."

North Carolina was the first place in America where English people lived. In 1587, Sir Walter Raleigh sent men, women, and children to settle there. They built a fort on Roanoke Island. A baby, Virginia Dare, was born. Then the leader of the colony sailed back to England for supplies. When he returned, the colonists were gone. Did all of them die? Did some move away? The Lost Colony remains a mystery to this day.

The Lightner Museum is one of the many old buildings in St. Augustine, Florida. St. Augustine, founded in 1565, is the oldest city in the United States. It is at about 30° north latitude, 81° west longitude.

along the coastal plains. **Swamps** are low, wet lands largely covered with water. Trees and grasses grow in the swamps. Many birds, fish, and small animals live there.

The states farthest south are often called the Sunbelt. This region gets a lot of light and heat from the sun all year. Most states in the South have long, hot summers. They have short, mild winters. They get a lot of rain in all seasons. Snow has sometimes fallen in every Southern state. Winters in western Texas and Oklahoma can be very cold and windy. But winters in the South are milder and shorter than winters in New England.

Long summers and heavy rains are good for crops. In the states farthest south, crops can grow almost all year. No other part of the nation has a better climate for farming. The warm, sunny climate also saves energy. Less fuel is needed for heat and light.

Resources

Fertile soil, sunshine, and rain are natural resources. So are minerals that can be burned

The Oklahoma state capitol has an oil well in its yard. Oklahoma City, the capital, is near 35° north latitude, 98° west longitude.

for energy. Texas is famous for oil wells. Texas and Louisiana lead the nation in producing petroleum and natural gas. The state of Oklahoma also has these fuels. Coal is found in Kentucky, Tennessee, and Virginia. Alabama has both coal and iron ore. So steel can be made in Alabama.

Farming is very important in the Southern States. Once, cotton was the South's main crop. The South was known as "the land of cotton." Cotton is still the leading crop in Texas and Mississippi. It is important in many states of the South. But now, many farmers raise cattle or soybeans instead of cotton. Texas and Oklahoma have huge cattle and sheep ranches. There, cattle are raised for meat and sheep for wool. Many Southern farmers also raise cattle on dairy farms. Poultry farms in the South supply many of the nation's chickens. Some farmers raise hogs for ham. Kentucky is famous for its beautiful racehorses.

All over the South, farmers grow fruits, vegetables, and grains. Corn, wheat, and soybeans grow in many Southern states. Along the Gulf Coast, farmers grow rice and sugar cane. They grow peanuts and pecans in Georgia and Alabama. They raise tobacco in North Carolina, South Carolina, Virginia, and Kentucky. Florida oranges and Georgia peaches are famous all over the nation.

Southern forests are a big source of wood and paper. Many Southern towns have furniture factories and paper mills. Once, farmers burned trees to clear land for farming. Now, they plant trees and harvest them like crops.

Manufacturing

Today in the South, more people are living in towns and cities. Fewer people are living on farms. Large machines do much of the farm work. There are more jobs for people in towns. Many factories have moved to the Southern States. The Southern States make cloth and clothing. They prepare and package foods. They make paper and furniture. They produce chemicals and make machines. Alabama manufactures steel. Texas and Louisiana **refine** petroleum. That means they make it into useful products such as gasoline and heating oil. Atomic energy is produced in Oak Ridge, Tennessee.

Places to Go

You can visit the past and the present in the Southern States. On Roanoke Island in North Carolina, you can see a play about Sir Wal-

ter Raleigh's Lost Colony. In Virginia, you can visit Jamestown and see how the early settlers lived. Then you can go on to nearby Williamsburg. This city was rebuilt to look as it did 200 years ago. You will find the grace and charm of the past in many Southern cities. St. Augustine, Florida, is the oldest city in the United States.

The French Quarter in New Orleans is also called the *Vieux Carre* (vee YUH cah RAY), or Old Square. The first Europeans to settle there were French. New Orleans is at 30° north, 90° west.

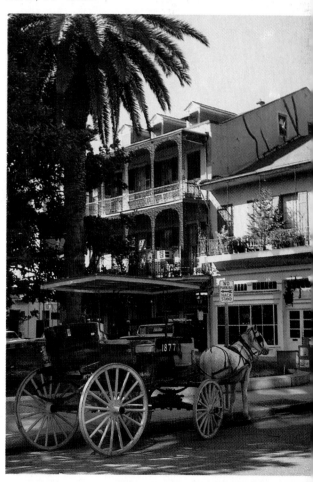

George Washington Carver

George Washington Carver was a great scientist. For years, he worked at Tuskegee Institute. It is a famous college in Alabama. Carver developed hundreds of new products from peanuts, sweet potatoes, and soybeans. He also taught farmers how to improve their soil and plant many new crops.

George Washington Carver was born a slave. He worked his way through college and became an artist as well as a scientist. He made his paints from clay and sweet potatoes. He made his paper from peanut shells. He made picture frames from corn husks. He was a genius who saw new uses for everything! Today, his birthplace is a national monument.

In Louisiana, you will not want to miss New Orleans. There, past and present come together in the French Quarter. It is an old part of the city that has been preserved. In Texas, remember the Alamo! The Alamo is a church and fort in San Antonio. In 1836, brave Texans died there fighting for their freedom. You may also visit some beautiful cities of the Gulf Coast. Mobile (moh BEEL), Alabama, and Biloxi (buh LOK see), Mississippi, are two of these.

The Southern States are also an important part of the space age. The Kennedy Space Center is in Florida. There, United States space rockets blast off. Mission control for the flights is in Houston, Texas, at the Lyndon B. Johnson Space Center. The Alabama Space and Rocket Center is in Huntsville, Alabama. There, visitors can find out how it might feel to travel to the moon.

Today, the cities of the South are growing. Seventeen Southern cities are among the 50 largest cities in the United States.

Atlanta, Georgia, is one of the great cities of America. It is a major center of transportation. Railways and highways come together there. Atlanta also has one of the world's largest, busiest airports.

THE SOUTHERN STATES

State name and nickname	Date state entered union	Area square miles	Area square kilometers	Number of people	State capital
Virginia (Old Dominion)	1788	40,815	105,711	5,636,000	Richmond
North Carolina (Tar Heel State)	1789	52,586	136,198	6,165,000	Raleigh
South Carolina (Palmetto State)	1788	31,055	80,432	3,300,000	Columbia
Georgia (Empire State of the South)	1788	58,876	152,489	5,837,000	Atlanta
Florida (Sunshine State)	1845	58,560	151,670	10,976,000	Tallahassee
Kentucky (Bluegrass State)	1792	40,395	104,623	3,723,000	Frankfort
Tennessee (Volunteer State)	1796	42,244	109,412	4,717,000	Nashville
Alabama (Yellowhammer State)	1819	51,609	133,667	3,990,000	Montgomery
Mississippi (Magnolia State)	1817	47,716	123,584	2,598,000	Jackson
Arkansas (Land of Opportunity)	1836	53,104	137,539	2,349,000	Little Rock
Louisiana (Pelican State)	1812	48,523	125,675	4,462,000	Baton Rouge
Oklahoma (Sooner State)	1907	69,919	181,090	3,298,000	Oklahoma City
Texas (Lone Star State)	1845	267,339	692,408	15,989,000	Austin

REVIEW

WATCH YOUR WORDS

1. A ___ is formed by soil that a river drops just before it flows into the sea.

    swamp   prairie   delta

2. ___ are low, wet lands.

    Sierras   Swamps   Plateaus

3. A ___ is wild land where no one lives.

    coast   peninsula   wilderness

4. A ___ is a long, flat boat.

    barge   canal   delta

5. Petroleum is made into gasoline by ___.

    conservation   refining   pollution

CHECK YOUR FACTS

6. List the 13 states in the Southern region.

7. The Louisiana Purchase (did/did not) double the size of the United States.

8. Which Southern state was once an independent nation?

9. Which Southern state was once an American Indian territory?

10. List three landforms found in the Southern States.

11. Where is the Piedmont Plateau?

12. What causes a delta to form?

13. What important mineral resources are found in Texas? In Alabama?

14. List four crops that are raised in the Southern States.

15. List three of the products made in Southern factories.

USE YOUR CHART

16. What Southern states joined the Union in the 1700s? List them.

17. Which Southern state has the most land?

18. Which two Southern states have the most people?

USE YOUR MAP

19. Which Southern states are on the Atlantic Coast?

20. Which Southern states are on the Gulf Coast?

21. Which Southern states are on the Mississippi River?

USE YOUR MAP SKILLS

22. Your teacher will give you an outline map and a regional fact sheet to fill out. Using the fact sheet, complete the map of the Southern States. Keep your map. You have three more to do.

SHARPEN YOUR THINKING

How can population growth help the South? What problems can it cause?

Lesson 5: The Midwestern States

Ohio   Michigan   Indiana   Wisconsin   Illinois
Minnesota   Iowa   Missouri   North Dakota
South Dakota   Nebraska   Kansas

FIND THE WORD

breadbasket

There are 12 states in the Midwestern region. This region is sometimes called the Middle West. Do not be fooled by this name. Some of these states are in the middle of the United States. But none of them is in the West. The Middle West was named long ago by people in the East. To them, the land around the Great Lakes was the West. Later, the land near the Pacific Ocean was called the Far West. So the Great Lakes region became the Middle West.

Look at the map of the Midwestern States on page 121. Six of these states border on the Great Lakes. The Missouri and Mississippi rivers flow through the states west of the lakes. About 59 million people live in the Midwestern States. That is 26 out of every 100 Americans.

The six Great Lakes states were once part of the Northwest Territory. The United States won the Northwest Territory from Great Britain in the Revolution. It included Ohio, Indiana, Illinois, Michigan, Wisconsin, and eastern Minnesota. Find these states on the map on page 121.

Missouri, Iowa, Kansas, Nebraska, and South Dakota were part of the Louisiana Purchase. So was western Minnesota and part of North Dakota.

During the 1800s, the lands of the Midwest were settled and became states. Ohio entered the Union first, in 1803. The Dakotas did not have enough people to be states until 1889. New settlers came there when the railroad was built. Many came all the way from Norway, Sweden, and Germany.

These people settled on the Great Plains 100 years ago. They built this sod house there. Sod is earth held together by roots of grass.

Land and Climate

Almost all the land in the Midwestern States is level. East of the Missouri River is the Central Lowland. This great area of level land is very fertile. The soil is rich and deep. The climate is good for crops. The summers are usually hot and wet. The winters are cold and snowy. Many crops grow in the Central Lowland.

West of the Missouri River are the Great Plains. The western parts of Kansas, Nebraska, and the Dakotas are on these plains. Much of the land on the Great Plains is dry grassland. Not enough rain falls there to grow crops. Farmers can use pipes and ditches to bring water to the land. Instead, many use the land to raise cattle and sheep.

There are two areas of hilly land in the Midwest. The Black Hills of South Dakota are mountains. Harney Peak in the Black Hills is higher than any Appalachian mountain. The Ozarks in Missouri are a region of hills and valleys. Actually, this area is a plateau.

The Midwestern States are not on the ocean. This makes their lakes and rivers very important. Waterways and canals link the rivers with the Great Lakes. Then the St. Lawrence Seaway provides an outlet to the Atlantic Ocean.

Fun Facts

Minnesota reaches farther north than any other state except Alaska.

Michigan is a land of 11,000 lakes. Four of the five Great Lakes wash Michigan's shores.

Indiana is famous for auto racing. The Indianapolis 500 is a 500-mile auto race. The race cars drive on the Indianapolis Motor Speedway. This speedway was built in 1909 to test new cars.

South Dakota has a dry region called the Badlands. Here, the forces of nature have worn the land into strange hills and hollows. The Badlands got their name because they were hard to cross.

Missouri was the home of Mark Twain. He wrote about the adventures of Tom Sawyer and Huck Finn on the Mississippi River. Mark Twain was once the pilot of a riverboat on the Mississippi.

Kansas is famous for corn. Actually, it grows more wheat than any other state. Most of the United States lies between Canada and Mexico. The center of these 48 states is Kansas.

Iowa was covered with tall prairie grass 100 years ago. Pioneers crossed the state in covered wagons. Now Iowa's prairies have become fields of corn.

Wisconsin was settled by the French 300 years ago. Later, people came from Germany to live there. Today, you will still hear German spoken in Wisconsin.

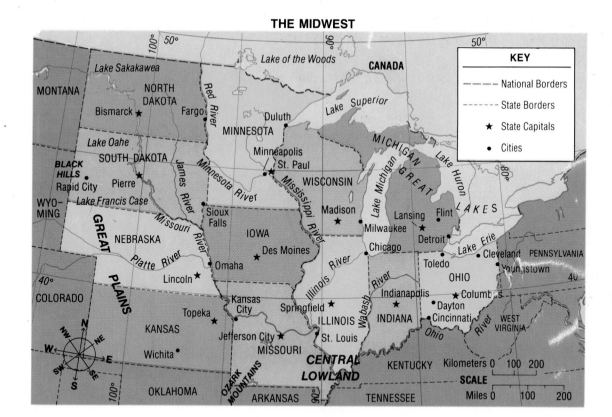

Many rivers in the region flow into the Mississippi. The Missouri flows into it from the west. The Ohio joins it from the east. Then the Mississippi keeps flowing south to the Gulf of Mexico.

Resources

The Midwest is the nation's most important farming area. It is called the breadbasket of the nation. A **breadbasket** is a region where much grain is grown. Farmers in the Midwestern States grow huge amounts of wheat and corn. So much food is grown here that some is sold to other nations. Soybeans, oats, and hay are other leading crops. In the Great Lakes states, farmers raise many fruits and vegetables.

Trees are still an important resource in northern Minnesota and Michigan. But these states used up much of their forests 100 years ago. Once, great forests covered much of the land around the lakes. Then settlers cut the trees down. Some were clearing the land to plant crops. Others worked for companies that sold wood. Now, Minnesota and Michigan are having to plant more trees.

Farmers in the Midwest also raise animals. Hogs, beef cattle, chickens, and turkeys are raised

121

Chicago, Illinois, is on Lake Michigan. The Chicago River flows through the city. Many tall buildings are on the river banks. Chicago is at 42° north latitude, 88° west longitude.

for their meat. Around the Great Lakes, many dairy farms are found. Wisconsin leads the nation in producing milk, butter, and cheese. Michigan, Minnesota, and Ohio are also dairy states.

Some states in the Midwest have important mineral resources. Illinois and Indiana produce large amounts of coal. Minnesota and Michigan are the nation's leading producers of iron ore. Missouri mines large amounts of lead. North Dakota produces petroleum. There are even gold mines in the Black Hills of South Dakota!

Manufacturing and Trade

Suppose you could fly in an airplane over the Midwestern States. You would see miles and miles of flat farmland. But you would also pass over great cities with large factories. Even in the Midwest, there are more jobs in factories than on farms.

Many states in this region prepare and package food. They pack meat and can vegetables. They grind grain to make flour and breakfast food. Metals and other minerals also provide factory jobs.

Illinois and Indiana make steel and refine petroleum.

Most of the nation's cars are made in the Midwest. Detroit, Michigan, is the center of the auto industry. Airplanes are built in Kansas. Space vehicles are made in Missouri. The Midwestern States also make mining equipment and farm machines.

The Midwestern States have very good transportation. Ships sail from the Atlantic Ocean through the St. Lawrence Seaway. That brings them to the Great Lakes. The Illinois waterway connects Lake Michigan with the Mississippi River. Goods can travel on this waterway from Chicago to St. Louis. Then they can go down the Mississippi River to the Gulf of Mexico. Goods can also be shipped north and east on this great water highway. Another important shipping route is the Ohio River.

Some of the nation's largest cities are on the Great Lakes. Find Chicago, Detroit, Milwaukee, and Cleveland on the map on page 121. What states are these cities in? What lakes are they on?

Places to Go

Chicago is the second-largest city in the United States. Chicago is a port city on Lake Michigan. It is a center for shipping, railways, highways, and airlines. It has the busiest airport in the

The largest carved figures in the world are on Mount Rushmore in South Dakota. George Washington's head is 18 meters (60 feet) tall. Mount Rushmore is at 44° north latitude, 103° west longitude in the Black Hills.

United States. Transportation provides many jobs in Chicago. There are also jobs in factories, offices, and city government. The world's tallest building is in Chicago. Goods made in this great city are sold all over the world.

THE MIDWESTERN STATES

State name and nickname	Date state entered union	Area square miles	Area square kilometers	Number of people	State capital
Ohio (Buckeye State)	1803	41,222	106,765	10,752,000	Columbus
Michigan (Wolverine State)	1837	58,216	150,779	9,075,000	Lansing
Indiana (Hoosier State)	1816	36,291	93,994	5,498,000	Indianapolis
Wisconsin (Badger State)	1848	56,154	145,439	4,766,000	Madison
Illinois (Land of Lincoln)	1818	56,400	146,076	11,511,000	Springfield
Minnesota (Gopher State)	1858	84,068	217,736	4,162,000	St. Paul
Iowa (Hawkeye State)	1846	56,290	145,791	2,910,000	Des Moines
Missouri (Show Me State)	1821	69,686	180,487	5,008,000	Jefferson City
North Dakota (Flickertail State)	1889	70,665	183,022	686,000	Bismarck
South Dakota (Sunshine State)	1889	77,047	199,552	706,000	Pierre
Nebraska (Cornhusker State)	1867	77,227	200,018	1,606,000	Lincoln
Kansas (Sunflower State)	1861	82,264	213,064	2,438,000	Topeka

St. Louis, Missouri, is very different from Chicago, Illinois. It is more like the cities in the Southern States. Just north of St. Louis, the Missouri River flows into the Mississippi. Fur traders and French people from New Orleans settled St. Louis. Today, visitors to

St. Louis can take a steamboat trip on the Mississippi. They can also go to the top of the Gateway Arch. For many pioneers, St. Louis was the "Gateway to the West." More recently, space capsules have been built in St. Louis.

Native peoples lived in North America long before the Europeans came. In Ohio, Indiana, Iowa, and Illinois, you can see great mounds of earth. They were built by American Indian peoples over 2,000 years ago. The mound builders were the first Midwestern farmers. In Ohio, they built one mound in the shape of a giant snake!

One of the most famous sights in the Midwest is Mount Rushmore in South Dakota. There, you can see George Washington, Thomas Jefferson, Theodore Roosevelt, and Abraham Lincoln. The faces of these Presidents are carved into the rock.

REVIEW

CHECK YOUR FACTS

1. List the 12 states in the Midwestern region.
2. Almost all the land in the Midwest is (level/hilly).
3. Why is the Midwest called the breadbasket of the nation?
4. List four crops grown in the Midwestern States.
5. Which state produces the most milk and cheese?
6. Which Midwestern states produce the most iron ore?
7. What rivers come together just north of St. Louis?

USE YOUR CHART

8. Which Midwestern state has the most land?
9. Which Midwestern state has the most people?
10. Which was the first Midwestern state to join the Union?

USE YOUR MAP

11. Which six Midwestern states border on the Great Lakes?
12. The Mississippi River forms part of the border of five Midwestern states. List them.
13. Name at least two rivers that flow into the Mississippi.
14. The Ohio River forms the southern border of three Midwestern states. List them.

USE YOUR MAP SKILLS

15. Your teacher will give you an outline map and a regional fact sheet to fill out. Using the fact sheet, complete the map of the Midwestern States. Keep the map. When you do two more, you will have all 50 states.

SHARPEN YOUR THINKING

Can you think of a better name for this region than the Middle West?

Lesson 6: The Mountain States

Montana Wyoming Colorado New Mexico
Idaho Utah Arizona Nevada

FIND THE WORDS

canyon   geyser   irrigate   dam

The eight Mountain States are huge. They are among the largest states in the nation. They are also in a region of great beauty. Here, you can see high mountains and deep valleys. You can see great forests and wide deserts. You can even see boiling water shoot out of the ground. Millions of people visit the Mountain States to see these sights. But only 12 million people live in this region. All six New England States would fit into any one of the Mountain States. And there would be room to spare! Yet the same number of people live in New England.

Even so, many people are moving to the Mountain States. Between 1970 and 1980, Nevada and Arizona were the fastest-growing states in the nation.

MOUNTAIN STATES

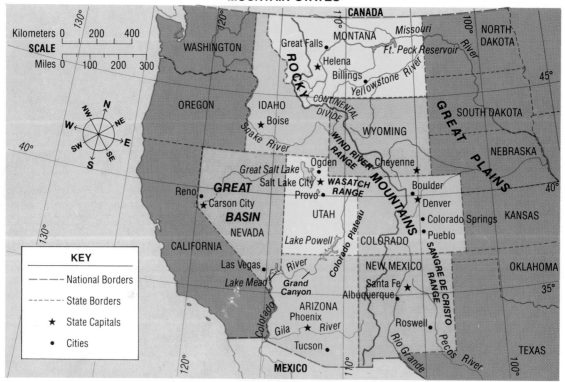

Land and Climate

Mountains and plateaus are the main landforms of the Mountain States. The Rocky Mountains stretch north to Alaska. They go through parts of Idaho, Montana, Wyoming, Utah, Colorado, and New Mexico. The highest mountain in this part of the Rockies is Mount Elbert. It is in Colorado. Mount Elbert is 4,400 meters (14,431 feet) above sea level.

Like the Appalachians, the Rockies have many different ranges. That means the mountains have different names in different places. The Bitterroot Range is between Idaho and Montana. The Wind River Range is in Wyoming.

A high ridge passes through the Rocky Mountains. It is like the backbone of the continent. This ridge is called the Continental Divide. All the rivers west of it flow toward the Pacific Ocean. All the rivers east of it flow toward the Atlantic Ocean.

East of the Rockies are the Great Plains. West of the Rockies is an area called the Great Basin. This area is a desert. Mountains and plateaus surround it.

One plateau in the area is called the Colorado Plateau. It is famous all over the world for the Grand Canyon. The Colorado River flows through the bottom of the canyon. From the rim of the canyon, the river seems small and

The Rocky Mountains stretch from Alaska to New Mexico. This is a scene near Sun Valley, Idaho (44° N latitude, 114° W longitude).

far away. Actually, the river carved the Grand Canyon out of the rock! It took many long ages for this to happen. The force of the running water wore part of the rock away. It cut a long, deep valley into the plateau. A deep, narrow valley with steep sides is called a **canyon.** The Grand Canyon is more than a mile deep.

The Grand Canyon is part of a national park in Arizona. Most of our largest national parks are in the Mountain States. Yellowstone National Park is in Wyoming, Montana, and Idaho. There, hot springs called **geysers** (GY zurz) shoot water and steam into the air. Yellowstone also has great forests. Animals such as buffaloes, moose, and bears live in the park.

Water is shooting up from a geyser in Yellowstone National Park. The park's location is 44–45° N latitude, 110–111° W longitude.

In the Mountain States, the climate is mostly dry. Summers are hot and dry. Winters are cold except in southern Arizona and New Mexico. There is snow in the mountains. To grow most crops, farmers in the Mountain States need irrigation. To **irrigate** land is to bring water there from somewhere else. Water flows to the fields through pipes and ditches.

To save water, large dams have been built on many rivers. A **dam** is a wall that blocks river water. It stops the water from flowing on to the ocean. Behind a dam, a lake will form to hold the water.

Resources

There are valuable minerals in the Mountain States. These states have silver and gold. They have copper and lead. Copper and lead are important in manufacturing.

Some mineral resources are burned for energy. Wyoming, Colorado, Montana, and Utah have large amounts of coal. Several of these states also have petroleum and natural gas. Water and sunlight are other sources of energy. Dams provide waterpower as well as water for irrigation. Both waterpower and energy from the sun can be used to make electricity.

Thanks to irrigation, crops can grow in the Mountain States. Most of these states grow wheat, hay, potatoes, and sugar beets. With irrigation, Arizona and Nevada can even grow cotton and fruit. Still, animals are more important than crops in most of this region. Many farmers raise sheep and cattle on large ranches. Wood from the forests is another natural resource.

Manufacturing, Business, and Trade

Mining and ranching are very important in the Mountain States. These states sell minerals and pack meat. They make wood products and sell wool. Their dairy cows supply milk and cheese. Factories make aircraft, spacecraft, and missiles in Utah and Arizona. In New Mexico, scientists study atomic energy and energy from the sun.

Places to Go

There are many exciting things to do in the Mountain States. You can visit the national parks. You can ski, swim, hike, camp, or canoe. You can see natural wonders such as canyons, caves, and deserts. You can go to places where American Indians lived hundreds of years ago. The Indians were pioneers in irrigation. They worked out very good ways to get water to their fields. Some built homes on the sides of cliffs.

Some of the nation's fastest-growing cities are in the Mountain States. Here, the city with the most people is Phoenix (FEE niks), Arizona. Phoenix is a city in the desert. Thanks to irrigation and air-conditioning, many people can live there. Second in population is Denver, Colorado. Denver is at the foot of the Rockies. It is on a mile-high plateau. Denver has a suburb called Aurora. In 1980, Aurora had over twice as many people as it had in 1970!

THE MOUNTAIN STATES

State name and nickname		Date state entered union	Area		Number of people	State capital
			square miles	square kilometers		
Montana (Treasure State)		1889	147,138	381,087	824,000	Helena
Wyoming (Equality State)		1890	97,914	253,597	511,000	Cheyenne
Colorado (Centennial State)		1876	104,247	270,000	3,178,000	Denver
New Mexico (Land of Enchantment)		1912	121,666	315,115	1,424,000	Santa Fe
Idaho (Gem State)		1890	83,557	216,413	1,001,000	Boise
Utah (Beehive State)		1896	84,916	219,932	1,652,000	Salt Lake City
Arizona (Grand Canyon State)		1912	113,909	295,024	3,053,000	Phoenix
Nevada (Silver State)		1864	110,540	286,299	911,000	Carson City

129

Fun Facts

Many Mountain states were wild and lawless in the early mining days. Tombstone, Arizona, was a well-known mining camp. There, Wyatt Earp fought the famous gunfight at the O.K. Corral. Later, many booming mining towns turned into ghost towns. When mines closed down, people left.

Wyoming is called the Equality State. Wyoming women got the vote in 1869. The United States did not give women the right to vote until 1920.

Idaho has more national forest land than any state except California.

In Arizona, one out of every five people is American Indian.

Colorado means "red" in Spanish. The state was named for the Rio Colorado, or "Red River." Montana means "mountain country."

Utah has the second-saltiest body of water on Earth. Only the Dead Sea is saltier than the Great Salt Lake.

New Mexico was the place where the first atomic bomb was exploded. This state has twice as many sheep and cattle as it has people.

Nevada's capital, Carson City, was originally a trading post on the California Trail. It was named for Kit Carson. He used to guide explorers and armies through the West.

REVIEW

WATCH YOUR WORDS

1. To____ land is to bring water there.
dam   irrigate   conserve

2. A ____ stops river water from flowing to the sea.
canal   harbor   dam

3. Water and steam shoot out of a hot spring called a____.
canyon   geyser   swamp

4. A river can cut a____out of rock.
swamp   delta   canyon

CHECK YOUR FACTS

5. List the eight Mountain States.

6. What are the main landforms of the Mountain States?

7. What national park has geysers?

8. How do farmers in the Mountain States get water?

9. List four mineral resources of the Mountain States.

USE YOUR CHART

10. Which was the first Mountain state to join the Union?

11. Which Mountain state has the most land?

12. Which two Mountain states have the most people?

USE YOUR MAP

13. In what state is the Grand Canyon?

14. What rivers flow through New Mexico?

15. In what state is the Great Salt Lake?

USE YOUR MAP SKILLS

16. Your teacher will give you an outline map and a regional fact sheet to fill out. Using the fact sheet, complete the map of the Mountain States.

Lesson 7: The Pacific States

Alaska   Washington   Oregon
California   Hawaii

The Pacific Ocean borders the West Coast of the United States. It is the largest ocean in the world. Five states have coasts that are washed by the Pacific waters. They are Alaska, Washington, Oregon, California, and Hawaii (huh WAH yee). Four of these states are on the continent of North America. The islands of Hawaii are far out in the ocean.

The Pacific States are special in many ways. California has more people than any other state in the nation. Alaska has the most land of any state. It also has the fewest people. Alaska is the state closest to the North Pole. Hawaii is the state closest to the equator.

History

California was discovered by a Spanish explorer in 1542. Spain started a colony there over 200 years later, in 1769. This colony was at San Diego (dee A goh).

THE PACIFIC STATES

State name and nickname		Date state entered union	Area		Number of people	State capital
			square miles	square kilometers		
Alaska (Last Frontier)		1959	586,400	1,518,776	500,000	Juneau
Washington (Evergreen State)		1889	68,192	176,617	4,302,000	Olympia
Oregon (Beaver State)		1859	96,981	251,181	2,674,000	Salem
California (Golden State)		1850	158,693	411,014	25,622,000	Sacramento
Hawaii (Aloha State)		1959	6,450	16,706	1,039,000	Honolulu

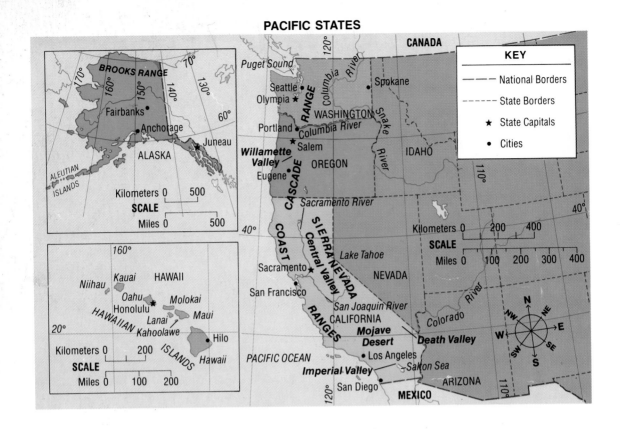

PACIFIC STATES

KEY
- — · — National Borders
- ------- State Borders
- ★ State Capitals
- • Cities

Soon, Spanish priests were starting many religious settlements, called **missions.** Missions and forts were built from south to north along the coast. Then, in 1777, the first California town was started. It was San Jose (hoh ZAY).

Later, California was ruled by Mexico. Then, in 1848, it became part of the United States. That same year, gold was discovered in California. The great California Gold Rush began. People came to California from all over the world. The population grew very fast. By 1850, California became a state.

In the 1840s, many settlers had begun to come to Oregon. They came in horse-drawn wagons along the Oregon Trail. It took them 6 months to travel from Kansas City, Missouri, to Oregon. By 1859, Oregon had enough people to become a state. Washington had to wait another 30 years. By 1889, the railroad had brought many new settlers there.

Alaska and Hawaii were the last states to come into the Union. In 1867, the United States bought Alaska from Russia. In 1900, Hawaii became a U.S. territory.

Waikiki (WY kee KEE) is a famous beach in Honolulu, Hawaii. Honolulu is near 21° north latitude, 158° west longitude.

Hawaii used to be a kingdom. Then, for a few years, it was a nation with a president. Next, it became a territory. Finally, in 1959, both Alaska and Hawaii became states.

Land and Climate

No two states are more different than Alaska and Hawaii! On a globe, you can clearly see where these states are. Find them on the map of the world on pages 312 and 313. On smaller maps, Alaska and Hawaii are often put at the bottom. Then, everything on the map can be shown in more detail.

Alaska is the largest state. It is more than twice the size of Texas. Alaska juts out from North America in the northwest. At about 168°

west longitude, it almost touches the Soviet Union. The upper part of Alaska is north of the Arctic Circle. There, the ground is always frozen. For most of the year, the Arctic Ocean is covered with ice. In the far southeast, Alaska gets more rain than snow. But most of Alaska has cold, snowy winters.

Hawaii is one of the smallest states. It is made up of eight large islands and many small ones. The island farthest south reaches to about 19° north latitude. That means it is close to the equator. Hawaii has a warm, sunny climate. It has palm trees and broad beaches of white sand. It has great tropical forests of ferns. Flowers bloom and fruits grow all year in the state of Hawaii.

Both Alaska and Hawaii have high mountains. Mount McKinley in Alaska is the highest mountain in North America. Both states also have volcanoes. A **volcano** is an opening in the earth. Hot, melted rock can shoot out of such an opening. So can ashes, smoke, and gases. The melted rock can build up around the opening. That way, it forms a mountain around the volcano. Material from a volcano can also push up from under the ocean. Then, it forms an island. Many of the islands of Hawaii were formed by volcanoes.

Washington, Oregon, and California share some of the same geography. Along the Pacific Coast are ranges of low mountains. They are called the Coast Ranges. Farther east are higher mountains. These higher mountains are called the Cascade Range in Washington and Oregon. In California, they are called the Sierra Nevada. Between the Coast Ranges and the higher mountains are three fertile valleys. The one farthest south is the great Central Valley of California. These valleys between the mountains have rich farmland.

Fun Facts

Point Barrow, Alaska, is farther north than any other point in the United States. It is just beyond 71° north latitude. There, the Arctic Ocean is frozen 9 or 10 months of the year. Ka Lae (kah LAH a), Hawaii, is farther south than any other point in the nation. It is at 19° north latitude.

The highest point in North America is in Alaska. Mount McKinley is 6,194 meters (20,320 feet) above sea level.

The lowest point in North America is in California. Death Valley is 86 meters (282 feet) below sea level. It is one of the hottest, driest places in the world. California also has the highest waterfall in North America. This is Yosemite (yoh SEM uh tee) Falls.

The place in the world where it rains most often is in Hawaii. It is Mount Waialeale (wy AH lee AH lee) on the island of Kauai (KOW eye). Sometimes it rains there as much as 350 days a year!

Crater Lake, Oregon, is the deepest lake in the United States. Oregon also has the continent's deepest canyon.

Washington has an active volcano. It is Mount St. Helens in the Cascade Range. Mount St. Helens used to have an elevation of 2,950 meters (9,677 feet). Now, it is only 2,530 meters (8,300 feet) above sea level. On May 18, 1980, the top of the mountain blew off! Steam and ashes shot up into the sky. The blast had more force than an atomic bomb. The great heat burned down forests. It killed millions of fish. Rushing rivers of mud buried people's homes. Towns in three states were covered with ashes. Mount St. Helens had really blown its top!

The top of Mount St. Helens is in the clouds. This volcano is in the state of Washington at 46° north latitude, 122° west longitude.

Along the Pacific Coast, Washington and Oregon have a marine climate. This climate area goes as far south as San Francisco. Warm, wet winds blow in from the ocean. These winds keep the air from getting very hot or cold. They bring a lot of rain to the coast. Then, at the snow-capped Cascade Range, the winds are cooled. Rain falls on the western side of the mountains. But the areas east of the mountains are dry. There, farmers have to irrigate their fields.

Great forests grow in Washington and Oregon because of the rain. California's northern coast has giant redwood trees. These trees have huge trunks. They can grow as tall as 117 meters (385 feet). They are among the oldest living things on Earth.

Here, Mount St. Helens is no longer quiet. It is creating its own clouds. You can see the heavy smoke shooting up into the air.

Farther south, the California coast has a Mediterranean climate. Cities like Los Angeles have warm, dry summers and warm, wet winters. In the dry southeast, California has deserts. Death Valley and the Mojave (moh HAH vee) Desert are there.

Resources

California produces more farm products than any other state. In the valleys, the land is irrigated. That way, California can grow huge crops of vegetables and fruits. No other state grows as much lettuce or as many tomatoes, carrots, and strawberries. Grapes, oranges, and lemons are major California crops. Cotton also grows in California.

Farther north, Oregon and Washington grow apples, peaches, pears, and cherries. They also grow many vegetables and raise wheat. Out in the Pacific, Hawaii grows pineapples and raises sugar cane. Only Alaska is not a farming state. But cattle are raised in all the states in the Pacific region.

There are also rich mineral resources in the Pacific States. California and Alaska have large amounts of petroleum and natural gas. In Alaska, petroleum is found in the northern part of the state. So a pipeline had to be built across the state. Oil can flow through the pipeline to an ice-free southern port. In California, much petroleum is found under the ocean close to the shore. Many people do not want to drill for this petroleum. They are afraid the oil might spill and spoil the beaches. Other people say that the nation needs the petroleum. They believe drilling is worth the risk.

Manufacturing, Business, and Trade

The Pacific States make money from the food they produce. They freeze, pack, or can fruit, vegetables, fish, and meat. They package and sell dairy products. They also manufacture wood and paper products from the forests. Redwood is used for building. It is valued for its beauty. Also, it does not easily rot.

Many jobs in Alaska depend on petroleum, wood, and fish. Many

The Alaska pipeline carries petroleum across fields of snow. The oil flows from the Arctic coast to an ice-free port near Anchorage. It travels south from about 70° north latitude to 61° north latitude. Anchorage is at 61° north latitude, 150° west longitude. Find it on the map on page 132.

There is much rich farmland in California's valleys. The land is irrigated so that huge crops can be grown. California produces more farm products than any other state.

people in Hawaii make their living on large farms. In Washington, Oregon, and California, airplanes and ships are built. In California, movies and television shows are made. Films from Hollywood are watched all over the world.

Places to Go

The Pacific States have many places to see. There are beaches, forests, lakes, and deserts. There are flat, fertile valleys. There are steep cliffs bordering the sea. In some parts of California, you can swim and ski on the same day!

Cities are growing in the Pacific States. The largest cities in this region are in California. Look at the map on page 132. Find Los Angeles, San Diego, and San Francisco. All these cities have Spanish names. Other large cities on the West Coast are Portland, Oregon, and Seattle, Washington.

San Francisco is a beautiful city in northern California. It is built on steep hills. The Golden Gate Bridge stretches across the entrance to the harbor. A great earthquake and fire destroyed San Francisco in 1906. In an **earthquake**, the ground shakes and trembles. This can cause buildings to fall down. But the people of San Francisco quickly built their city again. A famous part of San Francisco is called Chinatown. More Chinese-Americans live there than anywhere else in the nation.

People from all over the Earth live in the Pacific States. The native Alaskans are the Innuit (Eskimos). The native Hawaiians are the Polynesians. Later, people came to Hawaii from Japan, China, and the Philippines. Now people from Asia also live in Washington, Oregon, and California. People who speak Spanish live in California, too. American Indians, Mexicans, Europeans, Blacks, and Asians all helped to build the Pacific States.

REVIEW

WATCH YOUR WORDS

1. Hot, melted rock can shoot out of a____.
   geyser   volcano   swamp

2. A(n) ____ makes the ground shake and tremble.
   earthquake   geyser   dam

3. The first religious settlements in California were called____.
   forts   territories   missions

CHECK YOUR FACTS

4. List the five states that make up the Pacific region.

5. Which Pacific states are on the continent of North America?

6. Which state has more people than any other state?

7. Which state has the most land?

8. How are Alaska and Hawaii different? How are they alike?

9. What is a volcano?

10. Why do great forests grow in Washington and Oregon?

11. The land east of the Cascade Mountains is (wet/dry).

12. List five of the crops that grow in California.

13. Which Pacific state raises sugar cane and pineapples?

14. Which Pacific states raise apples, peaches, and pears?

15. Which Pacific states have a lot of petroleum?

USE YOUR CHART

16. Which is the smallest Pacific state?

17. Which Pacific state has the fewest people?

USE YOUR MAP

18. A river forms most of the border between Washington and Oregon. What river is it?

19. What large lake is northeast of the capital of California?

20. What range of mountains crosses northern Alaska?

21. On what island is Honolulu, Hawaii, found?

USE YOUR MAP SKILLS

22. Your teacher will give you an outline map and a regional fact sheet to fill out. Using the fact sheet, complete the map of the Pacific States. When you finish, you will have labeled all 50 states. Put your six maps together. Now your map of the United States is complete!

SHARPEN YOUR THINKING

Why do so few people live in Alaska? Why do so many live in California?

CHAPTER REVIEW

WATCH YOUR WORDS

1. The Pilgrims anchored their ship in a
   ___.
   delta   swamp   bay

2. The Statue of Liberty is on an island
   in New York___.
   wilderness   harbor   territory

3. The Middle Atlantic States have
   many___.
   ports   volcanoes   geysers

4. A___tree loses its leaves.
   softwood   hardwood   pine

5. The Mississippi River drops fertile
   soil to form a___.
   harbor   bay   delta

6. The Midwest is called the ___ of the
   nation.
   breadbasket   wilderness   delta

7. The Grand ___ is more than a mile
   deep.
   Geyser   Volcano   Canyon

8. There are hot springs called ___ in
   Yellowstone National Park.
   geysers   swamps   volcanoes

9. In 1906, a(n) ___ and fire destroyed
   San Francisco.
   volcano   earthquake   geyser

10. Mount St. Helens is a___.
    geyser   delta   volcano

CHECK YOUR FACTS

11. How many states are there in the
    United States?

12. What is the difference between a cap-
    ital and a capitol?

13. Where are the New England States?

14. Name three large cities in the Middle
    Atlantic States.

15. Is the land better for farming in the
    South or in New England?

16. Are the Southern States gaining or
    losing population?

17. Is most land in the Midwestern
    States hilly or flat?

18. How do the Mountain States compare
    with the New England States in size?
    In population?

19. How can farmers in a dry region
    grow crops?

20. Name two living and two nonliving
    resources of the Pacific States.

APPLY YOUR SKILLS

USE YOUR STATE CHARTS

21. What was the first state to join the
    Union?

22. What were the last two states to join
    the Union?

23. What are the largest and smallest states?

24. What state has the most people?

25. What states have the same nickname?

SHARPEN YOUR THINKING

26. Look at the map on page 111. Suppose
    the United States had not added on
    any land after 1783. How might your
    life be different?

27. In what states would you expect to hear
    Spanish spoken?

28. How did the discovery of the Cumber-
    land Gap help the nation to grow?

29. Why are rivers and lakes so important
    to the Midwestern States?

30. Alaska and Hawaii are often shown in
    boxes on maps of the United States.
    They are not in their right places. Ex-
    plain why.

UNIT REVIEW

WATCH YOUR WORDS

Use the words below to complete the unit summary. Use each term only once.

canal	Congress	geysers	Lakes
canyons	dams	Gulf	Seaway
capital	delta	irrigate	states
Capitol	federal district	isthmus	volcano

The United States is a nation made up of 50 __1__. Washington, DC, is the __2__. Washington is not in a state but in a(n) __3__. The __4__ is in Washington, DC. It is the building in which the __5__ meets.

Most of the United States is on the continent of North America. A narrow strip of land, called a(n) __6__, links North and South America. There, a(n) __7__ connects the Atlantic and Pacific oceans. Farther north, the St. Lawrence __8__ links the Atlantic Ocean with the five Great __9__. Another waterway connects the lakes with the Mississippi River. The Mississippi flows south to the __10__ of Mexico. It

drops rich soil to form a(n) __11__ before it flows into the sea.

North America has many natural wonders. Rivers have cut deep __12__ out of solid rock. Water shoots out of the ground from hot springs called __13__. When a(n) __14__ explodes, it can cover the land with ashes or melted rock. But other wonders have been made by human beings. People have built cities, highways, railroads, airports, and canals. They have built __15__ across rivers to hold the water back. Then they use the water to __16__ dry land. That way, they can live and grow food in the desert!

CHECK YOUR FACTS

1. What are the two major mountain systems of North America?

2. The highest mountains on the continent are in the (east/west).

3. List three areas of plains in North America.

4. What two rivers form the longest river in North America?

5. List two resources that can be renewed and two that cannot.

6. What three large nations take up most of North America?

7. Where is Central America?

8. The United States (is/is not) the world's largest nation.

9. How many states were there when the United States began?

10. Who were the first colonists to come to New England?

11. Where in the Middle Atlantic States do most people live?

12. Where is Independence Hall?

13. Where was the first lasting European settlement in the United States?

14. What was the Wilderness Road?

15. Which region is called the breadbasket of the nation? Why?

16. Describe the land in the Midwest.

17. What are the main landforms in the Mountain States?

18. What is the Continental Divide?

19. What state is farthest north?

20. List five different groups of people who live in the Pacific States.

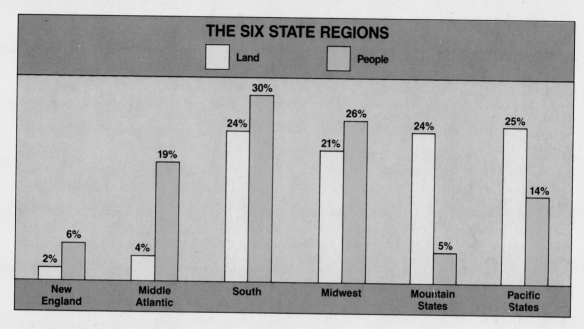

THE SIX STATE REGIONS

☐ Land   ☐ People

Region	Land	People
New England	2%	6%
Middle Atlantic	4%	19%
South	24%	30%
Midwest	21%	26%
Mountain States	24%	5%
Pacific States	25%	14%

USE YOUR CHART SKILLS

Use the bar graph above to answer the questions below.

1. Which region has the most land for the fewest people?

2. Which region has the most people on the least amount of land?

3. In what region are people crowded most closely together?

4. Which regions have the best balance between land and people?

5. Which regions cover about the same amount of land?

USE YOUR MAPS

6. Look at the political map of North America on page 87. Give the right intermediate direction: *northeast, northwest, southeast, southwest.*
   Alaska is ___ of Cuba. The Great Lakes are ___ of Alaska. Puerto Rico is ___ of Ottawa.

7. Look at the map of the United States on pages 70–71.
   a. Give the latitude of Juneau, Alaska, and St. Paul, Minnesota.
   b. Give the latitude of Columbus, Ohio, and Tallahassee, Florida.
   c. Give the longitude of Jackson, Mississippi, and Carson City, Nevada.
   d. Give the latitude and longitude of Houston, Texas.

SHARPEN YOUR THINKING

8. Why do you think the Middle Atlantic States have so many big cities?

9. Many factories have left the North and moved to the South. What reasons can you find for this?

10. How can people grow crops and build cities in very dry states such as Arizona and Nevada?

141

STUDYING YOUR STATE

You have studied your continent. You have learned about your government. And you have found out many things about all 50 states. Now, you may want to learn more about your own state. Here is a way to go about it.

Look for books and articles about your state in the library. You can find many facts in an encyclopedia or almanac. You can also write to agencies in your state for free materials.

Your state historical society can help you learn about state history. Your state department of transportation may send you a road map. Many states have a department of travel or tourism. It sends out leaflets to attract visitors to the state. You may be able to visit a state or local museum.

Be a detective. Try to find the answers to these questions. Soon, you will be an expert on your state.

HISTORY OF YOUR STATE

1. What early American Indian peoples lived in your state? What kinds of homes did they have? What artifacts did they leave behind?
2. Who were the first people from Europe to settle in your state? When did these settlers first arrive?
3. What part of your state was settled first? What attracted people to that region?
4. What is the oldest town or city in your state?
5. Was your state once a colony? Was it ever a territory or part of a territory? Was it ever part of Canada or Mexico? Was it once ruled by Great Britain, France, or Spain?
6. In what year did your state become a state?
7. What were the most important things that happened in your state? Make a time line. Put on the dates when these events happened.
8. Were any important battles fought in your state? If so, what were they?
9. Were any Presidents born in your state? What other great leaders lived there? Can you still visit the places where these leaders lived?
10. What are the people of your state like? From what parts of the world did they come?

GEOGRAPHY OF YOUR STATE

11. What landforms are found in your state?
12. Is your state on the Atlantic Ocean or Pacific Ocean?
13. What important rivers or lakes are in your state?
14. What are the highest and lowest points in your state?
15. What climate or climates does your state have? How does the weather change from season to season?
16. Does your state get much rain? If not, do farmers irrigate their fields?

NATURAL RESOURCES OF YOUR STATE

17. What crops are grown in your state?

18. Are animals raised in your state for milk, eggs, meat, or wool? Are horses raised there?

19. What important minerals are found in your state?

20. What sources of energy are found in your state? Does it have coal, petroleum, natural gas, waterpower, or nuclear power? Is sunshine used for solar energy?

21. Does your state have large forests?

22. Does the land, the water, or the climate attract visitors to your state?

23. What is your state doing to conserve its natural resources?

BUSINESS, TRANSPORTATION, AND TRADE

24. What kinds of factories are found in your state? What products are made there?

25. What are some other businesses in your state that make goods or supply services?

26. What kinds of jobs do people have who work for the city, county, or state?

27. What kinds of transportation are used to move people and goods in your state?

28. What products and resources does your state sell to other states?

GOVERNMENT OF YOUR STATE

29. What is the capital of your state?

30. What is the legislature called? How many members does it have?

31. Who is the governor of your state?

FUN FACTS ABOUT YOUR STATE

32. How did your state get its name? Its nickname?

33. What is the state motto? The state bird? The state flower? Is there a state animal?

34. Where and when is your state fair held?

35. What colleges, museums, and parks are in your state?

36. What places in your state attract the most visitors?

USE YOUR STATE MAP

37. How far does your state extend from north to south? From east to west? Use the distance scale to measure.

38. What two towns in your state are farthest apart? What roads would you take to get from one to the other?

39. How far is the state capital from where you live? In what direction would you travel to get there?

40. What U.S. highways go through your state?

41. What other states or nations border your state?

42. List the state parks, national parks, and national forests in your state.

43. Does your state map tell about places to visit?

PUT IT ALL TOGETHER

44. Draw or trace an outline map of your state.

45. Put the state capital and the five largest cities on the map.

46. Label important mountains, deserts, valleys, plains, and plateaus. Also label important bodies of water, such as oceans, lakes, and rivers.

CHAPTER 1

SOUTH AMERICA AND ITS PEOPLE

Lesson 1: Land and Climate

FIND THE WORDS

altiplano   jungle
llanos   pampas

"Towering, snow-capped mountains seem to rise out of the sea."

"There are rivers so wide you can't see across them!"

"There are forests so thick that the sun never shines on the ground!"

"One desert is so dry that sometimes it doesn't rain there for 10 years!"

Suppose friends told you about a land like that. Would you believe them? Would it even sound like a place on this planet? Well, it is. All these things describe the continent to the south of us. All of them are true of South America.

North America and South America share the Western Hemisphere. In many ways, these two continents are alike. Each of them has high mountains in the west. Each has lower mountains in the east. Look at the elevation maps on pages 73 and 147. Find the western and eastern mountains on each continent.

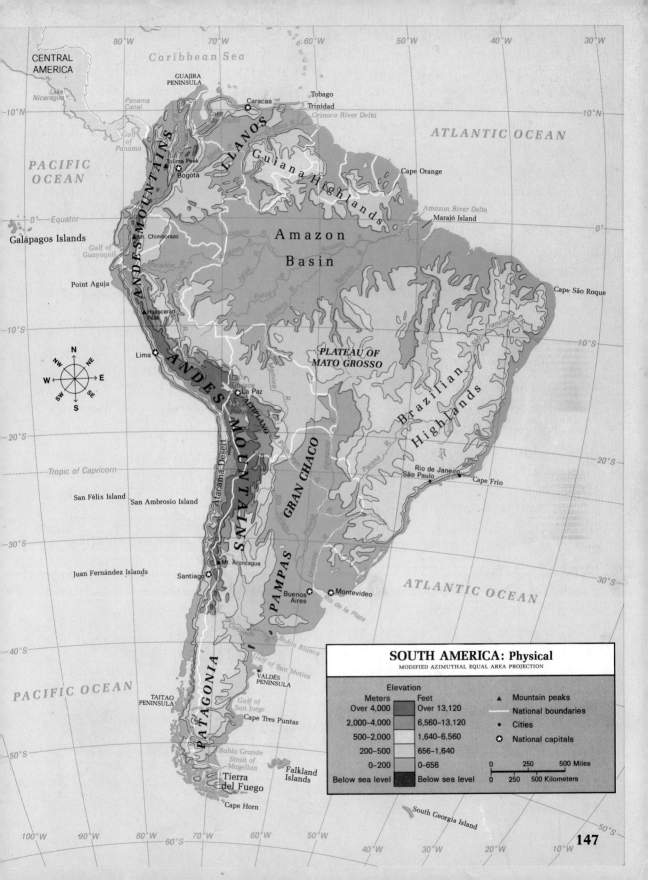

CENTRAL AMERICA

Caribbean Sea

GUAJIRA PENINSULA

Tobago

Trinidad

Caracas

Orinoco River Delta

ATLANTIC OCEAN

LLANOS

Cape Orange

Panama Canal

Lake Maracaibo

Tolima Peak

Guiana Highlands

Amazon River Delta

Marajó Island

Bogotá

Gulf of Panama

ANDES MOUNTAINS

PACIFIC OCEAN

Equator

Mt. Chimborazo

Amazon Basin

Galápagos Islands

Gulf of Guayaquil

Marañón

Amazon

Cape São Roque

Point Aguja

Purus

São Francisco

Huascarán Peak

PLATEAU OF MATO GROSSO

Lima

ANDES MOUNTAINS

La Paz

Lake Titicaca

Altiplano

Lake Poopó

Brazilian Highlands

Atacama Desert

GRAN CHACO

Rio de Janeiro

São Paulo

Cape Frio

Tropic of Capricorn

San Félix Island

San Ambrosio Island

Paraná R.

Juan Fernández Islands

Mt. Aconcagua

PAMPAS

Santiago

Buenos Aires

Montevideo

Rio de la Plata

ATLANTIC OCEAN

Colorado

Bahía Blanca

PACIFIC OCEAN

Gulf of San Matías

PATAGONIA

VALDÉS PENINSULA

TAITAO PENINSULA

Gulf of San Jorge

Cape Tres Puntas

Bahía Grande

Strait of Magellan

Falkland Islands

Tierra del Fuego

Cape Horn

South Georgia Island

SOUTH AMERICA: Physical
MODIFIED AZIMUTHAL EQUAL AREA PROJECTION

Elevation

Meters	Feet
Over 4,000	Over 13,120
2,000–4,000	6,560–13,120
500–2,000	1,640–6,560
200–500	656–1,640
0–200	0–656
Below sea level	Below sea level

▲ Mountain peaks
— National boundaries
• Cities
✪ National capitals

0   250   500 Miles
0   250   500 Kilometers

147

Each continent also has huge plains in the middle. And each has big rivers that flow through the plains. The rains that fall on the plains drain into the rivers.

These are some ways North America and South America are alike. In other ways, the two continents are very different. It is easier to live in North America than in South America. Only in the far north does North America have a harsh climate. In South America, much of the land and climate makes life difficult. As you read on, you will see why this is so.

Highlands of South America

South America has three main areas of highlands. They are the Andes Mountains, the Guiana Highlands, and the Brazilian Highlands.

The Andes Mountains run down the west coast of South America. On a map, this long line of mountains looks like a curving spine. Find the Andes (AN deez) on the elevation map on page 147.

The Andes are the longest system of mountains in the world. They are over 8,045 kilometers (5,000 miles) long. They are also the second-highest mountains in the world. Only the Himalayas (HIM uh LAY uhz) in Asia are higher. More than 45 peaks in the Andes are over 6,098 meters (20,000 feet) high.

The Andes Mountains are close to the Pacific coast. There is only a narrow plain between the ocean and the mountains. Part of this plain is the Atacama (AH tuh KAH muh) Desert. Find this desert on the climate map on page 151. The Atacama Desert is the driest place in South America. In fact, it is one of the driest deserts on Earth. Sometimes, no rain falls there for 10 years. That means it might not have rained there from the time you were born until now!

The Andes Mountains are very steep and rugged. This makes it hard for people to cross the mountains. It is hard to build roads and railroads there. It is also hard for people to live there.

The Andes Mountains are the longest system of mountains on Earth. They stretch from 12° north latitude to 56° south latitude. They are also the world's second-highest mountains.

Look at the elevation map again. Find the *altiplano* (AHL tee PLAH noh) in Bolivia. The **altiplano** is a plateau. It is a large area of high, flat land. In Spanish, *altiplano* means "high plain." People who live in the Andes live on plateaus like the *altiplano*. Or they live in valleys between the mountains. Plateaus and valleys are areas of flat land.

In the mountains, the climate changes as you climb up. The higher you go, the thinner the air gets. Remember, thin air holds less heat and wetness than heavier air does. So the higher you go, the cooler the climate is. Look at the climate map on page 151. Find the equator. It passes through the top part of South America. This means that most of South America is in the tropics. In the lowlands, the climate is very hot. So people prefer to live in the highlands. In the really high areas, the weather is cool all year.

Along the east coast of South America are two other areas of highlands. Look at the elevation map. Find the Guiana (gee AN uh) Highlands in the north. Then find the Brazilian Highlands to the south. Look at the map key. How high are these highlands? Are they as high as the Andes? How close to the Atlantic coast are they? Between these highlands and the ocean, do you see a narrow coastal plain?

Now look at the climate map. The Guiana Highlands are just north of the equator. Angel Falls, the highest waterfall on Earth, is there. Parts of the Guiana Highlands are covered by thick forests.

The Atacama Desert is the driest place in South America. This desert is in northern Chile near 70° west longitude. It stretches from about 20° to 30° south latitude.

Other parts are grasslands. The Guiana Highlands are not high enough to have cool air. So both the forests and the grasslands are very hot. Few people can make a living there.

In the Brazilian Highlands, much of the land is dry grassland. Few people live there, either, except along the coast. Most of South America's people live on plateaus or fertile plains along the coasts.

Lowlands of South America

South America also has three main areas of lowlands. They are the Amazon River valley, the llanos, and the pampas.

Look at the elevation map. Between the Andes, the Guiana Highlands, and the Brazilian Highlands is a huge area of lowlands. This great area is the Amazon River valley. Here the climate is hot and wet all year round.

The Amazon is the second-longest river in the world. It is almost 6,400 kilometers (4,000 miles) long. Only the Nile River in Africa is longer. But the Amazon carries more water than any other river on Earth. When the Amazon flows into the Atlantic, the river is 322 kilometers (200 miles) wide. You cannot even see across it!

The land in the Amazon River valley is covered by a thick rain forest. It is the largest rain forest in the world. Along the river banks, the underbrush is very thick. In the tropics, a very thick growth of plants and trees is called a **jungle.** To reach land from the river, people have to chop through the jungle with big knives. Then, when they get through the jungle, the rain forest seems strange. Tall trees grow so close together that no light reaches the forest floor. Without light, no small plants can root in the ground. Instead, there are huge tree trunks. There are also ferns and tangled vines.

The weather in the Amazon valley is always hot and wet. Because of this, few people live there. The soil in the Amazon valley is not good. The heavy rains wash out many of the minerals that crops need. The heat makes it hard for people to work. It makes

This picture shows the valley of the Amazon River. The Amazon is the second-longest river in the world. It joins the Atlantic at the equator.

CLIMATES OF SOUTH AMERICA

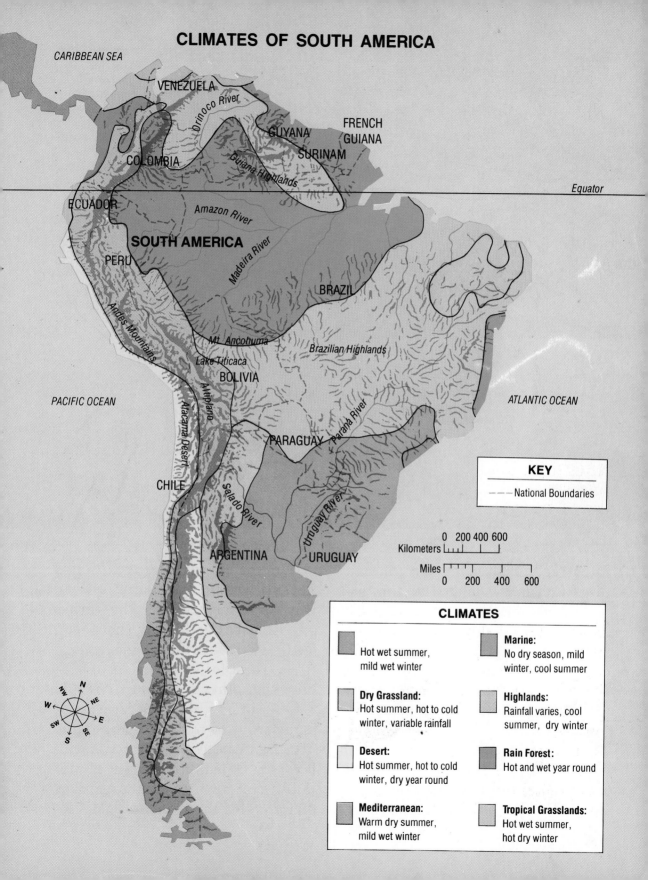

CARIBBEAN SEA

VENEZUELA

Orinoco River

GUYANA

FRENCH GUIANA

SURINAM

COLOMBIA

Guiana Highlands

Equator

ECUADOR

Amazon River

SOUTH AMERICA

PERU

Madeira River

BRAZIL

Andes Mountains

Mt. Ancohuma

Brazilian Highlands

Lake Titicaca

BOLIVIA

Altiplano

PACIFIC OCEAN

ATLANTIC OCEAN

Atacama Desert

PARAGUAY

Paraná River

CHILE

Salado River

Uruguay River

ARGENTINA

URUGUAY

KEY

‒‒‒ National Boundaries

0 200 400 600
Kilometers

Miles

0   200   400   600

N
NW NE
W   E
SW SE
S

CLIMATES

Hot wet summer, mild wet winter

Dry Grassland: Hot summer, hot to cold winter, variable rainfall

Desert: Hot summer, hot to cold winter, dry year round

Mediterranean: Warm dry summer, mild wet winter

Marine: No dry season, mild winter, cool summer

Highlands: Rainfall varies, cool summer, dry winter

Rain Forest: Hot and wet year round

Tropical Grasslands: Hot wet summer, hot dry winter

The Amazon rain forest is the largest rain forest in the world. This man used a bulldozer to clear away roots, limbs, and vines. Cleared land was used to build a road, the Trans-Amazon Highway. This east-west highway runs across Brazil from the Atlantic Ocean to Peru.

Cowboys in Argentina round up cattle on the pampas.

them get tired easily. People can try to clear the land. But the forest keeps growing back. People have to keep fighting the forest.

There is a second area of lowlands in northern South America. This is an area of treeless plains called the **llanos** (YAH nohs). In Spanish, *llano* means "plain." The Orinoco (OR uh NOH koh) River flows through these plains. Find the llanos on the map on page 147. They are in Venezuela.

On the llanos, the weather is hot all year. Most rain falls in the summer. Then, the grass grows fast. Cattle and sheep can feed on it. But during the winter, little rain falls. Then, the heat burns up the grass. Few people live in the llanos. There are not many ways to make a living there.

South of the Amazon River valley is a third large area of flat land. This is a region of grassy plains called the **pampas** (PAM puz).

In a South American Indian language, *pampa* means "plain." The pampas are in Argentina and Uruguay. They are one of the flattest, most fertile areas on Earth. The climate there is good for growing crops and raising animals.

Look at the map on page 147. Find the pampas. The Paraná and Uruguay rivers flow through these fertile plains. On the pampas, the climate is mostly warm all year. Winters are mild. Ranchers raise cattle and sheep on the pampas. Farmers grow huge crops of wheat, rice, oats, and corn.

Look again at the climate map on page 151. Notice that much of South America is warm or hot. Find the desert along the Pacific coast. Then find the desert in the south. It borders on the Atlantic.

Now you can see why much of South America is hard to live in. Many places are too high or too steep. Others are too hot, too wet, or too dry. The people of South America live where the land is flat and the soil is fertile. They live where the climate is comfortable. Soon, you will learn more about how they make a living.

REVIEW

WATCH YOUR WORDS

1. A high plain is a___.
   jungle   plateau   rain forest
2. The high plain in Bolivia is called the___.
   llanos   pampas   *altiplano*
3. A very thick growth of tropical plants and trees is a___.
   llanos   jungle   *altiplano*
4. The hot, treeless plains in Venezuela are called the___.
   llanos   *altiplano*   pampas
5. The fertile plains in Argentina are called the___.
   llanos   pampas   jungle

CHECK YOUR FACTS

6. Name two ways in which North America and South America are alike. Name two ways in which they are different.

7. Name the three highland areas of South America. Where are they?
8. Name three lowland areas in South America. Which lowland area is best for growing food?
9. Describe the climate of the Amazon valley. Why do few people live in this river valley?
10. Where in the Andes Mountains do people live? Why?

SHARPEN YOUR THINKING

11. Why do people in South America call a plateau an *altiplano*? Why do they say *llanos* and *pampas* for plains?

12. "Highest, longest, widest, strongest . . ." Pretend you are writing about South America for the *Guinness Book of World Records*. In what features is South America first or second in the world?

Lesson 2: Resources of South America

FIND THE WORDS

cacao   llama   alpaca
export   import

Much of South America's land may be hard to live on. But the continent is very rich in natural resources. Nonliving resources include fertile land and mineral wealth. Living resources include crops, animals, and products that grow in the forests.

Some land in the highlands and plains of South America is fertile. Fertile soil contains the minerals plants need to grow. On their fertile land, the South Americans grow large crops. Coffee trees produce beans used to make coffee. **Cacao** (kuh KAY oh) trees produce seeds used to make chocolate and cocoa. Sugar cane has thick stems from which we get sugar. And bananas also grow in South America. In places with mild climates, people grow wheat, oats, and corn. You could have a good breakfast with cereal, bananas, and cocoa from South America!

Some people in South America raise animals for a living. They raise cattle and sheep for milk,

Some South Americans grow bananas. They make money by selling bananas to other nations. Bananas are a South American export.

RESOURCES OF SOUTH AMERICA AND CENTRAL AMERICA

RESOURCES

- 🥣 Sugar Cane
- 🍌 Bananas
- 🛢 Petroleum
- ☕ Coffee
- 🐂 Beef Cattle
- ⬛ Iron Ore
- ▦ Copper
- 🧵 Cotton
- 🥤 Cacao
- 🌽 Corn
- 🐑 Sheep
- 🛢 Tin
- 🌾 Wheat
- ⬭ Silver

SCALE

Kilometers 0 — 1000

Miles 0 — 500 — 1000

Llamas live in the Andes Mountains. Their soft wool is used to make cloth and clothing.

meat, leather, and wool. They also raise llamas and alpacas. A **llama** (LAH muh) looks like a little camel without a hump. An **alpaca** (al PAK uh) looks like a sheep. Both llamas and alpacas have soft wool. South American farmers grow cotton, too.

Natural resources help South American people earn money. Much of what they raise is sold in other parts of the world. To sell goods to other countries is to *export* (ek SPORT) them. Goods sold to other countries are called **exports** (EK sports). Goods bought by one country from another are **imports** (IM ports). The United States *imports* (im PORTS) almost all its coffee from South America. Coffee is an export that helps South Americans earn money.

South Americans also grow crops for their own use. Corn, potatoes, and onions are among the crops they grow for themselves. Other living resources grow in the Amazon rain forest. Rubber trees grow there. Other trees produce nuts and furnish valuable wood for building.

Much of the best land in South America is owned by large landowners. A few landowners may own huge areas of land. Workers and their children live on this land. The workers are mostly poor. Many of them are South American Indians. Some small farmers in South America own their own land. But usually this is not good land.

Metals and other minerals are important South American resources. The first Europeans in South America were looking for gold and silver. They found great amounts of those metals in the Andes. But gold and silver are only a small part of South America's mineral wealth. There are also diamonds and emeralds on the continent. Tin is found in Bolivia. There is copper in Chile and Peru. There is iron in Brazil, Venezuela, and Colombia.

There is petroleum in Peru, Venezuela, Ecuador, and Colombia. This thick, dark-colored liquid is sometimes called black gold. Gasoline and fuel oil are made from petroleum. That is why this mineral is so valuable.

Look at the map on page 155. It shows the resources of South America. You can see that metals and other minerals are found throughout the continent. But most minerals are found in the highlands.

Unfortunately, there are problems with the mineral wealth of South America. First, the continent does not have much usable coal. Also, many countries do not have enough petroleum. Coal and petroleum can provide the energy to run factories and mines. Buying coal and petroleum from other countries is very costly.

Second, many minerals are in places that are hard to reach. Or they are far from places where people live. It is hard to get those minerals out of the ground. That means the minerals cost more to use. These two problems have made it hard for South Americans to develop their continent.

REVIEW

WATCH YOUR WORDS

1. ___ and ___ are South American animals with soft wool.
Cattle Llamas Kangaroos Alpacas

2. Chocolate and cocoa come from ___ seeds.
alpaca coffee cacao

3. We get gasoline and fuel oil from ___.
alpacas petroleum rubber

4. Coffee, bananas, and cacao are South American ___.
exports imports nonliving resources

5. In the United States, coffee is a(n) ___.
export import natural resource

CHECK YOUR FACTS
Look at the Map
6. Is silver found in the east or the west?

7. Are more sheep and cattle raised in the north or the south?

8. Are cotton and sugar cane grown on the west or the east coast?

9. Is more petroleum found in the northwest or the southeast?

10. Where do bananas grow?

Look at the Lesson
11. What are exports? What are imports?

12. List three crops that South America exports.

13. List three animals that South Americans raise.

14. What is petroleum? Why is it so valuable?

15. What are two problems in developing South America's resources?

Lesson 3: People of South America

FIND THE WORDS

conquer   conquistador   empire
descendants   ancestors

It is the year 1531. A small group of Spanish soldiers sails down the west coast of South America. Their leader is Francisco Pizarro (fran SIS koh pih ZAH roh). He has heard of a rich Indian empire. He and his soldiers are on their way to conquer it.

In 1532, the Spanish soldiers reach Peru. High in the Andes, they find the empire of the Incas (ING kuz). The Spanish soldiers have horses, swords, and guns. They capture the emperor. The Incas bring them a great treasure in gold and silver to set the emperor free.

Even so, Pizarro and his soldiers kill the emperor. Then they go on to conquer the Incan empire. To **conquer** is to defeat in battle. A Spanish conqueror was called by a Spanish word—**conquistador** (kohn kees tah DOR).

Afterward, the Spanish sent gold and silver back to Spain. They forced the Indians to work for them in mines and fields. And they set up certain ways of living in South America. Those ways of living are still followed today.

Earliest Peoples

People lived in the Western Hemisphere long before the Spanish came. Experts believe that the first Americans came from Asia. They think these people crossed at the Bering Sea. Look at the map on page 87. Find the Bering Sea. It is where Asia and North America almost touch.

The first peoples from Asia were bands of hunters. They were following herds of animals. Some of these people settled in North America. They lived in forests, deserts, and plains. Others kept going south. They traveled to Central America and South America.

Five thousand years ago, people in Central America had learned to farm. Some of these peoples went on to build great cities and nations. About 550 years ago, two groups began to build empires. An **empire** is a group of lands or nations under one government. The Aztecs built a great empire in Mexico. The Incas stretched their empire across the Andes Mountains. The Incan empire grew until it was 4,000 kilometers (2,500 miles) long!

To the Incas, riches were workers, crops, animals, and land. They used gold and silver for decoration. But gold and silver were

158

The Incas made this statue of a llama out of gold.

This is a South American Indian settlement. It is in the Andes Mountains of Peru.

riches to the Spanish. For this glittering wealth, the Spanish conquered the Incas' lands.

People from Many Lands

Today, the descendants of the first Americans live in North America and South America. We call them American Indians or Native Americans. Actually, each group has its own name and language. The American Indians are descendants of the early peoples from Asia. People's **descendants** are like their great-grandchildren. The early peoples from Asia were the ancestors of the American Indians. People's **ancestors** are like their great-grandparents.

Most South American Indians live in the highlands of the Andes Mountains. They live in the nations of Bolivia, Ecuador, and Peru. That is where the empire of the Incas used to be. At least half

the people in these nations are American Indians. Other South American Indians live in the rain forests of the Amazon River. Find these places on the climate map on page 151.

About 450 years ago, people from Europe began to come to South America. They came first from Spain and Portugal. These nations set up colonies in the new land. Nine South American nations used to be colonies of Spain. They are Venezuela, Colombia, Ecuador, Peru, Bolivia, Chile, Argentina, Uruguay, and Paraguay. Find these countries on the map on page 163. Then find Brazil. Brazil used to be a colony of Portugal. Today, many people in South America speak Spanish. But people in Brazil speak Portuguese.

People from Great Britain, the Netherlands, and France also came to South America. They, too, set up colonies in the new world. Guyana used to be a British colony. Suriname was Dutch. French Guiana was a colony of France. Today, it is a department of France. France's departments are like our states. Can you name the overseas state of our country?

Some Europeans came to South America to search for gold and silver. Others started businesses or farms. Today, people with European ancestors live all over South America. Most people in Argentina and Uruguay are descendants of people from Italy and Spain.

Some European settlers brought people from Africa to their colonies. They forced the Africans to work as slaves. Many Africans worked in sugar cane fields on the east coast. Others worked in mines. The Africans had to do the heavy work that Indians did elsewhere. Slavery went on for hundreds of years. Finally, in the nineteenth century, slavery was ended. Today, the descendants of the early Africans live all over South America. But most of the people with African ancestors live in Brazil.

Look at the pictures on page 159. Notice the many different faces of South Americans. People have come to South America from all over the Earth.

REVIEW

WATCH YOUR WORDS

1. Pizarro and his Spanish soldiers ___ the Incas.
   colonized conquered founded
2. What was a Spanish conqueror called?
3. The ___ of the Incas was 4,000 kilometers long.
   road canal empire
4. The American Indians are ___ of Asian peoples.
   ancestors conquerors descendants
5. Many people in Brazil have African ___.
   descendants ancestors landowners

CHECK YOUR FACTS
Look at the Lesson

6. Where did the first Americans come from?
7. Why did Francisco Pizarro go to South America?
8. What happened to the Indians when the Spanish came?
9. How did Africans first come to South America?
10. Why did Europeans come to South America?

Look at the Map

Look at the map on page 163. Where were the colonies of Spain? Use the cardinal and intermediate directions.

Lesson 4: Nations and Cities of South America

FIND THE WORDS

middle class
progress

Twelve nations and one state occupy the land of South America. You already know something about the land, climate, and people of each. You can learn more by looking at the map on page 163.

Find Brazil on the map. You can see that Brazil is the biggest country in South America. It takes up almost half the continent. Look at the borders of Brazil. How many countries touch Brazil?

Now find Chile. It is a long, narrow country. It is tucked between the Andes Mountains and the Pacific Ocean. Then go north and find Colombia. Colombia has coasts on both the Caribbean Sea and the Pacific Ocean. Play a game using the map for a treasure hunt. See how many other interesting facts you can find. Can you find the second-largest country? Can you find any countries that do not touch Brazil?

The chart on page 164 gives you more information about each nation. Which nations have more than 10 million people?

Where the People Live

Look at the population map of South America on page 164. Use your finger to trace around the edges of the continent. Most South Americans live along the coasts.

Much of the middle of South America is wilderness. Wilderness is wild or empty land where no one lives. There are few roads or railroads in the middle of South America. The middle of North America is very different. It has many big cities, such as Chicago, St. Louis, and Denver. It also has many roads and railroads.

About half of South America's people live in cities. South American cities are as big and busy as cities anywhere in the world. Find the cities on the population map. They are the largest cities in South America. Most of these big cities are near the ocean.

Common Problems

The nations and cities of South America share many problems. The most important problem is poverty. Many people in South American countries are poor. In South America, being poor can mean many things. It can mean

SOUTH AMERICA: Political

MODIFIED AZIMUTHAL EQUAL AREA PROJECTION

— National boundaries
• Cities
⊛ National capitals

0   250   500   750 Miles
0   250   500   750 Kilometers

CENTRAL AMERICA

Caribbean Sea

TRINIDAD AND TOBAGO

Barranquilla
Cartagena
Maracaibo
Barquisimeto
Valencia
Caracas

Lake Maracaibo

VENEZUELA

San Cristóbal
Medellín
Bucaramanga
Bogotá
Cali

COLOMBIA

Orinoco R.

Georgetown
Paramaribo
Cayenne

GUYANA
SURINAME
French Guiana (France)

PACIFIC OCEAN

⊛ Quito

ECUADOR
Guayaquil

Iquitos

Amazon R.

Manaus

Marajó Island

Belém
São Luís

Fortaleza

ATLANTIC OCEAN

Equator

Galápagos Islands (Ecuador)

Trujillo

PERU

Callao
Lima

Cuzco

BRAZIL

Recife
Maceió

Arequipa
La Paz

BOLIVIA

Sucre

Salvador

Brasília

Belo Horizonte

Iquique

Chuquicamata

Antofagasta

PARAGUAY

Salta

Asunción

Rio de Janeiro
São Paulo
Niterói

Tropic of Capricorn

Curitiba

San Félix Island (Chile)
San Ambrosio Island (Chile)

CHILE

San Miguel de Tucumán

Paraná R.

Córdoba
Santa Fe
Paraná
Rosario

Pôrto Alegre

URUGUAY

Juan Fernández Islands (Chile)

Valparaíso
Santiago

Buenos Aires
La Plata

Montevideo

Río de la Plata

ATLANTIC OCEAN

Concepción

ARGENTINA

Bahía Blanca

Colorado R.

Valdivia

PACIFIC OCEAN

N
NW NE
W E
SW SE
S

Punta Arenas

Strait of Magellan

Falkland Islands (U.K.)

South Georgia Island (Falkland I.)

163

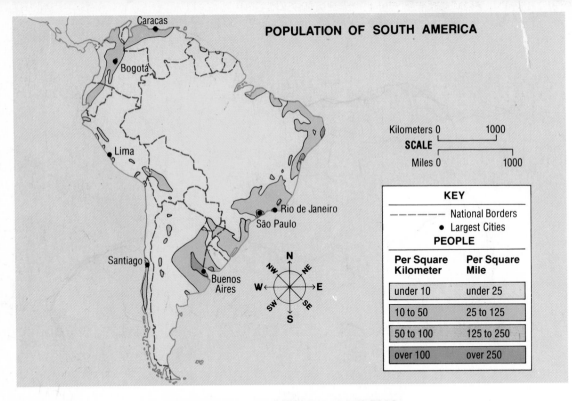

POPULATION OF SOUTH AMERICA

SCALE
Kilometers 0 — 1000
Miles 0 — 1000

KEY	
– – – –	National Borders
●	Largest Cities

PEOPLE

Per Square Kilometer	Per Square Mile
under 10	under 25
10 to 50	25 to 125
50 to 100	125 to 250
over 100	over 250

SOUTH AMERICAN NATIONS

Nations	Area		Number of people	Capital	Official language
	square miles	square kilometers			
ARGENTINA (AHR jun TEE nuh)	1,068,301	2,776,889	29 million	Buenos Aires	Spanish
BOLIVIA (buh LIV ee uh)	424,164	1,098,581	6 million	Sucre and La Paz	Spanish
BRAZIL (bruh ZIL)	3,265,075	8,456,508	133 million	Brasília	Portuguese
CHILE (CHIL ee)	292,135	756,626	12 million	Santiago	Spanish
COLOMBIA (kuh LUM bee uh)	439,737	1,138,914	30 million	Bogotá	Spanish
ECUADOR (EHK wuh DOR)	109,483	283,561	9 million	Quito	Spanish
GUYANA (gy AN uh)	83,000	214,969	1 million	Georgetown	English
PARAGUAY (PAR uh GWY)	157,048	406,752	4 million	Asuncíon	Spanish
PERU (puh ROO)	496,224	1,285,216	20 million	Lima	Spanish
SURINAME (SUR uh NAM)	63,037	163,265	⅓ million	Paramaribo	Dutch
URUGUAY (YUR uh GWY)	68,037	176,215	3 million	Montevideo	Spanish
VENEZUELA (VEN uh ZWAY luh)	352,144	912,050	15 million	Caracas	Spanish
Department of France					
FRENCH GUIANA (french gee AN uh)	35,135	91,000	¹⁄₁₀ million	Cayenne	French

Rio de Janeiro is a port city in Brazil at 23° south latitude, 43° west longitude.

The city of Santiago is the capital of Chile.

having no running water or electricity in your home. It can mean having tattered clothes and no shoes. It can mean not being able to go to the doctor when you are sick. If you are poor, there may not be a school for you to go to. Your parents may not have jobs. You may not have enough food.

Outside the cities, most of the people are small farmers. They work on land owned by big landowners. Many people move from the farm to the city to find better jobs. But most cannot find work.

The governments of all the countries want to develop their resources. They build public works, such as highways, railroads, dams, and power plants. They encourage people to start businesses and build factories. In these ways, the governments help provide jobs.

For many years, there were only two classes of people in South America. There were the rich and the poor. The rich owned the land. They ran the businesses and the government. The poor did the hard work. They had little to say about how their government was run. There was only a tiny middle class.

The **middle class** is made up of people who are neither rich nor poor. They are mostly people with good jobs. They work in offices, factories, shops, banks, and other businesses. Some of them are doctors, lawyers, and teachers. They are able to earn enough money to meet their needs.

165

Fun Facts

The driest place in the world:
Calama, in Chile, is in the Atacama Desert. Calama is the driest place in the world. No one has ever seen it rain there. In fact, in the Atacama Desert in Chile, it did not rain for about 400 years! Finally, in 1971, some rain fell there.

The river with the most water:
The Amazon River carries more water than any other river in the world. Only the Nile River in Africa is longer than the Amazon. This mighty river was named for the Amazons. In Greek myths, they were a nation of women who were warriors.

Earth's largest rain forest:
The largest rain forest on Earth is in the Amazon River valley. Trees grow so close together there that sunlight never reaches the ground.

Earth's longest mountains:
The Andes are the longest system of mountains in the world. They are over 8,045 kilometers (5,000 miles) long. Only the Himalayas in Asia are higher than the Andes.

Earth's highest waterfall:
Angel Falls in Venezuela is the highest waterfall on Earth. This waterfall was named for James Angel. He was an American pilot who found the falls in 1935. Angel Falls drops 979 meters (3,212 feet).

Earth's largest high-altitude lake:
Lake Titicaca is on the *altiplano* of Bolivia. It is 3,813 meters (12,506 feet) above sea level. It is also 209 kilometers (130 miles) long.

Here is a good way to tell how well a country is doing. Look at the size of the middle class. In the United States, most of the people are in the middle class.

Argentina, Uruguay, Chile, and Brazil are doing well. These countries have many people in the middle class. Also, the middle class in these countries is growing. That means that fewer people are poor.

Other countries in South America have a very small middle class. Bolivia, Ecuador, Peru, Suriname, and Paraguay are some of these countries. Many people in these countries cannot read and write. The governments of these countries are having trouble providing work. All over South America, the population is increasing. There are more people looking for work than there are jobs. So most people in poor countries will probably be poor for a long time.

The countries with a growing middle class are making progress. **Progress** (PROG ress) is improvement. It is action taken to reach a goal. Jobs for people are a sign of progress. Electricity, running water, schools, and doctors are signs of progress, too.

REVIEW

WATCH YOUR WORDS

1. A ＿＿ is a wild region where no people live.
   plain   wilderness   coast
2. The ＿＿ is growing in Argentina and Brazil.
   empire   wilderness   middle class
3. Jobs that allow people to meet their needs are signs of ＿＿.
   poverty   progress   wealth

CHECK YOUR FACTS

Look at the Maps

4. What is the largest country in South America?
5. List the countries that touch the borders of Brazil.
6. Where do most South Americans live?

Look at the Chart

7. What five countries have the most people?
8. What five countries have the fewest people?

Look at the Lesson

9. What is it like to be poor in South America?
10. Why do people move from the farm to the city?
11. What is the middle class?
12. How can a government help provide more jobs?
13. What are some signs of progress in South America?

SHARPEN YOUR THINKING

Many people live in the middle of North America. Why do so few live in the middle of South America?

CHAPTER REVIEW

WATCH YOUR WORDS

1. The ___ is a plateau in Bolivia, high in the mountains.
   pampas *altiplano* llanos
2. Hot chocolate comes from the ___ bean.
   coffee cacao alpaca
3. In Brazil, coffee is an ___ . In the United States, coffee is an ___ .
   import export artifact
4. Many people in Brazil are ___ of African peoples.
   ancestors artifacts descendants
5. Many people in Argentina had Spanish ___ .
   descendants ancestors llamas
6. Jobs and education are signs of ___ .
   progress resources empire

CHECK YOUR FACTS

7. Why is much of South America's land hard to live on?
8. List three important facts about the Andes Mountains.
9. List two important facts about the Amazon River.
10. What is the Amazon rain forest like?
11. What is the climate like in the Amazon River valley?
12. List three important things about the pampas.
13. South America has many resources. Name three animals, three plants, and three minerals.
14. Who was Francisco Pizarro?
15. Name three continents from which people came to South America.
16. Name four European countries that had colonies in South America.

APPLY YOUR SKILLS

USE YOUR CHART

Look at the chart on page 164.

17. How many nations are there in South America?
18. Which nation has the most land? Which has the most people?
19. Which nation is smallest in area?
20. How many nations have Spanish as their official language?
21. Where is Portuguese spoken?

USE YOUR MAP SKILLS

22. Draw a map of South America.
23. Label the Andes Mountains, the Atacama Desert, the Amazon River, the Amazon rain forest, and the pampas.
24. Color the Andes brown, the Atacama yellow, the Amazon blue, the rain forest green, and the pampas green.
25. Put red dots on the map to show where most of the people live.
26. Label these cities: São Paulo, Caracas, Rio de Janeiro, Buenos Aires, Lima, Santiago, and Bogotá.

SHARPEN YOUR THINKING

27. Where would you rather live—the *altiplano*, the pampas, or the rain forest? Why?
28. Why is it hard for South Americans to develop their resources?
29. Why don't people live in the middle of South America?
30. Do you think it is good for a country to have a large middle class? Why, or why not?

CHAPTER

2 LIVING IN A HIGH LAND

Lesson 1: Bolivia

FIND THE WORDS

coastline   **seaport**   **high-altitude**

Bolivia is one of the nations in South America. It is about the size of Texas and California combined.

There are several special things about Bolivia. First, this country has no coastline. A **coastline** is a natural boundary next to the ocean. Bolivia is not on the ocean. It has to ship its products from a seaport in Chile. A **seaport** is a town on the coast where ships can load and unload. One other nation in South America has no coastline and no seaports. Look at the political map on page 163. Can you find that other nation? What is it? Find Bolivia on the map, too.

Here is another special thing about Bolivia. Most of the people live on a very small part of the land. Look at the physical map on page 171. There are two very different kinds of land in Bolivia. There are high mountains in the

Lake Titicaca is the largest high-altitude lake in the world. It is 3,813 meters (12,506 feet) above sea level. Most people have never been that high except in an airplane. Lake Titicaca is at 16° south latitude, 69° west longitude.

west. There are grassy plains and rain forests in the east. Where do you think most Bolivians live?

Did you guess that they live in the west? If so, you guessed right! Most Bolivians live on a plateau high in the Andes Mountains. That plateau is called the *altiplano*. Most of the *altiplano* is about 3,660 meters (12,000 feet) above sea level. So most Bolivians live in a high land.

Another special thing about Bolivia is this. Bolivia has two capital cities! By law, the capital is Sucre (SOO kray). It is in the middle of the country. The other capital is La Paz (lah PAHZ). It is north and west of Sucre. Bolivia's courts of law are in Sucre. The congress and most of the government buildings are in La Paz.

La Paz is on the *altiplano*. It is Bolivia's largest city. La Paz is also one of the highest cities in the world. La Paz is 3,600 meters (11,800 feet) above sea level. At that elevation, the air is cold and thin. Visitors find it hard to breathe. But Bolivians are very comfortable living there.

The *altiplano*'s main resources are minerals. Tin, silver, and copper are found there. Minerals are Bolivia's most important exports. Land on the *altiplano* is not very fertile. A cereal grass called millet grows there. So do potatoes, onions, and some other vegetables.

Fish are another resource found on the *altiplano*. They come from Lake Titicaca (TEE tee KAH kah). Lake Titicaca is the largest high-altitude lake in the world. The term **high-altitude** means "high above sea level."

Bolivia has mountain valleys that are much more fertile than

BOLIVIA

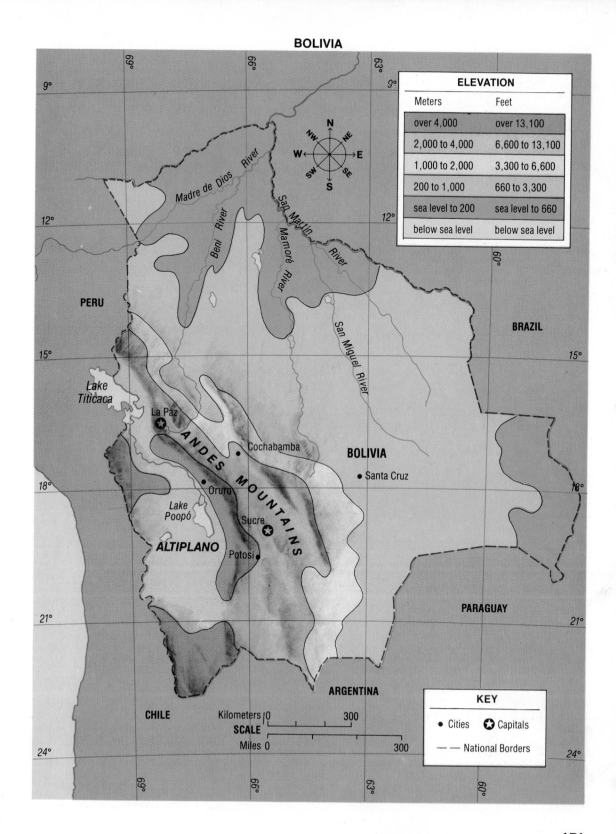

ELEVATION

Meters	Feet
over 4,000	over 13,100
2,000 to 4,000	6,600 to 13,100
1,000 to 2,000	3,300 to 6,600
200 to 1,000	660 to 3,300
sea level to 200	sea level to 660
below sea level	below sea level

N
NW NE
W E
SW SE
S

9°
12°
15°
18°
21°
24°

69° 66° 63° 60°

PERU

BRAZIL

Madre de Dios River

Beni River

San Martín

Mamoré River

San Miguel River

Lake Titicaca

La Paz

Cochabamba

BOLIVIA

Santa Cruz

Oruro

Lake Poopó

Sucre

Potosí

ANDES MOUNTAINS

ALTIPLANO

PARAGUAY

CHILE

ARGENTINA

SCALE
Kilometers 0 ———— 300
Miles 0 ———— 300

KEY

• Cities   ⭐ Capitals

– – – National Borders

Coffee grows in Bolivia's fertile valleys.

the *altiplano*. Coffee, sugar, fruit, and grains grow in the valleys. Sucre is in one of these valleys.

Bolivia needs to develop its resources in the east. The few people who live on the eastern plains raise cattle and goats. There is much fertile soil in the east. But little of the land is being farmed. There are also rich forests. And there are valuable minerals, such as iron ore, petroleum, and natural gas.

To use these rich lands, Bolivia needs better transportation. Now, there are few highways and railroads in the east. It is hard to get food and cattle from the east to the cities in the mountains. So it is hard for people in the east to sell their products. Many of the goods that are sold in Bolivia travel by air. Moving goods by airplane costs more than sending them by train, ship, or truck. Why do you think this is so?

REVIEW

WATCH YOUR WORDS

1. Every country that has the ocean as a boundary has a(n)____.
   altiplano   coastline   import

2. A(n) ____ is a town on the coast where ships can load and unload.
   export   *altiplano*   seaport

3. Lake Titicaca is the largest____lake in the world.
   fishing   high-altitude   polluted

CHECK YOUR FACTS

4. What are three special things about Bolivia?

5. Where do most Bolivians live?

6. What natural resources are found on the *altiplano*?

7. What natural resources do the mountain valleys have?

8. What natural resources are in the east of Bolivia? Why aren't these resources being used?

SHARPEN YOUR THINKING

9. Why would not having a coastline be a problem for a nation?

10. Why would it be hard to build roads and railroads across Bolivia?

Lesson 2: The People of the Altiplano

FIND THE WORDS

plantation   ranch   hacienda
criollos   campesino

Imagine a time over 1,400 years ago. At that time, a great city was built on the *altiplano*. This city was in Bolivia, near Lake Titicaca. It was about 4,000 meters (13,000 feet) above sea level. It was called Tiahuanaco (tee uh wuh NAH koh).

The people of Tiahuanaco built huge stone palaces and temples. They carved statues from great blocks of stone. One statue is called *Gateway to the Sun*. Pictures of the sun, of gods, and of giant birds are carved on it. The people of Tiahuanaco also wove beautiful cloth. They painted pottery. And they knew how to work with metals. Tiahuanaco lasted about 600 years as a great city. Experts think it was a religious center. Today, only its ruins remain.

Who built Tiahuanaco so long ago? Many think the ancestors of the Aymara built it. The Aymara (eye MAH ruh) are South American Indians. They lived on the *altiplano* long before the Incas came.

The Incas

Around the year 1100, the Incas came to the *altiplano*. They built their capital at Cuzco (KOOS koh) in Peru. Look at the political map of South America on page 163. Find Cuzco. You can see it is not far from Lake Titicaca.

Over 300 years went by. Then, in the 1400s, the Incas started to build their empire. They conquered other Indian groups in the Andes region. After a long struggle, they conquered the Aymara.

The Incas learned a lot from the people who lived on the *altiplano* before them. They also taught the Aymara some new ways of doing things. The Incas

The people of Tiahuanaco carved the *Gateway to the Sun*. The running figure at right is one of many carvings on the gateway.

The Incas wove wool and cotton cloth. Incan women knew almost all of the weaving methods and patterns used today.

were expert at planning and organizing. They counted their people. They made maps of their land. They built one road through the mountains and another along the coast. They dug canals to carry water to dry fields. They grew crops on the sides of mountains. They built stone cities that not even earthquakes could destroy. They wove wool and cotton cloth. They mined gold and silver. They knew how to make bronze from copper and tin. They were expert farmers and excellent soldiers. By the 1500s, the Incas ruled much of South America's west coast.

Some Aymara escaped to the mountains when the Incas came. Others stayed and learned Incan ways of fighting and farming. They helped build canals and roads. But most refused to learn the Incan language and religion. The Incas ruled the Aymara. But the Aymara way of life went on.

The Spanish

Then, in 1532, the Spanish came. Francisco Pizarro and his soldiers conquered the Incas. In 1538, his two brothers conquered the Aymara. Now the Spanish ruled all the American Indians of the *altiplano*.

Soon, the Spanish found the rich silver mines that the Incas had used. To get this silver, the Spanish forced Indians to dig in the mines. Many Indians died from too much work and too little food. Others died from European diseases. They caught these diseases from the Spanish.

The Spanish in South America made the Spanish in Europe rich. They sent silver and other treasure back to Spain. In return, the rulers of Spain gave the Spanish settlers land. The settlers used their lands to raise crops and animals.

A large farm where crops are raised is called a **plantation**. A large farm used to raise animals is called a **ranch**. In South America, a Spanish ranch or plantation was called a **hacienda** (HAH see EN duh). The Spanish settlers owned the haciendas. They had the best, most fertile land. They forced the Indians to work for them. Some hacienda owners became very rich.

Spain ruled the *altiplano* for almost 300 years. The king and queen of Spain lived far away.

WHERE WE ARE IN TIME AND PLACE

THE INCA EMPIRE

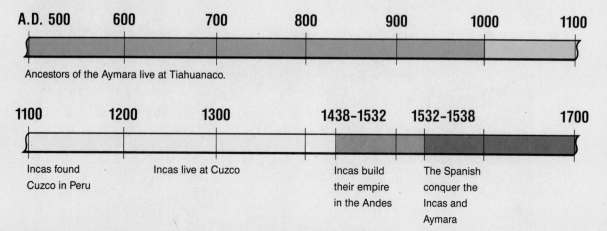

A.D. 500	600	700	800	900	1000	1100

Ancestors of the Aymara live at Tiahuanaco.

1100	1200	1300	1438–1532	1532–1538	1700

Incas found Cuzco in Peru

Incas live at Cuzco

Incas build their empire in the Andes

The Spanish conquer the Incas and Aymara

THE INCA EMPIRE

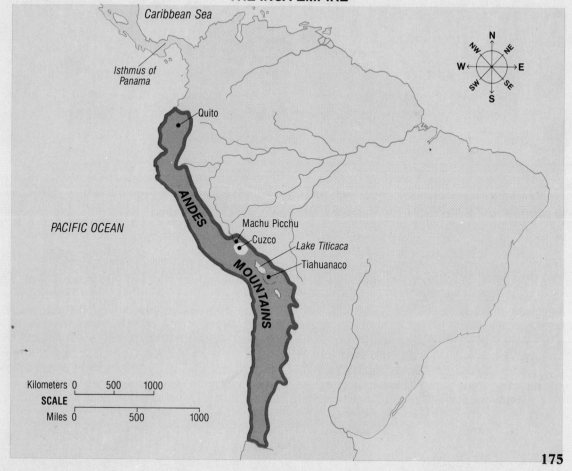

In 1911, Hiram Bingham made a great discovery. He was the son and grandson of missionaries. He taught at Yale University. And he had come to South America to explore Incan ruins.

He found what he called "the lost city of the Incas." It was the city of Machu Picchu (MAH choo PEEK choo). It was near the Incan capital of Cuzco in Peru.

Machu Picchu was built on a high ridge between mountain peaks. Bingham had never seen anything like it before. The city looked almost as if the Incas had just left it. It was built on many levels. More than 3,000 steps led from one level to another. Like other Incan cities, it had homes, temples, and palaces. It also had government buildings and a lookout tower. It was 2,058 meters (6,750 feet) above sea level.

To build this mountain city, the Incas first made models of clay. Then they cut and shaped large blocks of stone. They used ramps and rollers to move the stones. Then they fitted the stones very carefully together. Because they built so well, Machu Picchu has lasted for more than 800 years! People still visit it. How would you like to live there, on top of the world?

They sent Spanish officials to govern the *altiplano* for them. These officials made laws. They collected taxes. They controlled the army. The Spanish rulers and officials made decisions for the people of South America.

Independence

Many Spanish settlers wanted to make their own decisions. Many of them had been born on the *altiplano*. The *altiplano*—not Spain—was their home. They called themselves **criollos** (kree OHL yohs).

In 1809, fighting broke out between the Spanish soldiers and the criollos. The fighting lasted 16 years. Finally, the Spanish were defeated. The armies of the criollos won. These armies were led by two great generals. They were Simón Bolívar (see MOHN boh LEE vahr) and Antonio de Sucre (an TOH nee oh duh SOO kray).

A new, independent nation was born in 1825. It was called Bolivia in honor of General Bolívar. Its capital city was called Sucre after General de Sucre. Sucre was Bolivia's first president.

Independence for Bolivia made little difference to the Aymara. The Indians still dug silver in the mines. They still worked on the haciendas. They received little or no pay. Their lives were still ruled by others.

The *patrón* (pah TROHN), or boss, owned the land. The Indians

Left: Aymara mothers carry young children with them on their backs.
Right: These Aymara students go to school on the *altiplano*.

had to farm the land for the *patrón*. Indian families also took turns working as servants in the *patrón*'s home. They cooked meals and cleaned house. They milked cows and herded sheep and cattle. They cleaned the stables. They fixed the hacienda buildings. The *patrón* let the Indian families use small plots of ground. There, they could grow food for themselves. In some places, the *patrón* provided a school for the children. But the *patrón* could also beat the Indians and take their land away. Life was hard for these American Indians.

Finally, in 1952, the people of the *altiplano* won their freedom. Workers from the haciendas and the mines joined with poor people from the cities. They put their own leaders in charge of the government. This new government made many changes. Most of the hacienda lands were divided up. Now, families could own their little plots of land. New schools were built. Everyone over 20 got the right to vote. And the Indians got a new name. They were no longer the *patrón*'s servants. They were **campesinos** (KAM puh SEE nohz), or "small farmers."

Today, the *campesinos* are the largest group in Bolivia. About half of them are Aymara.

REVIEW

WATCH YOUR WORDS

1. A large farm where workers grow crops is a___.
   campesino   plantation   ranch

2. A large farm where herds of animals are raised is a ___.
   plantation   ranch   *campesino*

3. A large Spanish farm in South America was a___.
   hacienda   *campesino*   *patrón*

4. Some Spanish settlers on the *altiplano* fought for independence from Spain. They were___.
   campesinos   Incas   criollos

5. The Aymara people who became small farmers are___.
   criollos   *patróns*   *campesinos*

CHECK YOUR FACTS

6. How did the Incas change life on the *altiplano*? Name five things they did.

7. What happened to the Aymara and the Incas when the Spanish came?

8. Why did some Spanish settlers fight Spain?

9. Who was Simón Bolívar? Who was Antonio de Sucre? How did their people honor them?

10. What did an Indian family on a hacienda do for the *patrón*?

WRITE ABOUT IT

Pretend you are a *campesino*. You used to work for a *patrón*. Write a letter. Tell how your life changed in 1952.

Lesson 3: The Future of the Aymara

FIND THE WORDS

adapt   pack animal
memorize   civics

Since Incan times, the Aymara have kept their own culture. In their villages, they still follow customs from the old days. They pass on their dances, songs, and beliefs. They speak the Aymara language of their ancestors. They make artifacts, such as colorful blankets and shawls.

Over the years, the Aymara learned to live under many different rulers. To do this, they had to adapt. To **adapt** is to change when the conditions around you change. Aymara life is still changing.

The Village

In this lesson, we will visit an Aymara village. This village is on the shore of Lake Titicaca. Long ago, village people built their houses of mud brick, with roofs of straw. Now, most live in

In the villages, some Aymara follow their old ways. They cut wool from their llamas. Then they spin the wool into thread. After that, they use hand looms to weave the thread into cloth.

Once, the Aymara used llamas to carry goods to market. Now, they use trucks.

Bottom Left: Aymara farmers plant potatoes. Their ancestors were the first people in the world to grow potatoes.
Bottom Right: The Aymara sell their onions at a market in La Paz.

two-story houses with metal roofs. Once, people wove their cloth from the wool of llamas. Then, they sewed their clothes by hand. Now, they often buy their cloth. Many make clothes on sewing machines. Many also buy ready-made clothes in stores. Some are proud that they can dress the same way city people do.

This Aymara village is about 80 kilometers (50 miles) from La Paz. Once, the trip to La Paz was long and hard. Then, village people used llamas to carry their goods to market. An animal that carries a load on its back is called a **pack animal.** In Incan times, the armies used llamas to carry their supplies. Now, trucks carry goods between the village and the city. Many families in the village hope to own a truck someday. Village people can also get to the city on bicycles or on the bus.

Market Women

Most of the people in the village are small farmers. Their ancestors were the first people in the world to grow potatoes. Now, onions are the most important crop in the village. Both onions and potatoes grow well at high altitudes. The teenage village girls sell the onions in the city markets. Village families get most of their money from the onion sales.

Dolores Santiago always wanted to be a market woman. This is her story.

"I can still remember my childhood days. We were very poor. One day, a market woman came to our house. She wore new shoes and a brightly colored shawl. She had shiny black hair. Her eyes twinkled. She carried a big package. In it was my first pair of real shoes. I decided that I wanted to be a market woman.

"By the time I was 14, I was taking things to market for many families. I had to learn how to get the best price for their vegetables and weaving. It took a lot of work. People came to the market from many places. I had to learn how to speak Spanish.

"At first, my business was bad. People passed me by. I thought it was because I was new.

"One day, I watched the best market woman. She wore bright clothes. She sat in front of the prettiest building. She placed her goods so that they all looked interesting to shoppers.

"The next day, I wore my prettiest clothes. I left early and got there before the others. I sat in front of a big blue-and-white building. Then, I took extra time to fix my goods.

"That day, I sold more things than ever before!"

Market women learn how to arrange their fruits and vegetables. An attractive display helps a market woman make more sales.

181

Tin is one of Bolivia's most important resources.
Here a woman sells tin goods at the market.
To speak to customers, she had to learn Spanish.

The Aymara are proud of their village school.
At the school, students learn to read and write
in Spanish. They also learn arithmetic.

The Village School

In 1958, the people of the village built a school. There, students learn to read and write in Spanish. In Bolivia, people need to know Spanish to get good jobs.

The village school has no maps or globes. There are not many books. The teacher teaches the lesson and writes things on the board. Often, students say things over and over until they know them. To learn this way is to **memorize.** Students also learn to write down what the teacher says. They see and say what they have to learn.

The class spends most of its time on arithmetic and civics. **Civics** is the study of the rules and rights of people in a nation. The class also studies history, geography, and health.

Sometimes, parents visit the school. While they watch, the teacher asks the students questions. The students give the answers. Then the parents know that their children are learning.

Many young Aymara have left their quiet villages. They look for jobs in busy modern cities like La Paz. La Paz is at 16° south latitude, 68° west longitude. It is more than 2 miles above sea level.

Life in the City

Life has changed for the Aymara in many ways. The village people are still poor. But now they own land. They take their own crops to market. They learn to read and write. They own radios and other products from all over the world. They take a greater part in their local government. They also learn more about their country and the world.

Life in the villages has gotten better. Still, most young people are moving to La Paz. They want to find jobs in the city. This is not easy. Some cannot find work. Others get jobs that pay very little. They clean streets, carry heavy boxes, or work as servants. Many of them have not yet learned Spanish.

Other village people learn new ways of living in the city. They learn Spanish. They dress like city people. Some drive taxis and trucks. Others work in factories or stores. Many start businesses, making clothes or baking bread. Often, people already in the city help others from their village. They help newcomers get a job and find a place to live. They visit their village often. That way, they stay close to their families.

For thousands of years, the Aymara have been farmers. Much of their culture is built on farming life. Their way of life has lasted through Incan rulers. It has lasted through Spanish conquerors. It has lasted through haciendas and *patrones*. Will the Aymara way of life last in the city?

City life for the Aymara is a mixture of old and new. The Aymara
come to the city to find jobs. City life is different from life
in the village. Even in the city, though, many Aymara keep their
rich culture alive. Their past is still part of their present.

REVIEW

WATCH YOUR WORDS

1. To change when conditions around
   you change is to____.
   conquer escape adapt

2. The Incan armies used the llama as
   a(n)____.
   export pack animal
   nonliving resource

3. To say something until you know it
   is to____it.
   memorize repeat forget

4. ____ is the study of rights people
   have and rules they follow.
   History Civics Science

CHECK YOUR FACTS

5. What were Aymara houses like in
   the past? What are they like now.

6. How did the Aymara get their
   clothes in the past? How do they
   get their clothes today?

7. How did the Aymara take their
   goods to market in the past? How
   do they get their goods to the city
   now?

8. The Aymara's ancestors were the
   first people to grow a certain vegetable. What was it?

9. List three things that students
   study in the Aymara village school.

10. Why is it important for a market
    woman to know Spanish?

SHARPEN YOUR THINKING

How is the Aymara school like your
school? How is it different?

CHAPTER REVIEW

WATCH YOUR WORDS

1. Bolivia and Paraguay do not have ____ .
   resources   exports   coastlines

2. Sheep and cattle are raised on a____.
   plantation   ranch   *campesino*

3. Sugar cane is raised on a____.
   ranch   llano   plantation

4. Small farmers, or ____ , are the largest group in Bolivia.
   campesinos   conquistadores   criollos

5. The Aymara survived because they could____.
   conquer   adapt   memorize

CHECK YOUR FACTS

6. Where in Bolivia do most people live?

7. How high is the *altiplano?*

8. What is Sucre? For whom was it named?

9. What is La Paz? Tell three special things about it.

10. What resources are found on the *altiplano?* Name three living resources and three nonliving resources.

11. Where was the empire of the Incas? List five things the Incas did.

12. What work did the American Indians do for the Spanish?

13. Why did the criollos fight the Spanish army?

14. Who was Simón Bolívar?

15. When was Bolivia born as a nation? When did the Aymara get the vote?

APPLY YOUR SKILLS

FIND THE TIME LINE

16. List the events below in the right order. Start with the one that happened first. End with the one that happened last.

   —The Spanish conquered the Incas and the Aymara.
   —The Indians got votes and land.
   —People built Tiahuanaco.
   —The criollos won their independence from Spain.
   —The Incas conquered the Aymara.

WRITE ABOUT IT

17. Write the story of the Aymara. First, tell who they are and where they live. How long have they lived there? Then, tell about their history. Who conquered them? What work did they have to do? How did they win their freedom? Finally, tell how their life changed in 1952.

SHARPEN YOUR THINKING

18. How could Bolivia develop its resources in the east?

19. How did the Aymara keep their culture alive?

20. Have you ever learned to do something by watching someone who did it well? Is this a good way to learn?

21. How can your parents tell that you are learning?

22. Why is it important for people in Bolivia to learn Spanish? Why is it important for you to learn English?

UNIT REVIEW

WATCH YOUR WORDS

Use the words below to complete the unit summary. Use each term only once.

adapt   cacao   conquistador   exports   llamas   petroleum
altiplano   coastline   descendants   haciendas   middle class   progress
ancestors   conquer   empire   imports   pack animals   seaport

High in the Andes Mountains is a plateau called the __1__. There, long ago, the city of Tiahuanaco was built. We think the __2__ of the Aymara built it. Then, about 500 years ago, the Aymara were defeated by the Incas. They became part of the great Incan __3__. The Incas built long roads. They used woolly __4__ as __5__ to carry loads. Then, Francisco Pizarro came with his Spanish soldiers to __6__ the Incas. Pizarro was a conqueror, or __7__. The Spanish settlers made the Indians work for them on large farms called __8__. The __9__ of those Indians still live in Bolivia. The Aymara survived many rulers because they could __10__, or change.

Products that South American nations sell to other countries are __11__. One such product is __12__, from which we get cocoa and chocolate. Another such product is coffee. The United States brings in, or __13__, coffee from South America. Bolivia sells tin to other nations. But Bolivia does not have a __14__. Therefore, it has to ship its goods from a __15__ in Chile. Many South American nations do not have enough __16__ to meet their energy needs. The nations making the most __17__, or improvement, have a growing __18__.

CHECK YOUR FACTS

1. What are the longest, and second-highest, mountains in the world?
2. What is the driest place in South America?
3. What is the climate like in the highlands of South America?
4. What river carries the most water?
5. Name three plants and three animals that South Americans raise.
6. Name three minerals that are found in South America.
7. What are exports? What are imports?
8. What five European countries had colonies in South America?
9. Where are most of the big cities in South America?
10. Name three signs of progress.

KNOW YOUR PEOPLE

Match the name with the clue.

11. The Aymara   A. conquered the peoples of the Andes in the 1500s.

12. The Incas   B. was the first president of his country.

13. Francisco Pizarro C. ruled an empire in the Andes.

14. Simón Bolívar   D. lived on the altiplano before the Incas.

15. Antonio de Sucre   E. had a country named for him.

SKILL DEVELOPMENT

USE YOUR CHART SKILLS

1. Copy the chart below on a separate sheet of paper. Then fill in the blanks.

Nations	Area	Number of people	Capital	Official language
ARGENTINA	1,068,301 sq. mi.		Buenos Aires	
BOLIVIA		6 million		Spanish
BRAZIL	3,265,075 sq. mi.		Brasília	
COLOMBIA		30 million		Spanish
PERU	496,224 sq. mi.		Lima	
VENEZUELA		15 million		Spanish

2. Answer these questions based on your chart.
  a. Which two nations have the most land?
  b. Which three nations have the most people?
  c. Which nation has two capitals?

USE YOUR MAPS

3. Look at the elevation map of South America on page 147. What is the elevation of the Andes Mountains? Of the pampas?

4. Look at the resource map of South America on page 155. In what places is petroleum found?

5. Look at the political map on page 87. Where did early peoples cross from Asia to North America?

6. Look at the political map of South America on page 163. How many countries do not touch Brazil?

7. Look at the population map of South America on page 164. Which areas have the most people?

USE YOUR MAP SKILLS

8. On a separate sheet of paper, draw an outline map of Bolivia. Use the map on page 171 as a guide. Put these things on your map:
  a. the Andes Mountains
  b. the *altiplano*
  c. the eastern plains
  d. La Paz and Sucre
  e. Lake Titicaca
  f. the border with Peru
  g. the border with Chile
  h. the border with Argentina
  i. the border with Paraguay
  j. the border with Brazil

FIND THE TIME LINE

9. Make a time line for Bolivia. Put these dates on it. Then write what happened on each date.
1100   1538   1825   1952

SHARPEN YOUR THINKING

10. Which thing in the list below is not a plant?
cacao   coffee   alpaca   banana

11. Which thing in the list below is not an animal?
cow   sheep   llama   llano

12. Which thing in the list below is not land?
pampas   llanos   *campesino*   *altiplano*

13. Which thing in the list below is not a farm?
plantation   criollo   hacienda   ranch

14. Which place in the list below is not hard to live in?
jungle   wilderness   desert   pampas

1 AFRICA AND ITS PEOPLE

Lesson 1: Land and Climate

FIND THE WORDS

rapids	inland	barren
source	silt	mouth
rainy season		dry season

More than 500 years ago, ships left Portugal, a country in Europe. They sailed down the Atlantic coast of Africa. The captains of those ships were looking for a way to the riches of India. They were trying to find a way around Africa.

Along the coast of Africa, they found few harbors for their ships. A harbor is a place on a coast protected from the open sea. There,

ships can anchor safely. There, people and goods can be easily moved between ship and shore.

The land in Africa seemed to rise very steeply from the shore. Often, there were deserts or rain forests along the coast. Also, the rivers often had **rapids,** or rocky places. The rocks make the water flow very fast. Rapids and waterfalls kept ships from sailing up the rivers very far.

These were the kinds of land and rivers the explorers found. Thus, it was hard for them to travel inland in Africa. **Inland** means beyond the coast, toward

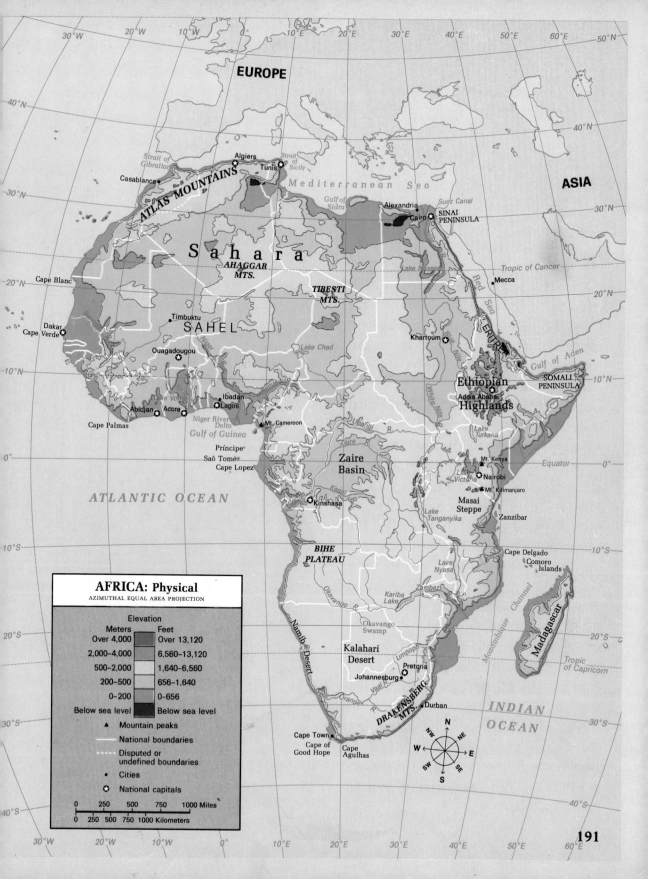

AFRICA: Physical

AZIMUTHAL EQUAL AREA PROJECTION

Elevation

Meters	Feet
Over 4,000	Over 13,120
2,000–4,000	6,560–13,120
500–2,000	1,640–6,560
200–500	656–1,640
0–200	0–656
Below sea level	Below sea level

▲ Mountain peaks
— National boundaries
--- Disputed or undefined boundaries
• Cities
✪ National capitals

0   250   500   750   1000 Miles
0 250 500 750 1000 Kilometers

191

the middle of the land. Europeans couldn't get to the middle of Africa. So they called Africa the Dark Continent. They called it that because they knew little about it.

Not until the 1800s did Europeans begin to explore all of Africa. But Africa had great empires long before the Europeans came. You will learn about two empires of west Africa in the next lesson.

Look at the elevation map of Africa on page 191. Notice that most of the continent is made up of plateaus. Sometimes there are narrow plains along the coast. But Africa's coast has few natural harbors. It has few rivers that ships can sail. This is because the highlands are close to the ocean.

Africa is the second-largest continent on Earth. Only Asia is larger. Yet much of the land in Africa is not useful to people. The climate is either too hot and dry or too hot and wet. Still, more than 500 million people live in Africa. In this lesson, we will look at Africa's land and climate.

The equator crosses Africa almost in the middle. So most of Africa lies in the tropics. This makes Africa the hottest continent on Earth. Remember, climates near the equator are tropical climates. In tropical deserts, savannas, and rain forests, the weather is hot almost all year.

An oasis is a place in a desert with water and fertile land.

At the mouth of the Nile is a fertile delta. The delta was formed from silt dropped by the Nile. The Nile flows into the Mediterranean Sea at about 32° north latitude.

NILE RIVER DELTA

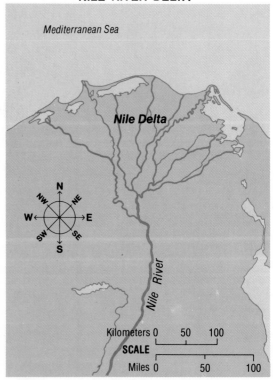

Mediterranean Sea

Nile Delta

Nile River

Kilometers 0   50   100
SCALE
Miles 0   50   100

192

The Nile is the longest river on Earth.
Its water is used to irrigate fields.

The Sahara

A great desert, the Sahara, stretches across most of northern Africa. In the language of the Arabs, *Sahara* (suh HAR uh) means "desert." The Sahara is the largest desert on Earth.

On the Sahara, days are very hot. Nights are cool. Almost no rain falls in the Sahara. The land is mostly barren. **Barren** land is land on which no plants will grow. Here and there in the desert are sand dunes. There are also some mountains in the Sahara.

Few people live in the Sahara. Most of those who do live there live in oases (oh A seez). An *oasis* (oh A sis) is a place in a desert with water and fertile land. In Africa, the Nile River flows through the Sahara. The valley of the Nile is the largest oasis in the world.

The Nile

The Nile River is the longest river on Earth. The Nile has two branches, the White Nile and the Blue Nile. The White Nile begins at Lake Victoria at the equator. The Blue Nile begins at Lake Tana in Ethiopia (EE thee OH pee uh). That means Lake Victoria and Lake Tana are the sources of the Nile. The **source** of a river is the place where it starts. The two branches of the Nile join at Khartoum (kahr TOOM) in the Sudan. From there, the Nile flows north to the Mediterranean Sea.

Notice that the Blue Nile starts in the eastern highlands. In the summer, heavy rains fall there. Then the river carries the rain water north. So, once a year, the Nile in Egypt would fill up and overflow. The river also carries along soil that is full of minerals. This rich soil is called **silt.** When the river flooded the land, it left this rich soil on top. That made the banks of the Nile very fertile.

Still, the river carried some of the floodwater on to the sea. That water was lost. To save it, the people of modern Egypt built a dam. Now, the Aswan High Dam holds back the floodwaters. Now, farmers can get water for their fields all year long. But their fields no longer get the Nile River silt.

The place where a river flows into the ocean is called the **mouth.** Sometimes, at the mouth of a river, there is a delta. A delta is an area of rich soil, or silt. It is usually shaped like a triangle. The delta of the Nile is north of Cairo (KY roh) in Egypt.

The Savannas

Now look at the climate map on page 195. Suppose you are traveling from north to south in Africa. First, you cross a narrow strip of land along the Mediterranean Sea. There, the land is fertile and the climate is comfortable. Next, you go through the desert. Then, you come to tropical grasslands, or savannas. Almost half of Africa is savanna land. Savannas have a few trees and bushes.

Savannas have only two seasons. In the **rainy season,** the weather is hot and wet. The land is green. The rivers fill up and sometimes overflow. The farmers grow their crops during the rainy season. In the **dry season,** the weather is hot and dry. Little or no rain falls. The grass dies, and the fields turn brown. Some of the rivers dry up.

The Rain Forests

South of the savannas are tropical rain forests. Rain forests cover much of the Atlantic coast near the equator. They also stretch far inland. Find the rain forest area on the climate map. The weather is hot and wet there all year. It is hard for people to live and work in such a climate.

Elephants and zebras visit a water hole on the African savanna. Savanna lands are grasslands.

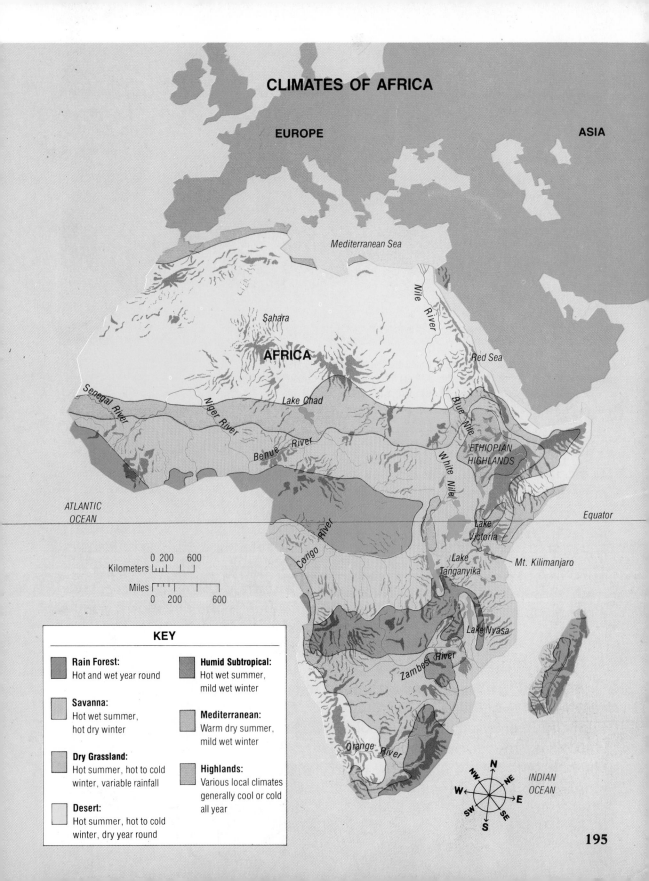

CLIMATES OF AFRICA

EUROPE

ASIA

Mediterranean Sea

Nile River

Sahara

AFRICA

Red Sea

Senegal River

Niger River

Lake Chad

Blue Nile

Benue River

ETHIOPIAN
HIGHLANDS

White Nile

ATLANTIC
OCEAN

Equator

Congo River

Lake
Victoria

Lake
Tanganyika

Mt. Kilimanjaro

0   200   600
Kilometers

Miles

0   200   600

Lake Nyasa

Zambesi River

Orange River

INDIAN
OCEAN

N
NW   NE
W   E
SW   SE
S

KEY

Rain Forest:
Hot and wet year round

Savanna:
Hot wet summer,
hot dry winter

Dry Grassland:
Hot summer, hot to cold
winter, variable rainfall

Desert:
Hot summer, hot to cold
winter, dry year round

Humid Subtropical:
Hot wet summer,
mild wet winter

Mediterranean:
Warm dry summer,
mild wet winter

Highlands:
Various local climates
generally cool or cold
all year

195

Mount Kilimanjaro is the highest mountain in Africa. It is near the equator, at 3° south latitude, 37° east longitude. Because of its high elevation, there is snow on top all year.

The South

South of the rain forests are more savannas. Still farther south, you come to the Kalahari (KAH luh HAH ree) Desert. Finally, you reach the southern tip of Africa. There, the weather changes more from season to season. There are more areas of fertile land.

The Highlands

All along the eastern part of Africa are highlands. They stretch from the Red Sea down the whole continent. In the highlands are plateaus with fertile land. The climate on the plateaus is cool and comfortable. It is not too wet or too dry. People can grow grain crops, such as wheat. Coffee also grows in the eastern highlands. On the highland plains of Kenya, there are many wild animals. Lions, elephants, zebras, giraffes, and leopards are found there.

Running through the eastern highlands is the Great Rift Valley. This valley is a huge break in the land. It is very wide and deep. It is also 2,900 kilometers (1,800 miles) long.

Some large, deep lakes have formed in this valley. Among them are Lake Nyasa (ny AS uh) and Lake Tanganyika (TANG guh NYEE kuh). Lake Tanganyika is almost a mile deep. Other important lakes in Africa are Lake Victoria and Lake Chad. Find these lakes on the elevation map. These are natural lakes. Then find Lake Nasser. It is an artificial lake. Lake Nasser formed behind the Aswan High Dam. It holds the floodwaters of the Nile.

Near Lake Victoria is Mount Kilimanjaro (KIL uh mun JAHR oh). It is the highest mountain in Africa. Mount Kilimanjaro is almost 5,900 meters (19,340 feet) high. Even though it is near the equator, there is snow on top all year. Why do you think this is so?

REVIEW

WATCH YOUR WORDS

1. The place where a river starts is its ___.
   mouth   source   rapids

2. The place where a river flows into the ocean is its ___.
   rapids   source   mouth

3. The rocky places in rivers are called ___.
   highlands   mouths   rapids

4. The rich soil a river carries is called ___.
   sand   silt   savanna

5. A ___ is a protected place on a coast where ships can anchor.
   plateau   harbor   valley

6. The ___ of the Nile is shaped like a triangle.
   source   valley   delta

7. Land on which no plants will grow is ___.
   barren   fertile   rain forest

8. To go toward the middle of a continent is to go ___.
   inland   east   south

9. Farmers grow crops in the savannas during the ___.
   dry season   rainy season
   baseball season

10. The grass on the savannas dies during the ___.
    rainy season   floods   dry season

CHECK YOUR FACTS

11. Name three kinds of land in Africa that have tropical climates.

12. What is the largest desert on Earth? Where is it?

13. What is the longest river on Earth? Where is it? What are its branches?

14. What large lake in Africa lies on the equator?

15. Why did the people of Egypt build the Aswan High Dam?

USE YOUR MAP SKILLS

Plan a trip down the west coast of Africa. Start at the Mediterranean Sea. Go to the tip of the continent. What climates will you pass through? What clothes and supplies will you need?

SHARPEN YOUR THINKING

How would a ship sail from Portugal to India today? Would it have to sail around Africa? Is there now a shorter way?

Lesson 2: People: Past and Present

FIND THE WORDS

**Muslim   Islam   pyramid
pharaoh   subsistence farming
herding   nomad**

Many different peoples live in Africa. This makes it hard to talk about Africans in a general way.

Even so, it is possible to divide Africans into five main groups. These groups are Blacks, Arabs, Hamites, Europeans, and Asians.

Blacks

Blacks are by far the largest group of Africans. In fact, we often use the word *African* to mean *Black.* Most Black Africans live south of the Sahara. Some live in small villages. Others live in large, modern cities. Blacks are a majority in almost all the countries where they live.

There are many important Black peoples in different parts of Africa. Bantu peoples live in central and southern Africa. The San live in the Kalahari Desert. White settlers in South Africa called the San the Bushmen.

These peoples, and many more, are Blacks. But they often look very different from one another. More important, different Black peoples in Africa have different beliefs. They speak many different languages. Their histories differ. They follow different ways of life.

Most Africans are Blacks. But there are many different Black peoples in Africa. Each group has its own language, customs, and beliefs.

Arabs

Most of the Arabs in Africa live north of the Sahara. Their ancestors conquered this area over a thousand years ago. Most Arabs are Muslims. Many Blacks in Africa are Muslims, too. A **Muslim** (MUZ lum) is someone who believes in the religion called **Islam** (IS lam). This religion was founded in the 7th century by the prophet Muhammad (moh HAM uhd). Muhammad lived in southwestern Asia 1,400 years ago. He was born in the city of Mecca (MEK uh). Today, many people in Africa and Asia are Muslims.

Hamites

The Hamites live in north Africa. They were named for Ham, a son of Noah in the Bible. These people came to Africa from Asia long ago. They look much like Europeans. Some Hamites are Muslims. Most Hamites in Ethiopia are Christians. The Christian Hamites belong to the Coptic Church.

Europeans

Europeans began coming to Africa about 150 years ago. In most of the continent, they are a very small minority. Only in the nation of South Africa are there very many Europeans. There, 4 million of the 28 million people have European ancestors.

There are many Arabs in northern Africa. These Arabs are trading in a market in Morocco. They dress in loose, light-colored robes to protect themselves from the sun.

Asians

Asians live in east Africa. Most came to Africa from India and Pakistan. They form a minority in many countries that border the Indian Ocean.

Three Empires

You have probably heard of the most famous African empire. It was the kingdom of ancient Egypt in the valley of the Nile. The ancient Egyptians were Hamites. Their empire lasted for 3,000 years.

The Egyptians built great stone **pyramids** (PIR uh midz) in the desert. These pyramids were tombs where kings, queens, and nobles were buried. A king of ancient Egypt was called a **pharaoh** (FEHR oh). Ancient Egyptians believed in life after death. They thought people could take things with them to the afterlife. Important people had their jewelry, furniture, dishes, and statues buried with them. The ancient Egyptians also had a system of picture writing. Their writing, paintings, and artifacts tell us what their life was like.

Two other great empires were founded in west Africa. They were Black African empires. The first was the empire of Ghana (GAH nuh). It lasted for over 700 years. Traders met in Ghana to trade salt and other goods for gold. They did this by the "silent trade." The traders never met face to face. First, one set of traders left piles of goods by the river. Then, the second set of traders left gold beside the goods they wanted. If the price was right, the first traders took the gold. They left the goods they had sold. If the gold wasn't enough, they took away some goods. Then they tried the trade again. The two sets of traders trusted each other. They were on their honor to be honest.

The king of Ghana charged a tax on the trade. That way, he made his empire rich. He also built a great army. In 1066, William the Conqueror defeated England with 25,000 soldiers. That same year, Ghana had 200,000 soldiers. Suppose William had gone to Ghana. His army would have been outnumbered eight to one!

Right: The ancient Egyptians carved this huge stone statue of a sphinx. It has a human head and a lion's body.

Below: The people of ancient Egypt built great pyramids in the desert. Egyptian pyramids were tombs. Kings, queens, and nobles were buried there.

WHERE WE ARE IN TIME AND PLACE

THREE AFRICAN EMPIRES

3100 B.C.	2700 B.C.	2050 B.C.	1570 B.C.
Upper Egypt and Lower Egypt unite	Old Kingdom begins in Egypt	Middle Kingdom begins in Egypt	New Kingdom begins in Egypt

1200 B.C.	332 B.C.	31 B.C.
Moses leads the Hebrew people out of Egypt	Alexander the Great conquers Egypt	Rome conquers Egypt

4 B.C.	A.D. 500s–1200s	A.D. 1200	A.D. 1312–1337
Birth of Jesus Christ	Empire of Ghana	Empire of Mali conquers Ghana	Mansu Musa is emperor of Mali

EMPIRES OF AFRICA

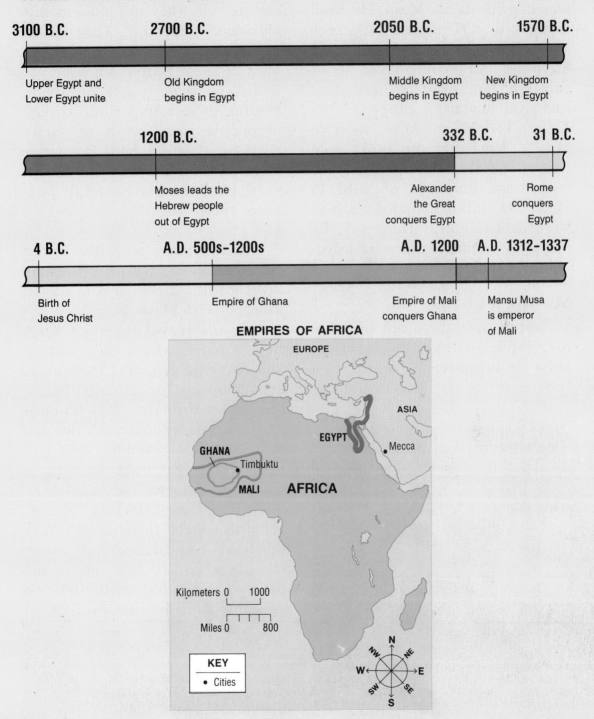

EUROPE

ASIA

GHANA

Timbuktu

EGYPT

Mecca

MALI

AFRICA

Kilometers 0   1000

Miles 0   800

KEY
• Cities

Next, the empire of Mali (MAH lee) became great. Mali had rich gold mines. One emperor of Mali was named Mansu Musa. He lived in the city of Timbuktu (TIM buck TOO). Look at the elevation map on page 191. What river flows through Timbuktu? Where does this river join the ocean?

In 1324, Mansu Musa went to Mecca. Mecca is the most holy city of the Muslims. Mansu Musa took huge amounts of gold to Mecca. He brought many teachers back to Timbuktu. That way, he made his empire a center of learning and trade.

Making a Living

Today, over three out of every four Africans live by farming. Most do **subsistence farming.** To subsist is to stay alive. Subsis-

tence farmers grow just enough food for their own needs. They usually have little or nothing left over to sell. They use old and simple ways of farming. They do not have modern farm machinery. Most of these people are poor.

In the drier parts of Africa, **herding** is very important. Groups of people raise herds of cattle, goats, or sheep. A herd is a group of large animals that are all the same kind. To herd animals is to keep them together while they find grass to eat.

Some herders who live in dry places are called nomads. A **nomad** (NOH mad) is a person who travels from place to place. Family groups of nomads travel together. They live in tents, which they fold up and carry with them. They move about, looking for grass and water for their animals. The nomads herd sheep and goats. On the desert, they use camels to carry loads. They get milk from their goats and camels. They can drink the milk or use it to make cheese. They also make their clothes from sheep wool and camel hair. Now, not many nomads are left in the desert. Long dry spells left no grass for their animals to eat.

Families of nomads stop at oases for food and water. Here, a father shows a child how to carve a camel saddle.

AFRICA'S LARGEST CITIES

City	Number of people
Cairo, EGYPT	5,278,000
Alexandria, EGYPT	2,409,000
Kinshasa, ZAIRE	2,202,000
Algiers, ALGERIA	1,523,000
Casablanca, MOROCCO	1,506,373
Lagos, NIGERIA	1,404,000
Addis Ababa, ETHIOPIA	1,125,340
Accra, GHANA	1,045,381
Ibadan, NIGERIA	1,009,000
Nairobi, KENYA	827,775
Dakar, SENEGAL	798,792
Cape Town, SOUTH AFRICA	697,514
Johannesburg, SOUTH AFRICA	654,232

Not all of Africa's people are farmers or herders. Many millions of Africans live in cities. Some African cities are among the largest in the world. Cairo is the largest city in Africa. It is the capital of Egypt. This great city is thousands of years old. Most other African cities are very young. Nairobi (ny ROH bee) was started less than 100 years ago. It is the capital of Kenya. Now, Nairobi is a center of manufacturing and trade.

Dakar, Senegal (15° north latitude, 17° west longitude)

Cairo, Egypt (30° north latitude, 31° east longitude)

Fun Facts ... about Africa

The hottest place in the world:
Africa is the hottest continent on Earth. The hottest place in the world is Dallol, Ethiopia. For 6 years, the average yearly temperature there was 34°C (94°F). It was hot in the summer and in the winter, too!

The largest desert in the world:
The Sahara is the largest desert on Earth. At its longest, it stretches more than 4,830 kilometers (3,000 miles) from the Atlantic Ocean to the Red Sea. At its widest, it covers more than 1,930 kilometers (1,200 miles) from north to south. Overall, the Sahara covers more than 9,065,000 square kilometers (3,500,000 square miles).

The longest river in the world:
The Nile is the longest river on Earth. It is about 6,695 kilometers (4,160 miles) long. For hundreds of years, the source of the Nile was a mystery. Long ago, people thought this great river began in the "Mountains of the Moon."

The largest oasis in the world:
The valley of the Nile is the largest oasis on Earth. The most fertile part of the valley is the Nile delta.

REVIEW

WATCH YOUR WORDS

1. Egyptian kings, or ___ , were buried in tombs called___.
   pyramids   savannas   artifacts   pharaohs

2. The religion that Muhammad founded is called___.
   Hamite   Coptic   Islam

3. A person who believes in Islam is a___.
   Coptic   Muslim   Kalahari

4. Herders who keep moving from place to place are called___.
   Hamites   traders   nomads

5. In ___ , farmers usually grow only the food they eat.
   subsistence farming   herding   the Sahara

CHECK YOUR FACTS

6. Which is the largest group of Africans? Where do most of these people live?

7. Name four other groups of African peoples.

8. Who was Muhammad? What did he do?

9. Name two empires that were founded in west Africa. Which one was ruled by Mansu Musa?

10. What is the largest city in Africa? What country is it in?

SHARPEN YOUR THINKING

Most African farmers are poor. Many farm the same way their ancestors did. How could African farmers raise more food?

USE YOUR MAP SKILLS

Mansu Musa traveled from Timbuktu to Mecca. How far is Timbuktu from Mecca if you cross the Red Sea? How far is it if you go by land? Use your distance scale.

Lesson 3: Resources and Their Use

FIND THE WORDS

fertilizer   commercial farming
raw material   finished goods

The continent of Africa has many resources. But they are not spread evenly over the continent. Some parts of Africa are rich in resources. Other areas have very few resources.

One important mineral resource is petroleum. Fuel oil comes from petroleum. We use petroleum to heat our homes and to run our cars.

In north Africa, there is a lot of petroleum in Algeria and Libya. South of the Sahara, petroleum is found in Nigeria. Algeria, Libya, and Nigeria sell petroleum as an export. The money they earn is helping them become modern. Some petroleum is also found farther south, in Angola. Look at the resource map on page 206. Find the petroleum on the map.

Phosphates (FOSS fayts) are also mineral resources. They are salts used to make fertilizers. A **fertilizer** is spread on the soil. It adds minerals to help crops grow. Phosphates are found in Morocco.

Look again at the resource map of Africa. It shows where the mineral wealth of Africa is found.

Petroleum is found along the coast of Nigeria. These Africans are collecting petroleum from wells in the ground. The coast of Nigeria is between 4° and 6° north latitude. It is between 3° and 8° east longitude.

RESOURCES OF AFRICA

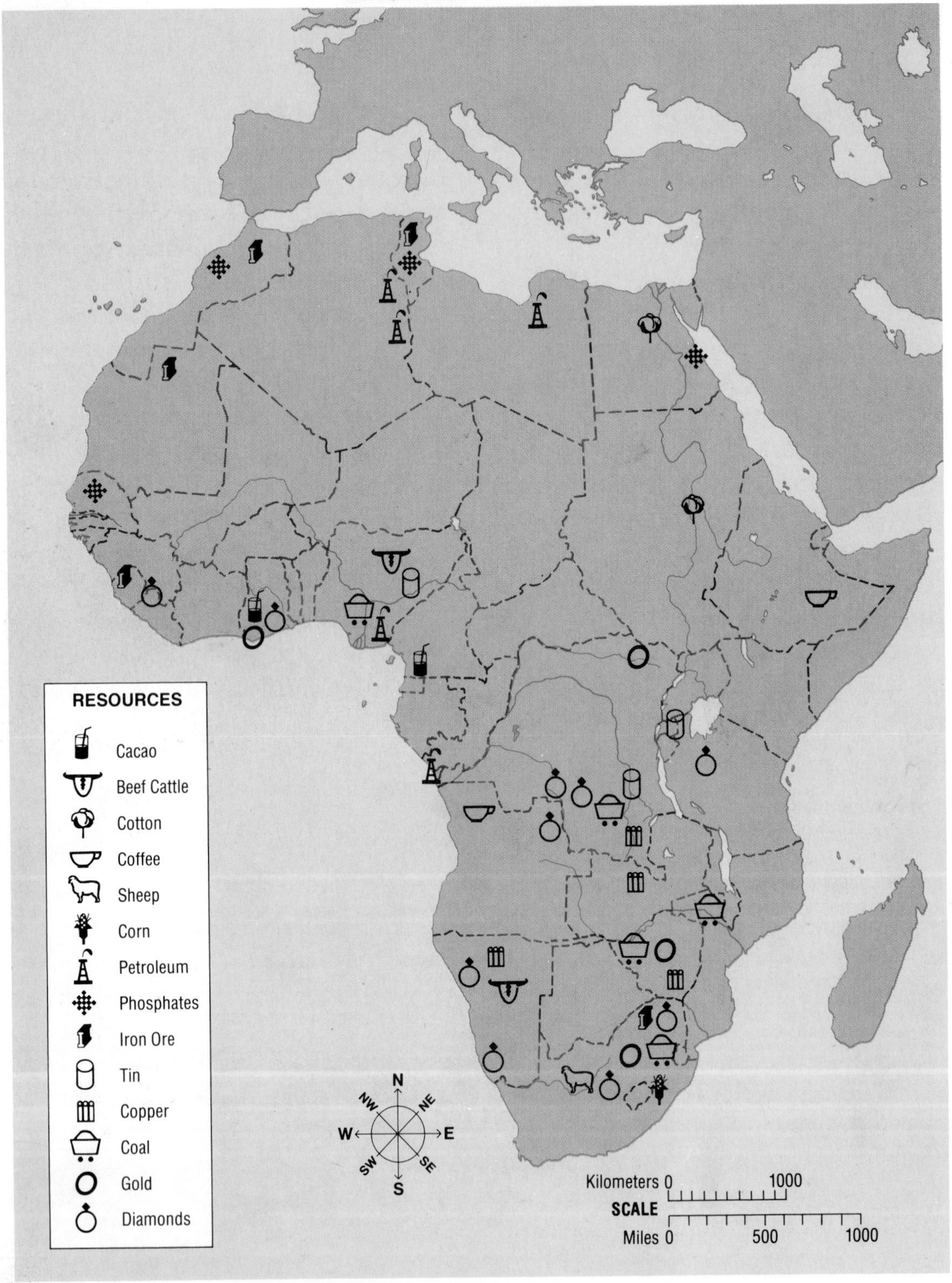
RESOURCES
Cacao
Beef Cattle
Cotton
Coffee
Sheep
Corn
Petroleum
Phosphates
Iron Ore
Tin
Copper
Coal
Gold
Diamonds
N
NE
E
SE
S
SW
W
NW
Kilometers 0
1000
SCALE
Miles 0
500
1000

There is copper in southern Africa, in Zambia and Zaire (zah IR). South Africa is rich in gold, diamonds, and coal. Find the parts of Africa that have the most minerals. Then look at the part of Africa just south of the Sahara. The nations here do not have much mineral wealth.

All African nations are trying to make better use of their mineral resources. However, most of Africa's minerals are exported. Only South Africa has enough industry to use its mineral resources at home.

Another natural resource is farmland. In north Africa, people farm the land along the Mediterranean Sea. This is the only part of north Africa that gets enough rain for crops. Here, farmers grow fruits such as olives, dates, and grapes.

Most of the farmland in Egypt is in the delta and valley of the Nile. That is where most of Egypt's people live. Cotton is grown there. In the Nile valley, much of the land is irrigated. To irrigate dry land is to bring water there from somewhere else. The water is used to wet the land so crops will grow. People dig ditches or lay pipes to carry the water. In north Africa, they get the water from the Nile. Remember that the Aswan High Dam holds back the Nile's floodwater. This water is

These farmers are irrigating their fields in an old-fashioned way. They take water from the Nile and empty it into a canal.

stored in Lake Nasser. It can be used all year to irrigate dry land.

South of the Sahara, Africans do two kinds of farming. One kind is called **commercial farming.** It is done on large farms called plantations. In commercial farming, crops are grown to be sold. Cacao beans, from which we get cocoa and chocolate, are grown in Ghana. Coffee is raised in the highlands of east Africa. Peanuts

In commercial farming, large crops are grown to be sold. Tea is grown on this farm in South Africa.

and cotton are grown in some savanna lands. All these crops are African exports.

The other kind of farming is subsistence farming. It is done on small, family farms. In subsistence farming, families grow food to feed themselves. They do not raise crops to sell. Most of the farming south of the Sahara is subsistence farming.

Many resources in Africa are not used in ways that improve people's lives. This is so because of the kinds of products Africa exports. Most African nations sell their resources as raw materials. A **raw material** is a natural product that has not been improved by manufacturing. Resources are worth less as raw materials than as finished goods. **Finished goods** are products that have been manufactured. They are in the form in which you can use them. For example, logs are raw materials. Tables made from the logs are finished goods.

Iron comes from a mine in the form of iron ore. Iron ore is a raw material. It is not very useful as it is. In a steel mill, the ore is melted down. It is made into steel sheets or pipes. The steel sheets or pipes can then be used in cars or buildings. These finished goods are worth much more than the raw material.

Here is another example. Cotton picked from a plant is a raw material. People use it to make cotton thread and cotton cloth. The thread and cloth are worth more than the raw cotton. A shirt made from the cloth and thread is worth even more. At each of these steps, people had to do work. This work added value to the material. So, after each step, the material was worth more.

Nations would rather sell finished goods than raw materials. Selling finished goods gives them more value for their resources. Manufacturing more finished goods will help African nations meet two of their goals. They can provide more work for their people. And they can get more money for what they sell.

REVIEW

WATCH YOUR WORDS

1. A___adds minerals to soil.
   raw material   fertilizer   resource
2. To ___ dry land is to bring water to it.
   fertilize   farm   irrigate
3. In___, farmers raise crops to sell.
   subsistence farming   herding
   commercial farming
4. Logs, cotton, and iron ore are___.
   finished goods   nonliving resources
   raw materials
5. Shirts and tables are___.
   finished goods   raw materials
   natural resources

CHECK YOUR FACTS

Look at the Map

6. Are there more minerals in middle Africa or southern Africa? In the west or the east?

7. Where in Africa are gold and diamonds found?
8. Where in Africa are both sheep and cattle raised?

Look at the Lesson

9. How do farmers in the Nile River valley get water to grow crops?
10. What is the difference between commercial farming and subsistence farming?
11. Name three crops that African farmers export.

SHARPEN YOUR THINKING

What makes finished goods worth more than raw materials? In your answer, give an example. Choose a raw material. Then tell what finished goods people make from it.

Lesson 4: Nations of Africa

FIND THE WORDS

unity   culture group
civil war

Almost 500 million people live in Africa. They live in 51 different nations. Each nation has its own land and people. Each has its own capital city and government leaders. At one time, most African nations were European colonies. That meant they were ruled by nations in Europe. Today, most of these colonies have become independent nations. This means the people rule themselves, just as people do in the United States.

Most African nations have small populations. Look at the chart below. First, it shows the five African nations that have the most land. Then, it shows the five African nations that have the most people. One nation is on both lists. Which is it? Find these nine nations on the map of Africa on the next page.

NINE AFRICAN NATIONS

Nations with the most land	Area		Number of people
	square miles	square kilometers	
SUDAN (soo DAN)	967,500	2,505,813	21 million
ALGERIA (al JIR ee uh)	919,595	2,381,741	21 million
ZAIRE (zah IR)	905,567	2,345,409	32 million
LIBYA (LIB ee uh)	679,362	1,759,540	4 million
CHAD (CHAD)	495,755	1,284,000	5 million
Nations with the most people	Area		Number of people
	square miles	square kilometers	
NIGERIA (ny JIR ee uh)	356,669	923,768	88 million
EGYPT (EE jipt)	386,643	1,001,400	47 million
ETHIOPIA (EE thee OH pee uh)	472,434	1,223,600	32 million
ZAIRE (zah IR)	905,567	2,345,409	32 million
SOUTH AFRICA (south AF ruh kuh)	434,674	1,125,800	32 million

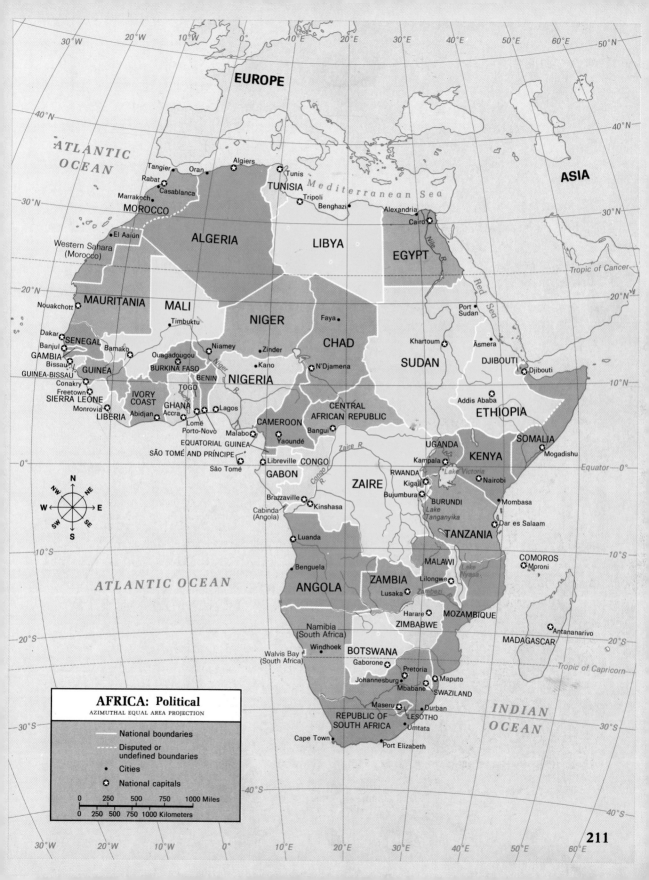

AFRICA: Political

AZIMUTHAL EQUAL AREA PROJECTION

— National boundaries
- - - Disputed or undefined boundaries
• Cities
✪ National capitals

0   250   500   750   1000 Miles
0 250 500 750 1000 Kilometers

EUROPE

ASIA

ATLANTIC OCEAN

Mediterranean Sea

Tangier • Oran • Algiers ✪ Tunis ✪
Rabat ✪ • Casablanca
Marrakech •
MOROCCO
• El Aaiún
Western Sahara (Morocco)

TUNISIA
Tripoli • Benghazi •

ALGERIA

LIBYA

EGYPT
Alexandria •
Cairo ✪
Nile R.

Tropic of Cancer

Nouakchott ✪
MAURITANIA

MALI
Timbuktu •

NIGER
Niamey ✪
Zinder •
Kano •

CHAD
Faya •

Khartoum ✪
SUDAN

Port Sudan •

Āsmera ✪

Red Sea

DJIBOUTI
Djibouti ✪

Dakar ✪ **SENEGAL**
Banjul ✪ Bamako ✪
GAMBIA
Bissau ✪ **GUINEA**
GUINEA-BISSAU
Conakry ✪
Freetown ✪
SIERRA LEONE
Monrovia ✪ **LIBERIA**

Ouagadougou ✪
BURKINA FASO
BENIN
TOGO
IVORY COAST
Abidjan •
GHANA
Accra ✪
Lomé ✪
Porto-Novo ✪

Niger R.
NIGERIA
N'Djamena ✪

CENTRAL AFRICAN REPUBLIC
Bangui ✪

ETHIOPIA
Addis Ababa ✪

SOMALIA
Mogadishu ✪

Lagos •
Malabo ✪
CAMEROON
Yaoundé ✪
EQUATORIAL GUINEA
SÃO TOMÉ AND PRÍNCIPE
São Tomé ✪
Libreville ✪ **CONGO**
GABON

Zaire R.
ZAIRE
Brazzaville ✪
Kinshasa ✪
Cabinda (Angola)
Congo R.

UGANDA
Kampala ✪
RWANDA
Kigali ✪
BURUNDI
Bujumbura ✪
Lake Victoria
KENYA
Nairobi ✪
Mombasa •

TANZANIA
Dar es Salaam •
Lake Tanganyika

Luanda ✪

Benguela •

ANGOLA

ZAMBIA
Lusaka ✪

MALAWI
Lilongwe ✪
Lake Nyasa

COMOROS
Moroni ✪

ATLANTIC OCEAN

Zambezi R.
Harare ✪
ZIMBABWE

MOZAMBIQUE

Namibia (South Africa)
Windhoek •
Walvis Bay (South Africa)

BOTSWANA
Gaborone ✪

MADAGASCAR
Antananarivo ✪

Tropic of Capricorn

Pretoria ✪
Maputo ✪
Johannesburg •
Mbabane ✪
SWAZILAND
Maseru ✪
LESOTHO
Durban •
REPUBLIC OF SOUTH AFRICA
Umtata •
Cape Town ✪
Port Elizabeth •

INDIAN OCEAN

N
NW NE
W   E
SW SE
S

211

African nations share many of the same goals. They are working for a better future for their peoples. One important goal is national unity. Many African nations are trying to increase unity within the nation. **Unity** is a feeling of oneness or togetherness. Government leaders want people to feel that they belong to their nation

Government workers in Africa want to get people to try new ways.

and their nation belongs to them. But sometimes people do not feel like part of a larger whole.

There are hundreds of different peoples in Africa. These peoples are sometimes called culture groups. People in a **culture group** speak their own language. They have their own beliefs and way of living. Different culture groups may live in the same nation. But they may not feel that they belong together.

Here is one reason. Language can keep people apart. Africans speak more than 800 different languages. Within a single nation, 20 different languages may be used. It is hard for people to work together if they do not speak the same language. A nation needs at least one language that everyone can understand.

Here is another reason. The people of Africa did not draw up their own national boundaries. Europeans drew those boundaries years ago when they set up their colonies. Then the colonies won their freedom. Even so, most boundaries did not change. Now, members of the same culture group may live in two or more different nations. They would rather be in the same nation. Also, culture groups that were always enemies may be in the same nation. They would rather be apart.

These problems have caused several civil wars in Africa. A **civil war** is a war between different groups in the same nation.

Unity is not the only goal of African nations. Another goal is to develop Africa's resources. Some African nations are among the poorest countries in the world.

Other African nations make money from petroleum or other exports. Among these nations are Nigeria, Libya, Algeria, and Zaire. South Africa is the richest nation in Africa. It has gold, diamonds, and coal mines. It also has huge farms and many factories.

All over Africa, governments are trying to make life better for their people. To do this, they are building schools and roads. They are trying to improve farming. They want businesses to build more factories and to open more mines. But all these things cost money. And most African nations do not have much money. To help African nations, other nations could lend them money. They could also send people to help.

African peoples value their past. They are loyal to their culture groups. They are proud of their beliefs. They honor their ancestors. Becoming more modern will change their way of life. Do you suppose all Africans want this to happen?

REVIEW

WATCH YOUR WORDS

1. ___ is a feeling of being part of a larger whole.
   Progress   Unity   Culture

2. People in a ___ share language and beliefs.
   culture   continent   country

3. Members of a ___ in Africa feel that they belong together.
   nation   colony   culture group

4. A ___ is fought between different groups in the same nation.
   battle   world war   civil war

5. Today, most African nations are ___ .
   colonies   rich   independent

CHECK YOUR FACTS

Look at the Chart

6. Which two African nations have the most land?

7. Which two African nations have the most people?

8. Which nation is larger, Zaire or South Africa?

Look at the Lesson

9. How did today's African nations get their boundaries?

10. Why have there been civil wars in Africa?

11. What are African governments doing to make life better for their people? Name three things.

SHARPEN YOUR THINKING

Suppose every person in your class spoke a different language. How could one teacher teach all of you? How could you use the same books? How could you understand the same program on TV?

CHAPTER REVIEW

WATCH YOUR WORDS

1. The coast of Africa has few____.
   rapids   harbors   beaches

2. People exploring Africa found it hard to travel____.
   north   west   inland

3. Much land in the Sahara is____.
   barren   fertile   savanna

4. In dry areas, people ____ cattle, goats, and sheep.
   export   import   herd

5. Herders who move from place to place and live in tents are____.
   ancestors   subsistence farmers   nomads

6. Lake Victoria and Lake Tana are the ____of the Nile River.
   mouths   sources   deltas

7. The delta of the Nile is at the ____ of the river.
   mouth   savanna   source

8. More money can be made from ____ than from____.
   raw materials   rain forests
   sand dunes   finished goods

9. Islam is the religion of the____.
   Muslims   Hamites   Christians

10. People who feel like part of a larger whole have____.
    civil war   culture groups   unity

CHECK YOUR FACTS

11. Why was it hard for Europeans to explore Africa?

12. What kind of land is most of northern Africa?

13. Which way does the Nile River flow? What are its branches?

14. Savannas have two seasons. What are they?

15. What are the five main groups of people in Africa?

16. How do subsistence farming and commercial farming differ?

17. Name three African nations that have petroleum.

18. Why do people irrigate land? How do they do it?

19. Name three great African empires of earlier times.

20. Name two goals that the nations of Africa share.

APPLY YOUR SKILLS

USE YOUR MAP SKILLS

21. Draw an outline map of Africa.

22. Africa is surrounded by two oceans and two seas. Label them.

23. Label the Sahara, the equator, the rain forests, and the savannas.

24. Label the Nile River.

25. Draw in boundaries for nations with coasts on the Mediterranean Sea. Label these nations.

SHARPEN YOUR THINKING

26. Why are harbors useful?

27. Lands near the equator get a lot of sunlight. Why did Europeans once call Africa the Dark Continent?

28. Why did ancient Egyptians have their furniture buried with them?

29. Why isn't the southern tip of Africa the hottest part?

30. Suppose every state in the United States was an independent nation. Suppose people in every region spoke a different language. How would your life change?

CHAPTER 2 LIVING ON A SAVANNA

Lesson 1: Burkina Faso

FIND THE WORDS

**landlocked   warrior   assembly
sorghum   baobab**

Burkina Faso (bour KEE nah FAH soh) is a nation in west Africa. It is near the equator. It lies between the modern nations of Mali and Ghana. Find Burkina Faso on the map of Africa on page 211. What hemispheres is it in?

Like Bolivia in South America, Burkina Faso has no coastline. It is **landlocked.** That means it is surrounded by land. Six other African nations surround Burkina Faso. Four of them are on the coast.

The climate in Burkina Faso is hot, dry, and sunny for much of the year. There are deserts in the north. Some grasses and a few small trees and bushes grow there. There are savannas and small forests in the south.

Once, Burkina Faso was a colony of France. Then, in 1960, it became an independent nation. Burkina Faso is a small nation. It is the same size as one of our states: Colorado. It has fewer people than New York City has. About 6½ million people live in

Burkina Faso. Most of them are farmers and live in villages. But about 180,000 people live in the capital city, Ouagadougou (WAH guh DOO goo).

Burkina Faso is a poor nation. The soil is thin and does not hold water well. This makes it hard for people to farm. There are few factories in the cities. This makes it hard for people to find jobs.

Burkina Faso imports food, clothes, metals, and machines. That means it buys these goods from other nations. It exports cotton, peanuts, and live animals. That means it sells these things to other nations. Burkina Faso has to pay for what it imports. It does not earn nearly as much for what it exports. This is another reason why the nation remains poor.

BURKINA FASO

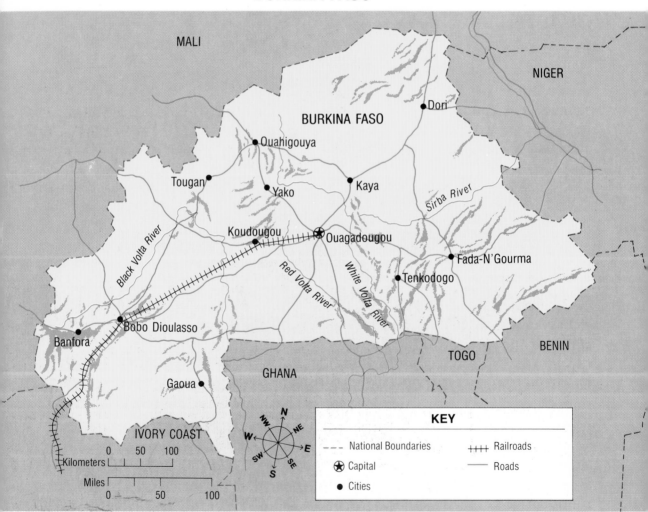

Many people leave Burkina Faso to work in other nations. They go south to the Ivory Coast and Ghana to find jobs. Then they send money home to help their families.

Several culture groups live in Burkina Faso. The Mossi (MAW see) people are the largest group. About half the people in the country are Mossi. Each culture group has its own language. The language of the Mossi people is called Moré (MOR ay).

Many people in Burkina Faso speak two or more languages. Besides their own language, they may also speak French. Sometimes, people also speak the language of groups that live nearby. That way, neighbors can understand each other.

The words *Burkina* and *Faso* come from two different languages. Together, they mean "land of the upright people." Burkina Faso used to be called Upper Volta. The Volta River's sources are there.

The Mossi people have their own leaders and ways of doing things. The Mossi once ruled over a large kingdom. They had strong armies. Other people feared their **warriors,** or fighters. The Mossi king lived in Ouagadougou. He was called the Moro Naba (MOH roh NAH buh). Later, the Mossi became part of the Mali empire.

When Burkina Faso became independent, the people elected a National Assembly. An **assembly** is a group of people who meet to make laws. In the United States, we call such a group a *legislature.*

A Mossi market is a place for buying and selling goods. It is also a place for friends to meet.

The Mossi sell fruit and vegetables in the market.

Do these baobab trees look upside down to you?

The Mossi like to help each other. These young Mossi are carrying a new roof.

In the villages, most Mossi people work in the fields. Families do subsistence farming. They grow the food they eat. They do not have much left over to sell. Village people make thread out of the cotton they grow. Then they weave the thread into cloth.

Since the weather is usually hot, the Mossi are almost always outdoors. In the hottest part of the day, they sit under sun shelters. That way, they have some shade.

Mossi children are like all children. They like to play games. One game they play is like hopscotch. They play a string game like our game of cat's cradle. They also play ball and guessing games.

In a Mossi village, a person almost never feels alone. Everyone knows everyone else. The Mossi like to do things together and help each other. Members of a family work together. Groups of families sometimes work together, too.

The Mossi sit under sun shelters during the hottest part of the day. Burkina Faso is near the equator, between 10° and 15° north latitude.

Fun Facts

Did you know that part of Ghana used to be called the Gold Coast? Europeans used to go there to trade for gold. They went to the Ivory Coast to trade for ivory. Ivory comes from elephant tusks, or teeth.

A favorite meeting place is the market. The market is a place for buying and selling. There, people can buy and sell fruit, vegetables, and grain. Thread and cloth are also sold at the market. Mossi women sell a drink called *dolo*. It is made from **sorghum** (SOR gum), a grain that tastes like corn. Syrup is also made from the sorghum plant. Have you ever heard of sorghum molasses?

At the market, the Mossi talk with friends. They meet people from other villages. They tell stories and make each other laugh. One story they tell is about the **baobab** (BAY oh bab) tree. The branches of this tree are bare and twisted. They look more like roots than branches. The Mossi say that one day God became angry with the baobab. They say God pulled the tree up and put it back upside down!

REVIEW

WATCH YOUR WORDS

1. A ___ country is surrounded by land.
   barren   independent   landlocked

2. The Mossi kingdom once had strong armies of___.
   farmers   warriors   pharaohs

3. Another name for a legislature is an___.
   assembly   empire   export

4. *Dolo* and syrup are made from ___.
   cotton   sorghum   peanuts

5. The ___ tree looks like it is upside down.
   baobab   softwood   hardwood

6. Cotton and peanuts are ___ of Upper Volta.
   imports   exports   seaports

CHECK YOUR FACTS
Look at the Map

7. Name the capital of Burkina Faso.

8. What six nations surround Burkina Faso?

9. Name two ways you could get from Ouagadougou to Koudougou.

Look at the Lesson

10. Name three things that Burkina Faso imports.

11. Give two reasons why Burkina Faso is not rich.

SHARPEN YOUR THINKING

Each culture group in Burkina Faso speaks its own language. Suppose each group also learned to speak French. How would this help Burkina Faso?

Lesson 2: Life in the Village

Burkina Faso has two seasons. It has a dry season. It also has a rainy season.

The period from November to May is the dry season. This is the time when people in the United States have fall, winter, and spring. In the first half of the dry season, the weather is cool. In the second half, the weather gets very hot. All the grass dies. Often the animals have very little to eat. They get thin and grow weak.

The dry season causes problems for people living on Africa's savannas. It is hard to farm land that is dry most of the year. The Mossi dig wells to find water. Digging a well is hard work. Several families may work together to dig a well. Then all of them use it.

In the dry season, the Mossi get water from their wells. With this water, they can grow vegetables in small gardens. But without rain, they cannot grow crops in the fields. This can be a hard time of year for the Mossi.

The rainy season begins in late May or early June. It ends in October. When the rains come, the weather gets cooler. The rains make the grass and the crops grow. The animals can find more food, and they get fatter. The people plant crops in the fields when the rains begin. They have to grow all their crops during the rainy season.

Growing food in Burkina Faso is not easy. Farmers do most of the work by hand. When the rainy

In the dry season, the Mossi get water from their wells. Digging a deep well is hard work.

Top left: Preparing food. *Top right:* The rainy season. *Bottom right:* A family garden.

season starts, a farm family clears its fields. First, the Mossi wait for the rains to soften the hard ground. Then, they begin to loosen the soil. They do this with an iron blade on a short wooden handle. Then, they plant their seeds.

Families plant some crops near their homes. They plant other crops in fields far from the village. Family members walk to these fields during the rainy season.

Farmers in Burkina Faso raise cereal plants and vegetables for their own use. They plant corn, millet, sorghum, and rice. They grow tomatoes, onions, eggplants, and beans. They also raise chickens and gather fruits and nuts.

Some farmers grow cotton and peanuts to sell. They may also sell sheep and goats. They use the money to buy seeds and other things they need.

As the crops grow, the Mossi families weed the fields. First, they pull up the weeds. Then, they loosen the soil around the crops. This is the hardest work of the growing season.

When the crops are grown, the people harvest them. To **harvest** crops is to gather them in. Harvesting the crops is the last job of the growing season. Again, the whole family works together. First, the men cut down the stalks of grain. Then, the women cut the heads of grain off the stalks. The children take care of the babies. They also carry water to the workers in the fields.

The women carry the grain home to be dried and stored. They take the stalks, too. They can burn stalks as fuel for cooking. They can also feed stalks to the animals during the dry season. The Mossi waste little of what they grow.

Drought

Sometimes, the rainy season does not come when it is due. Then there is a drought (DROWT). A **drought** is a long period of time with little or no rain. Burkina Faso has had many droughts. So have many other nations in Africa.

A drought causes many problems. Rivers dry up. Grass dies. Soil blows away. Animals die because they have no water to drink. Food will not grow without water to wet the soil. So the people become very hungry. A **famine** (FAM in) happens when people in a place do not have enough food for a long time. Then, many people get sick and weak. Some of them

The houses in this Mossi compound have cone-shaped roofs.

die. A long drought can even turn savanna land into desert. This is one way that nature's forces change the surface of Earth.

In the 1960s and 1970s, west Africa had a bad drought. Herders and farmers left their homes. They had to live in camps near the cities. Thousands of people died. The people who lived had to adapt. They had to change because conditions around them changed. Nomads had to settle down. Herders began to farm. Farmers and herders found work building roads. They began to ride bicycles. Many farmers and herders got used to city life. The change in their land and climate changed their ways.

The Compound

Members of a Mossi farm family live in a family compound. A **compound** is a group of houses built close together. Each house is made of mud brick and has a straw roof. Each house or group of houses has a **courtyard.** This is a roofless area with walls around it.

A compound has different work areas. Women cook in their own courtyards. There is a place to grind flour and make dough. There are other places to wash clothes. There may also be a place where women can make *dolo.* Outside the compound are places to keep animals and places to store grain. There is also a small family field around each compound.

This child is working in the compound. She has ground up grain to make flour. Now she is using flour to make dough.

A Mossi family usually has two meals a day. Breakfast might be cereal, fried cakes, or beans. The main meal might be a very thick cereal served with a vegetable sauce. To honor a special guest, the Mossi will serve chicken. But Mossi families eat very little meat.

All members of a Mossi compound have special jobs. Men and boys build the houses. Women pave the floors and put plaster on the walls. The children take care of the family's animals.

A Mossi village is made up of groups of family compounds. The compounds of a village are spread out over a wide area. The most important compound is that of the village chief. Visitors to a village go to see the chief as soon as they arrive. This is a Mossi custom.

REVIEW

WATCH YOUR WORDS

1. A group of houses for a Mossi family is a____.
   compound   courtyard   village

2. A roofless area with walls around it is a____.
   village   compound   courtyard

3. To gather in crops is to____them.
   plant   weed   harvest

4. A____is a long time with no rain.
   desert   harvest   drought

5. When people do not have enough food to live, there is a____.
   rainy season   famine   desert

CHECK YOUR FACTS

6. When is the dry season in Burkina Faso?

7. How do the Mossi find water during the dry season?

8. When do the Mossi plant their crops?

9. Name two crops that some Mossi farmers sell.

10. What is the last job of the growing season?

SHARPEN YOUR THINKING

Farmers in Burkina Faso do most of their work by hand. How do most farmers plant, weed, and harvest in the United States?

Lesson 3: Cities and Change

FIND THE WORDS

illiterate   **profit**
unemployed   **official language**

Today, many Mossi young people are leaving their villages. They are moving to the cities. Why? There are several reasons.

Life in Mossi villages has been hard for many years. There has been very little rain and not enough food. Also, there are not many ways to earn money in the villages. Some young people sell crops that they raise on their own. But usually, they give all the money to their families. In the cities, young people hope to earn money for themselves.

Most people in the villages are **illiterate.** That means they do not know how to read and write. In Burkina Faso, only 1 person in 14 can read and write. Many children do not get to go to school. There are not many elementary schools in Burkina Faso. Children can go to school only if there is a school nearby.

There are about 40 high schools in Burkina Faso. The high schools are in the cities. There is only one university. It is in the capital city, Ouagadougou. Ouagadougou has several other kinds of schools. One school trains people for government jobs. Another school trains nurses. Still another trains veterinarians, or animal

Village young people in Burkina Faso must go to the city to attend high school. This is a French high school in Burkina Faso. The first word on the gate is *lycée*. *Lycée* (lee SAY) means "high school" in French. Does the Philippe Zinda Kabore High School look like schools you know?

doctors. There are also schools that teach people trades.

Many young people move to the cities hoping to go to school. All of them hope to find a job. Those who get jobs do not make much money. But they still send some money home to help their families. They also go home to visit as often as they can. On these visits, they tell friends about city buildings and traffic. They tell about the food in French and African restaurants. Some friends in the village cannot imagine movies and television. They want to visit stores in the city. They want to see the many things for sale.

After hearing such stories, more and more young people leave the

This African blacksmith is in business for himself. He provides a service.

farms. This has caused the population of cities to grow very fast. Now there are more people in cities looking for jobs. But there are no more jobs than before.

It is hard to get a good job in the city. It is important to have gone to school. It is important to know French. But many young people have not been to school. They do not speak French. They cannot read and write. So they have to take jobs with long hours and low pay. Some young men load sacks of sugar on carts in the market. Others help build buildings. They dig with shovels and picks. They also push carts loaded with sand and cement.

Most young women work in *dolo* factories. Some find jobs in homes. Young men also work in homes. In homes, workers clean, wash, iron, and do errands. They may also cook and take care of the garden.

Some young people go into business for themselves. They buy goods at one price and sell them for more. That way, they make a profit. A **profit** is the extra money left from a sale after expenses are paid. Some young people sell magazines, newspapers, or cold sodas. Others sell vegetables that they grow in small gardens. Still others shine shoes on the streets.

Many young people try to find work but are not successful. They are **unemployed.** That means they

Kaboré Lazare goes to high school at night. He is preparing for the future.

Campaoré Poko owns a large *dolo* business. She also buys and sells cattle.

do not have a job. These people may become unhappy. They may wonder if coming to the city was a mistake.

Kaboré Lazare (kuh BAW ray luh ZAH ruh) is a young man about 19 years old. He left his family farm and moved to Ouagadougou. Now he works as a waiter 6 days a week. He works 8 hours a day. After work, he studies for 2 hours. Then he goes to high school in the evening. He is learning to speak French. He already knows English. Going to school is very important to Lazare. He is learning many new things. He is working hard to prepare himself for a better job.

Mossi women work and study in the cities, too. Women who go to school and learn French sometimes can get good jobs. Some are trained for jobs in government. Others become teachers or nurses. Sometimes, women in the cities have men working for them. In the villages, Mossi men are always in charge. In the cities, both men and women have to change old ways of thinking.

Campaoré Poko (CAHM pah oh ray POH koh) has a large *dolo* business in the city. She hires many young city women. They make and sell *dolo* for her. Compaoré Poko has become rich. She owns her own home. With the money from her *dolo* business, she buys and sells cattle. The Mossi people respect Campaoré Poko because she runs her business well.

Changing to new ways was good for Kaboré Lazare and Campaoré Poko. But change is hard for most people. The older Mossi like to do things as their ancestors did them. They think the young people should stay on the family farms.

Government leaders also want to change Burkina Faso. They want it to be a united nation. They want the people to learn French. That way, everyone would have at least one language in common. The government has made French the official language of Burkina Faso. The **official language** of a nation is the one used by the government and the schools.

The leaders also want the people to learn better ways of farming. They want the people to use better methods of health care. But the older Mossi want to see someone using the new ways, first. If the new ways make things better, they may try them, too.

REVIEW

WATCH YOUR WORDS

1. The ____ in the cities of Burkina Faso is growing.
   famine   drought   population

2. A person who cannot read or write is ____.
   unemployed   landlocked
   illiterate

3. A person without a job is ____.
   illiterate   unemployed   inland

4. In Burkina Faso, it is important to know the ____.
   pharaoh   official language
   unemployed

5. A ____ is the money left from a sale after expenses.
   profit   price   harvest

CHECK YOUR FACTS

6. Why do many Mossi young people move to the cities?

7. Why are many Mossi people not able to read and write?

8. What kinds of jobs can people from a Mossi village get in the city?

9. Why do the Mossi have respect for Campaoré Poko?

10. Name three things that government leaders want people in Burkina Faso to do.

SHARPEN YOUR THINKING

Young people usually like new things. Older people sometimes prefer old ways of doing things. Why do you think this is true? Are new ways always better than old ways?

CHAPTER REVIEW

WATCH YOUR WORDS

Match each word to the right meaning.

1. assembly
2. compound
3. courtyard
4. drought
5. famine
6. harvest
7. illiterate
8. landlocked
9. profit
10. unemployed

A. surrounded by land
B. to gather in the crops
C. a long period with no rain
D. a group that meets to make laws
E. without a job
F. not able to read and write
G. a group of houses built close together
H. a lack of food that makes people sick and weak
I. a roofless area with walls around it
J. money left from a sale after expenses

CHECK YOUR FACTS

11. Where is Burkina Faso? What is its capital city?
12. Why do many people leave Burkina Faso?
13. What is the largest culture group in Burkina Faso?
14. What is *dolo?* What is it made from?
15. How long does the dry season last in Burkina Faso?
16. What happens during a drought? Name three things.
17. What are three jobs that Mossi children do in the compound or fields?
18. Name three jobs that people can train for in Ouagadougou.

19. How is Kaboré Lazare preparing himself for a good job?
20. Why do Burkina Faso's leaders want the people to learn French?

APPLY YOUR SKILLS

FIND THE TIME LINE

21. List the events below in order.
    —The families weed the fields.
    —The rains soften the ground.
    —The women carry the grain and stalks home.
    —Farm families plant seeds.
    —The people harvest their crops.

USE YOUR MAP

Look at the map on page 216.

22. Give the right cardinal direction (north, south, east, or west):
    Niger is __a__ of Burkina Faso. Burkina Faso is __b__ of Ghana. The railroad runs __c__ and __d__ from Ouagadougou to Ivory Coast.
23. Name two things on the map that were made by people.
24. Name two things on the map that are natural features.

SHARPEN YOUR THINKING

25. How does the climate of Burkina Faso affect the way farm families live?
26. Why are the Mossi careful not to waste anything they grow?
27. Suppose all the young Mossi move to the cities? What will happen to the farms?
28. Think about life in a Mossi village. What might city people miss?
29. How could the Mossi learn to farm in better ways?

UNIT REVIEW

WATCH YOUR WORDS

Use the words below to complete the unit summary. Use each term only once.

commercial	finished goods	nomads	rainy season
deserts	harbors	pharaohs	rapids
drought	herding	profit	raw materials
dry season	inland	pyramids	savanna
famine	irrigate	rain forests	subsistence

Africa was hard for Europeans to explore. This continent had few __1__ where ships could anchor. It was also hard to get past the coast and go __2__. Ships could not sail up rivers that had waterfalls and __3__. Hot, barren __4__ and thick, wet __5__ made it hard to cross Africa.

Now, we know much more about Africa. We know that almost half of Africa is tropical grassland, or __6__. We know the savannas have two seasons. Farmers plant their crops during the __7__. They cannot grow crops in the fields during the __8__. Most farm families in Africa grow only enough food to feed themselves. This is called __9__ farming. In places that are too dry to farm, people live by __10__ animals. Herders who move from place to place are called __11__.

Sometimes, the rains do not come when they are due. A long time with no rain is called a __12__. Fields dry up and animals die. People do not have enough food. This lack of food is a __13__.

In the valley of the Nile, farmers __14__ their fields. They use water from the Nile to wet the land. That way, crops will grow. Along the Nile, you will also see great __15__. These are the tombs of the ancient Egyptian kings, or __16__.

There are also large farms in Africa. Here, crops are grown to be sold. This is called __17__ farming. Africa needs more large farms and factories. Factories improve __18__, such as cotton and logs. These materials are worth much more as __19__, such as shirts and tables. Then, the goods can be sold for a __20__.

CHECK YOUR FACTS

1. What is the second-largest continent on Earth?

2. What is the hottest continent on Earth? Do you remember which continent is the coldest?

3. What is the Sahara? Where is it?

4. What is the Nile? How long is it?

5. What are savannas? How do the seasons change on savannas in Africa?

6. What is the climate like in Africa's rain forests? In the eastern highlands?

7. Name three animals found in Kenya.

8. What is Africa's highest mountain?

9. Divide Africans into five main groups of people. Then name a part of Africa where each group lives.

10. Name three great African empires.

11. How do most Africans make a living?

12. Name three large cities in Africa.

13. Name three African nations that export petroleum.

14. Where in Egypt do most people live?

15. What does Burkina Faso import? What does it export? Does Burkina Faso make a profit? Why, or why not?

SKILL DEVELOPMENT

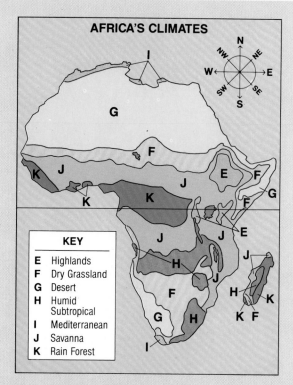

AFRICA'S CLIMATES

KEY
- **E** Highlands
- **F** Dry Grassland
- **G** Desert
- **H** Humid Subtropical
- **I** Mediterranean
- **J** Savanna
- **K** Rain Forest

USE YOUR MAP SKILLS

The map above shows Africa's climate zones. Use it to answer questions 1–6. Refer to the climate map on page 195.

1. Where are Africa's deserts?
2. Where are Africa's rain forests?
3. Are the dry grasslands near or far from the deserts?
4. Where are the savannas?
5. Where are highland climates found?
6. Name the climates along the Nile.
7. Draw or trace an outline map of Africa. Put these things on the map and label them:
   A. the equator and the Sahara
   B. the Atlantic Ocean, Mediterranean Sea, Red Sea, and Indian Ocean
   C. the White Nile, the Blue Nile, the Nile, and the Nile delta

USE YOUR MAPS

8. Look at the elevation map of Africa on page 191. Where is most of the land at or near sea level?
9. Look at the political map of Africa on page 211.
   A. What African nations have coastlines on the Red Sea?
   B. What African nations does the equator pass through?

KNOW YOUR RIVERS

Match the word with the clue.

10. delta
11. mouth
12. rapids
13. silt
14. source

A. rocky places in a river
B. the place where a river begins
C. a triangle of rich soil at a river mouth
D. the place where a river flows into the sea
E. rich soil that a river carries

SHARPEN YOUR THINKING

15. In the United States, we say "up north" and "down south." But in Egypt, Upper Egypt is south. Lower Egypt is north. Why is this so?
16. Suppose the desert spread farther south. What would happen to the people, the animals, and the land?
17. Pretend you are president of a new African nation. The people of your nation belong to two culture groups. They speak different languages. They do not get along. You want them to work together. What will you do?

231

ARCTIC OCEAN

North Cape

Barents Sea

Iceland
▲Mt. Hekla

40°W

70°N

30°W

20°W

10°W

0°

10°E

20°E

30°E

40°E

50°E

KOLA
PENINSULA

White
Sea

Vestfjorden

Norwegian
Sea

Arctic Circle

Prime Meridian

ATLANTIC
OCEAN

30°W

LAPLAND

KJØLEN MTS.

SCANDINAVIAN PENINSULA

Gulf of Bothnia

Lake
Ladoga

Faeroe Is.

Shetland Is.

Orkney Is.

Outer Hebrides

British Isles

PENNINE
CHAIN

Dublin

Irish Sea

St. George's Channel

50°N

Oslo

Helsinki

Leningrad

Stockholm

Gulf of Finland

Gotland

Baltic
Sea

North Sea

JUTLAND

NORTH EUROPEAN PLAIN

Dnepr Lowland

Amsterdam

London

Brussels

Berlin

Warsaw

English Channel

BRITTANY
PENINSULA

Paris

ARDENNES

Bonn

Prague

CARPATHIAN MTS.

20°W

Bay
of Biscay

JURA MTS.

Lake
Constance

CENTRAL
MASSIF

ALPS

Vienna

Budapest

Hungarian
Basin

TRANSYLVANIAN
ALPS

40°N

PYRENEES
MTS.

Milan
PLAIN OF LOMBARDY

Venice

DINARIC ALPS

Belgrade

Bucharest

Duero R.

MESETA

Madrid

APENNINE
PENINSULA

APENNINES

BALKAN MTS.

Sofia

Lisbon

IBERIAN
PENINSULA

Corsica

Rome

BALKAN
PENINSULA

Istanbul

PINDUS MTS.

Naples
Mt. Vesuvius

Sardinia

Balearic Is.

▲Mt. Olympus

Aegean
Sea

Tyrrhenian Sea

Strait of Gibraltar

Athens

30°N

Sicily

Ionian
Sea

AFRICA

Malta

Crete

Mediterranean Sea

10°W

10°E

20°E

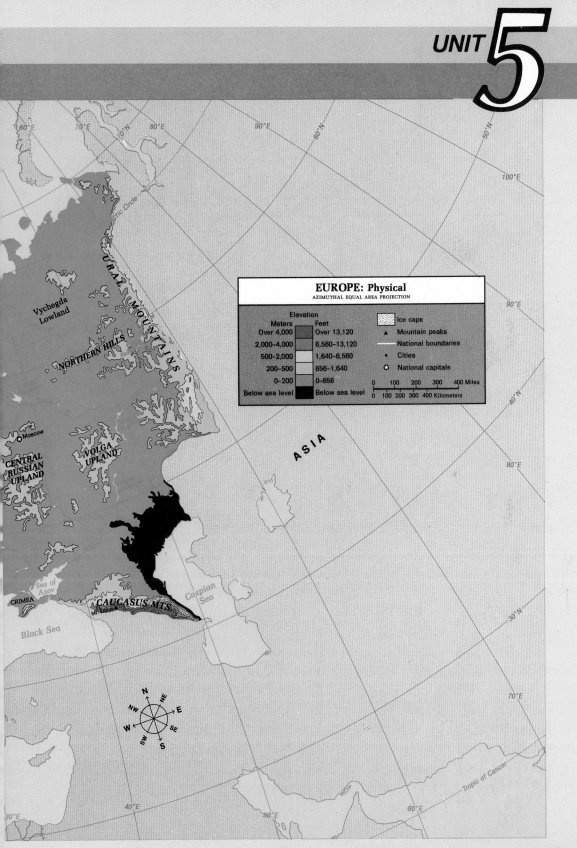

EUROPE: Physical

AZIMUTHAL EQUAL AREA PROJECTION

Elevation

Meters	Feet
Over 4,000	Over 13,120
2,000–4,000	6,560–13,120
500–2,000	1,640–6,560
200–500	656–1,640
0–200	0–656
Below sea level	Below sea level

Ice caps
▲ Mountain peaks
— National boundaries
• Cities
✪ National capitals

0   100   200   300   400 Miles
0 100 200 300 400 Kilometers

URAL MOUNTAINS

Vychegda Lowland

NORTHERN HILLS

Moscow

CENTRAL RUSSIAN UPLAND

VOLGA UPLAND

ASIA

CRIMEA

Sea of Azov

CAUCASUS MTS.
Mt. Elbrus

Caspian Sea

Black Sea

Tropic of Cancer

N NE E SE S SW W NW

CHAPTER 1 EUROPE AND ITS PEOPLE

Lesson 1: Land and Climate

FIND THE WORDS

**mainland   island   peninsula
sea   uplands**

Europe! What do you think of when you hear that name? Castles in Spain? April in Paris? The isles of Greece? Skiing in the Alps? London fog? Maybe you think of the capitals of Europe—great cities like London, Paris, and Rome. In fact, Rome gave us our word *romance*. And Europe is full of romantic, faraway places. Many Americans have ancestors who came from Europe. Much of our history is there.

234

Europe and Asia are part of the same big mass of land. Even so, we think of Europe and Asia as two continents. Those two continents are separated by the Ural Mountains. Find the Ural Mountains on the map of Europe on pages 232 and 233.

Europe is only one of seven continents of Earth. Yet, when writers from Great Britain and Ireland say "the Continent," they mean Europe. Actually, they mean the mainland of Europe.

The **mainland** of a continent or country is the chief mass of land. Islands may be counted as part of a continent. But islands are not part of the mainland.

Some people call Europe "a continent of peninsulas and of islands." What do you suppose this means?

An **island** is a piece of land completely surrounded by water. It is smaller than a continent. Australia is completely surrounded by water, but we call it a continent. It is a large mass of land. Ireland is completely surrounded by water, and we call it an island. It is much smaller than Australia.

Look at the map of Europe again. How many islands can you find? Only the largest islands are shown on the map. There are many small islands as well.

A **peninsula** is a piece of land almost surrounded by water. In

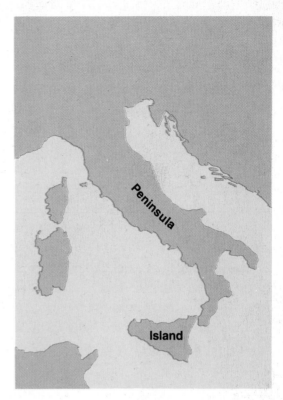

Italy is a peninsula. It is almost surrounded by water. Sicily is an island. It is completely surrounded by water.

fact, the word *peninsula* means "almost island." In the United States, Florida is a peninsula. In Europe, the main part of Italy is a peninsula. It is shaped like a boot. Spain and Portugal are on a peninsula. So are Norway and Sweden. Find these peninsulas on the map of Europe.

Do you know the difference between an ocean and a **sea?** *The* sea means the same thing as the ocean. But *a* sea is smaller than an ocean. A sea can be part of an ocean. The North Sea is part of the Atlantic Ocean. The Barents

Sea is part of the Arctic Ocean. Or, a sea may be surrounded by land. Look at the map of Europe. Find the Mediterranean (MED uh tuh RAY nee un) Sea. Did you know that *Mediterranean* means "middle of the dry land"? How many other seas can you find?

The Caspian (KASS pee un) Sea is like a huge salt lake. It is the largest inland body of water in the world. The lowest part of Europe is the surface of the Caspian Sea. It is 28 meters (92 feet) below sea level! How can a sea be below "sea level"? An inland sea can be lower than the level of Earth's oceans.

Oceans, seas, and rivers have been very important to Europe. For centuries, people from Europe sailed out to explore the world. They traded with faraway lands. They used ships to carry people and goods. Their waterways were like our highways. The best "road" from one place to another might be the sea or river.

Sometimes, a river forms a natural boundary between nations. The Rhine River separates France and West Germany. Find the Rhine River and the Danube (DAN yoob) River on your map. Then look farther east and find the Volga River.

Norway is part of the northern highlands region of Europe. There are many mountains and high hills along Norway's coast. Norway extends from 58° to 71° north latitude. Thus it goes as far north as Alaska in the United States. In fact, the name *Norway* means "northern region" in the Old Norse language. Like Alaska, Norway has its northernmost coast on the Arctic Ocean. The part of the Arctic Ocean near Norway is the Barents Sea.

Highlands and Lowlands

Europe is a small continent. It is not quite as large as our country, the United States. It is less than half the size of our continent, North America. Australia is the only continent smaller than Europe. But Europe has many different kinds of land. We will learn about four regions of Europe.

In the north of Europe are the northern highlands. These highlands stretch from Iceland through Norway, Sweden, and Finland.

South of the northern highlands is the European (YOOR uh PEE un) plain. This plain goes from one side of the continent to the other. It stretches from the west coast of France to the Ural Mountains. The land of the plain is flat or gently rolling. Much of the soil is fertile. In fact, the plain is fine for farming and for factories. Many people live close together on the European plain.

Farther south are the central European uplands. This region is central because it is near the middle of Europe. It is called the **uplands** because of its hills and plateaus. Portugal and Spain are in this uplands area.

Finally, there is the Alpine (AL pyn) region. This region was named for its most famous mountains, the Alps. It includes steep

People from all over the world visit the Swiss Alps. They hike in summer and ski in winter.

mountains, high hills, and fertile river valleys. Look at the physical map on pages 232 and 233. Find the mountain groups that make up the Alpine system. They go across the continent, from west to east.

The Pyrenees (PIR uh neez) Mountains are a natural boundary between France and Spain. The Alps form a semicircle around the peninsula that Italy is on. The parts of the Alps in Switzerland are called the Swiss Alps. The parts in Italy are called the Italian Alps.

Now find Greece. It is on the peninsula east of Italy. This is called the Balkan Peninsula. The Balkan Mountains are here. The Balkans stretch from the Mediterranean Sea east to the Black Sea.

North of the Balkans are the Carpathians (kahr PAY thee unz). They form a smaller semicircle than the Alps. East of the Balkans are the Caucasus (KAW kuh sus) Mountains. They are between the Black Sea and the Caspian Sea. The Caucasus Mountains separate Europe from southwest Asia. The highest mountain in Europe, Mount Elbrus (EL broos), is in the Caucasus. All these mountain chains are part of the Alpine mountain system.

CLIMATES OF EUROPE

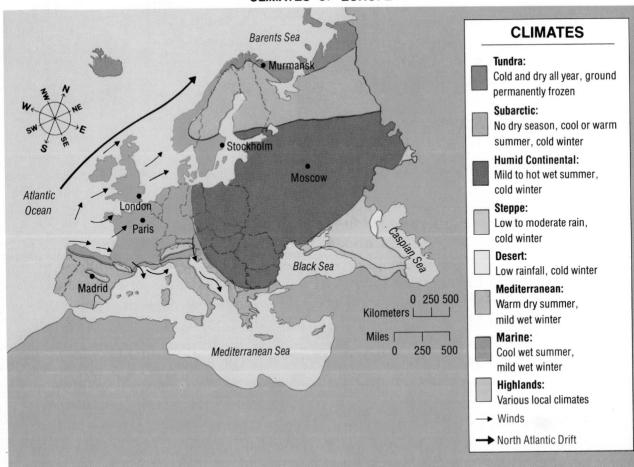

CLIMATES

Tundra: Cold and dry all year, ground permanently frozen

Subarctic: No dry season, cool or warm summer, cold winter

Humid Continental: Mild to hot wet summer, cold winter

Steppe: Low to moderate rain, cold winter

Desert: Low rainfall, cold winter

Mediterranean: Warm dry summer, mild wet winter

Marine: Cool wet summer, mild wet winter

Highlands: Various local climates

→ Winds

➡ North Atlantic Drift

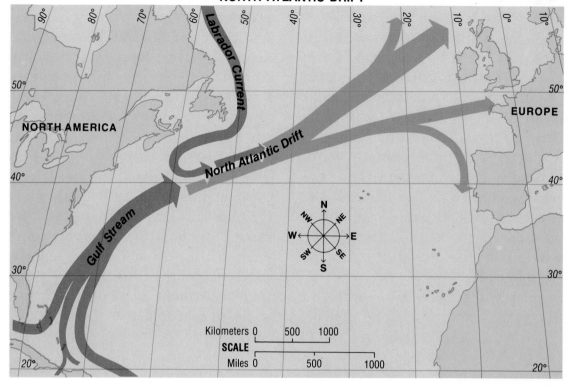

The North Atlantic Drift is a current of warm ocean water. Winds blow off this warm water. They keep the climate of western Europe mild. London, England, and Red Bay, Labrador, are both at 52° north latitude. Still, London has a much warmer climate, thanks to the North Atlantic Drift.

Europe's Climates

Europe stretches all the way from the Mediterranean Sea to the Arctic Ocean. Southwest Europe has a warm, dry, Mediterranean climate. This climate is named for the warm Mediterranean Sea. Northeast Europe has subarctic and tundra climates. Here, it is usually cool or very cold. The climate is also cool in the high mountains of Europe. But in most parts of Europe, the climate is mild. Look at the climate map of Europe on the facing page. You can see that western Europe has mild, wet winters.

This seems odd. It is not what you would expect. If you look at a globe, you will see why. Southern Europe is at the same latitude as the northern United States. Rome, Italy, is as far north as Boston, Massachusetts. That means Great Britain is as far north as Labrador in Canada.

Even Norway has a fairly mild climate. Why isn't Europe colder?

Western Europe owes its mild climate to the North Atlantic Drift. This is a current of warm ocean water. It starts at the Gulf of Mexico as the Gulf Stream. The Gulf Stream flows northeast. It joins with a cold current from Labrador and warms it. Then, the combined current flows across the North Atlantic Ocean. Winds blow off this warm ocean water. These winds keep the climate in western Europe mild.

The warm Atlantic winds do not reach eastern Europe. There, the weather changes more from season to season. Winters in eastern Europe can be bitter cold. Rivers ice over. Snow stays on the ground until spring. In the Soviet Union, winters are colder and summers are hotter than in western Europe.

As you can see, much of Europe is a good place to live. It has a lot of flat land and fertile soil. Europe has mild, pleasant climates. It has many rivers and seas. Unlike Africa, it has many good seaports. Europe may be a small continent in size. But many of Earth's people live there.

REVIEW

WATCH YOUR WORDS

1. A small body of land surrounded by water is a(n)___.
   peninsula   sea   island
2. Part of an ocean may be called a ___.
   river   sea   lake
3. The meaning of the word ___ is "almost island."
   Mediterranean   peninsula   mainland
4. By "the Continent," English writers mean the___of Europe.
   mainland   islands   country
5. Hills and plateaus are___.
   lowlands   mountains   uplands

CHECK YOUR FACTS

6. How many continents does Earth have? How does Europe rank in size?
7. How did the Mediterranean Sea get its name?
8. Why are oceans, seas, and rivers important to Europe?
9. Name four land regions in Europe.
10. What gives western Europe a mild climate? Explain.

SHARPEN YOUR THINKING

11. How is an inland sea like an island? How is it different?
12. How is a continent like an island? How is it different?

Lesson 2: Resources of Europe

FIND THE WORDS

deposit   developed   market

There are many resources on the continent of Europe. But the people do not have some important resources that they need. Europe has large areas of fertile soil. So Europeans farm much of their continent.

Many European farmers raise a lot of food on their land. They know and use modern ways of farming. They use fertilizer and modern farm machinery. They also grow many different kinds of foods. Some parts of Europe are good for special crops. In France and Italy, farmers grow grapes. Olives grow on trees in Spain, Greece, and southern Italy. Many European nations grow potatoes, sugar beets, and grains. Many farmers also raise cattle for milk and cheese. Fish are an important resource, since Europe has many bodies of water.

Even so, most European nations cannot produce enough food to feed their people. These nations have to buy food from other countries. Great Britain has to import half its food. France is different. French farmers produce more food

Great Britain is an island nation. The British catch many fish off their shores.

than the French people need. Thus, France can export food to other nations.

In several parts of Europe, there are large coal deposits. A mass of a mineral found in the ground is called a **deposit.**

Coal is important in Great Britain, France, East and West Germany, and Poland. There are iron mines near the coal deposits in France and in East and West Germany. This is very useful. Both

NONLIVING RESOURCES OF EUROPE

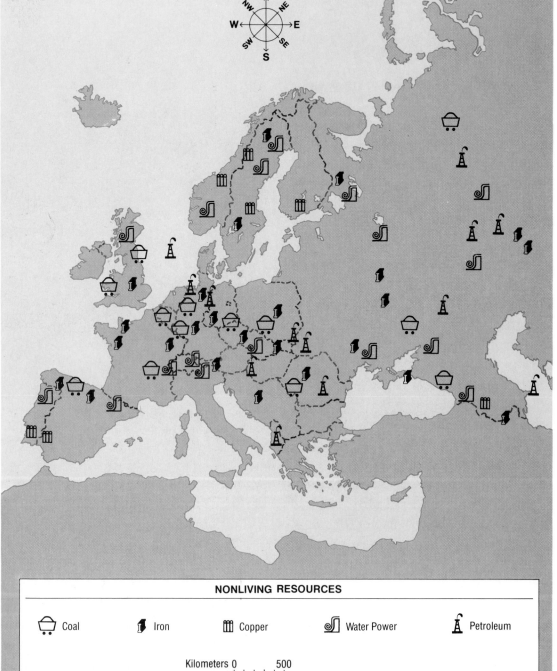

NONLIVING RESOURCES

Coal	Iron	Copper	Water Power	Petroleum

Kilometers 0   500
SCALE
Miles 0   500

coal and iron are needed to make steel. So steel is made in this region. Farther east is the Soviet Union. It is very rich in coal and iron ore. Thus, a lot of steel is made there, too. Iron ore is also found in Sweden and northern Spain. Look at the resource map of Europe. Notice the areas where coal and iron ore are found.

Many European nations burn coal to make electricity. In Norway, Sweden, and the Alps, water power runs electric power plants. Petroleum, or fuel oil, is another source of energy. Petroleum has been found beneath the North Sea. It is found in the Soviet Union. But most European nations have little or no petroleum. They have to import it.

Like North America, Europe is a highly developed continent. A **developed** region is one that has many factories. The people of a developed region make good use of their natural resources. Many more people live in cities than in the country. More people work in factories, offices, stores, and repair shops than on farms.

Here is one way to tell how developed a nation or region is. Find out how many people work on farms. The fewer farm workers there are, the more developed the region is. Suppose only 10 or 20 workers out of every 100 work on farms. Such a region is developed.

Top: Fine grapes are grown in Italy. *Bottom:* Many people in West Germany work in factories.

The nations of Europe have many factories. European people use modern ways to manufacture goods. But Europeans have to import many raw materials for their factories. Europeans do not grow cotton. They don't raise enough sheep for the wool they need. So they have to import cotton and wool to manufacture cloth and clothes. They have to import metals like aluminum to build and run modern factories.

For centuries, a few European nations ruled most of the land on Earth. Europeans needed many raw materials for their factories.

Remember the nations of Europe that had colonies in Africa and South America? Those continents had raw materials that Europeans needed.

Europeans also wanted markets for the goods they made. A **market** is a place where goods can be sold. The people who buy the goods are also called the market. Colonies were ready-made markets for manufactured goods.

European nations have lost their colonies. But Europe is still one of the most developed regions on Earth. And Europeans still use resources from all over the world.

REVIEW

WATCH YOUR WORDS

1. Most of the nations of Europe ___ petroleum.
   export   deposit   import
2. European nations got ___ from their colonies.
   finished goods   raw materials
   factories
3. People who buy goods are called the ___.
   market   colonies   Europeans
4. A ___ region has many jobs in its cities.
   tundra   farming   developed
5. A mass of a mineral in the earth is a ___.
   bank   deposit   crop

CHECK YOUR FACTS

6. Name four foods that Europe's farmers grow.
7. Name four things that Europeans import.
8. Why is it good if coal and iron ore are found near each other?
9. How can you tell if a region is developed?
10. How were colonies useful to Europe? Name two ways.

SHARPEN YOUR THINKING

Europe imports food, raw materials, and petroleum. It exports finished goods. Suppose war broke out and stopped this trade. What do you think would happen?

Lesson 3: People of Europe

FIND THE WORDS

**Indo-European literate rival
free trade tariff**

Europe is the second-smallest continent. It covers only 7 percent of Earth. But Europe has over 15 percent of the world's people. These facts tell you that Europe is crowded.

More than 700 million people live in Europe today. That is a lot of people for so little space. Look at the population map of Europe below. The map shows you that the people of Europe are not spread evenly over the continent. Great Britain, the European plain, and northern Italy have the most people. These areas have the most factories, too. People like to live in places with good land and a comfortable climate. They also live where they can get good jobs. The far north of Europe and the high mountains have the fewest people.

People build factories where they can get power to run machines. Coal, gas, and petroleum

POPULATION AND INDUSTRY IN EUROPE

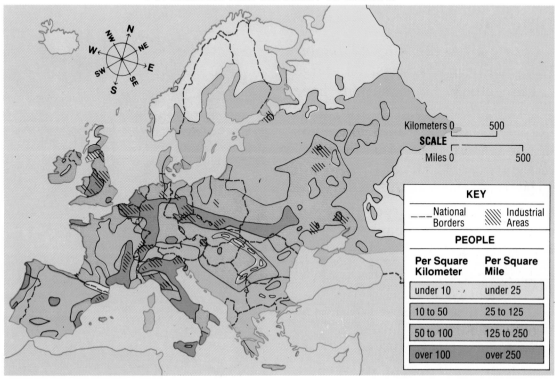

KEY	
——— National Borders	\\\\\\ Industrial Areas

PEOPLE	
Per Square Kilometer	**Per Square Mile**
under 10	under 25
10 to 50	25 to 125
50 to 100	125 to 250
over 100	over 250

SCALE
Kilometers 0 — 500
Miles 0 — 500

can be burned to supply this power. The forces of moving wind and water can supply power, too. So can energy from the sun and nuclear (NOO klee ur) energy. All these forms of energy can be changed into electricity. The electricity makes the machines work.

Then workers are needed to run the machines. Raw materials are needed to make finished goods. Transportation is needed to move workers and goods around. Level lands tend to have good sources of power. They tend to have good transportation. They often have useful raw materials. So level lands are good places for factories and people.

Europeans: Alike and Different

Europe has 27 major nations. Each nation has at least one large culture group. Some nations have several culture groups within their borders. And sometimes, members of one culture group live in different nations. Each culture group has its own language, history, customs, and beliefs. From this, you might think Europeans are very different from one another. But Europeans also have many things in common.

Most Europeans are White. The people of northern Europe tend to have light skin and blond hair. In southern Europe, many people

have slightly darker skin and dark hair. However, nations like Spain, Italy, and Greece have blond people, too. Recently, people from other continents have been moving to Europe. Nations like Great Britain and France now have some Black and Asian peoples.

Most Europeans are Christians. Many people in southern Europe are Catholics. Many in northern Europe are Protestants. Jewish people also live in many nations of Europe. The Jewish people have been very important in European history. Some Muslims, too, have

moved to Europe from the Middle East. As you can see, in Europe, many people are religious.

Still, in some parts of Europe, people are not allowed to worship freely. They are taught not to believe in God. This is especially true in the Communist countries of eastern Europe.

The people of Europe speak about 50 different languages. Yet almost all these languages belong to the same family. Most are **Indo-European** languages. Languages in this family are spoken all the way from India to western

Many different peoples are Europeans. Each culture group in Europe has its own language, history, and customs.

Europe. English and German are Indo-European languages. So are French, Spanish, and Italian. So are Greek and Russian. And there are many more.

Most Europeans are **literate.** That means they can read and write. Most have good schools. Most get good health care. Most also have good food and get enough to eat. This means that most Europeans can expect to live at least 70 years. In some parts of the world, people live only 40 years or so.

Rivals and Partners

For hundreds of years, some Europeans were rivals. A **rival** competes with another person or group for something they both want. *Rivals* used to be people who got their water from the same *rīvus,* or stream. Great Britain, France, Germany, and Spain have often been rivals. They were rivals for land, power, and wealth. Sometimes, they fought wars with one another.

Since World War II, many European peoples have been trying

MAIN LANGUAGES OF EUROPE

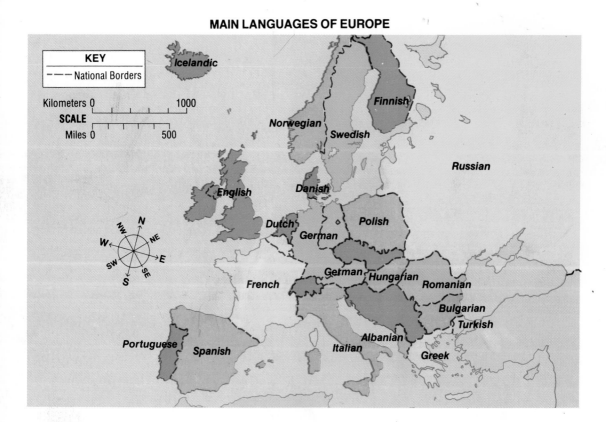

to work together. Many nations of western Europe are now partners in the Common Market. They work together to help Europe's businesses grow. These nations practice free trade with one another. **Free trade** means that there are no taxes on imports. A tax on imported goods is called a **tariff** (TAIR if). Governments often put tariffs on goods from other countries. That way, the imports won't be cheaper to buy than goods made in their own country. The Communist nations of eastern Europe do not belong to the Common Market. They have their own trading group. This group is called COMECON.

Today, many Europeans are planning their futures together. People from western Europe no longer rule the world. But Europeans still have descendants all over the Earth. They have carried their languages to every continent. They have spread their culture and beliefs all over their planet. They have changed the world with their discoveries and inventions. They may be crowded together in a small space. But they have been among the most creative people in history.

REVIEW

WATCH YOUR WORDS

1. People who can read and write are ___.
   literate   illiterate   Indo-European

2. English, French, and Spanish are ___ languages.
   Alpine   Mediterranean
   Indo-European

3. Groups that compete against each other for the same goal are ___.
   partners   rivals   nations

4. ___ raise the price of imported goods.
   Common Market countries
   Europeans   Tariffs

5. Member nations have ___ within the Common Market.
   tariffs   free trade   rivals

CHECK YOUR FACTS

6. Where in Europe do most people live?

7. Why are level lands good places for factories? Give three reasons.

8. Name three ways in which Europeans are alike. Then name three ways in which they are different.

9. Why do most Europeans live for a long time?

10. Western Europe and eastern Europe have different trading groups. What are these two groups called?

SHARPEN YOUR THINKING

11. Do you think free trade is always a good thing? Why, or why not?

12. In Europe, people who speak different languages live close together. What problems could this cause? What is good about it?

Lesson 4: Nations of Europe

FIND THE WORDS

ministate   industry
industrial   Communist   ally

There are 27 nations in Europe. There are also 7 **ministates,** or tiny nations. Two nations of Europe have most of their land in Asia. These two nations are Turkey and the Soviet Union, or U.S.S.R.

The largest and smallest nations on Earth are in Europe. The Soviet Union is the world's largest nation. It is more than twice as large as the United States. Vatican City is the world's smallest nation. This ministate is in Italy. It lies within the city of Rome.

Nations as we know them have existed in Europe only a few hundred years. Look at the map of Europe's nations. This map shows the political boundaries of today. These boundaries have changed many times in Europe's history. The names of some of Europe's nations have changed, too. We still say "Russia" when we mean the Union of Soviet Socialist Republics. We still speak of "Germany," although that nation has been split in two. We still say "England" for the United Kingdom of Great Britain and Northern Ireland. The new names are longer.

Empires of the Past

The nations of Europe have fought many wars and battles over land. Through history, the map of Europe has changed many times. Once, much of western Europe was part of the Roman Empire. First, the city of Rome conquered the rest of Italy. Soon, the Romans ruled all the lands around the Mediterranean Sea. At last, Rome spread its empire over three continents. The Roman Empire stretched from the Caucasus Mountains to the Atlantic Ocean. It went south to the Sahara and north to the North Sea.

The Romans built roads all over their empire. These roads linked different parts of Europe together. People said that "all roads lead to Rome." The Romans carried a great culture to the lands they conquered. They spread their laws and their language, Latin. The French, Spanish, Italian, and Portuguese languages all come from Latin. After Rome became Christian, the Romans also spread the Christian religion.

The Roman Empire lasted hundreds of years before it fell. Over the centuries, other empires and kingdoms joined parts of Europe together. Later, wars split these empires apart.

EUROPE: Political

AZIMUTHAL EQUAL AREA PROJECTION

--- National boundaries
• Cities
✪ National capitals

| 0 | 100 | 200 | 300 | 400 Miles |
| 0 | 100 | 200 | 300 | 400 Kilometers |

251

Many nations built empires overseas. Europeans have always been explorers. In the year 1000, Leif Ericson (LEEF AIR ik sun) sailed from Norway to North America. About 500 years later, Columbus sailed to America from Spain. The Europeans were finding lands they had not known about before. They called the Western Hemisphere *the New World.* Spain, Portugal, France, the Netherlands, and Great Britain set up colonies there. Eventually, the tiny British Isles ruled lands on six different continents. People said, "The sun never sets on the British Empire!" As Earth rotated, some British lands were always turning toward the sun.

Nations of Today

Europeans no longer control most of the lands on Earth. The people in the colonies wanted to govern their own countries. Most colonies gained their independence. Yet the nations of Europe are still important. Four important western nations are France, Italy, West Germany, and Great Britain. We will study them.

France is a fortunate nation in many ways. The soil is fertile. The climate is mild and varied. The farmers grow more than enough food to feed the people. France also has iron and coal. Industries use minerals like these to make goods. An **industry** (IN duss tree) is a branch of manufacturing and trade. Nations that manufacture many goods are called **industrial** (in DUSS tree ul) nations. Today, France is one of the great industrial nations of the world.

The French people are highly educated. Through history, France has produced many great artists and thinkers. France has also been a good friend to the United States. The French helped the United States win independence from Great Britain.

The French have taken their language and culture all over the Earth. People speak French from Canada to Algeria to Vietnam. Once, France ruled many foreign colonies. Today, France controls only a few lands outside Europe. But French paintings, perfume, food, and fashions are famous. Paris is the capital of France. It is one of the most beautiful cities in the world.

Italy did not become one nation until 1870. Before then, it was divided into smaller countries. The city of Rome no longer rules the western world. But Rome is still a great city. It is the capital of Italy. Visitors to Rome can see ruins from the time of the Roman Empire. They can also visit Vatican City. It is the home of the pope. The pope is the head of the Roman Catholic Church.

EIGHT EUROPEAN NATIONS

Nations with the most land	Area		Number of people
	square miles	square kilometers	
FRANCE	211,208	547,026	55 million
SPAIN	194,882	504,741	38 million
SWEDEN	173,780	450,089	8 million
NORWAY	149,158	386,317	4 million
FINLAND	130,558	338,145	5 million
Nations with the most people	Area		Number of people
	square miles	square kilometers	
WEST GERMANY	96,016	248,678	61 million
ITALY	116,319	301,266	57 million
GREAT BRITAIN	94,249	244,102	56 million
FRANCE	211,208	547,026	55 million
SPAIN	194,882	504,741	38 million

Italy does not have many natural resources. The nation has to import many materials to run its factories. Also, Italy has many mountains. These highlands cannot be farmed. So Italy imports some of its food. Even so, Italy is an important modern nation. Its factories make large amounts of steel and many cars. The art and music of Italy are world-famous.

Italy has had many changes in government. No one group has been strong enough to rule alone. So several groups have had to join to run the government. Often, the groups have trouble getting along.

West Germany has recovered from defeat in World War II. Today, it is the leading nation of western Europe. It has more people and factories than any other western European nation. Only three nations in the world produce more goods than West Germany. They are the United States, the Soviet Union, and Japan.

West Germany also has many of the resources needed to run its factories. It has plenty of coal and iron. It also has very modern equipment. After World War II, much of the nation was rebuilt. Thus, many factories are new.

Paris is the capital of France. The Eiffel (EYE ful) Tower is its most famous landmark.

Paris: 49° north, 2° east
Rome: 42° north, 13° east
Berlin: 53° north, 13° east
Bonn: 51° north, 7° east
London: 52° north,
            0° longitude

Vatican City in Rome is the world's smallest nation. It is ruled by the pope. St. Peter's Church, shown here, is the largest Christian church in the world.

Germany was divided into two separate nations after World War II. Today, West Germany is part of western Europe. It has a democratic government. East Germany is part of eastern Europe. It has a Communist (KOM yuh nist) government. In a **Communist** country, the government owns and runs all the businesses.

Berlin used to be Germany's capital city. Today, the capital of West Germany is Bonn. Berlin is split in two. West Berlin is like an island in the middle of East Germany. The Soviet Union controls East Berlin. West Berlin is controlled by the United States, Great Britain, and France. The United States, Great Britain, France, and the Soviet Union were allies in World War II. An **ally** is someone who works with you, not against you. Today, the United States and the Soviet Union are not allies. In fact, in 1961, the Communists built a wall in Berlin.

The Berlin Wall divides the Communist part of Berlin from the free part.

West Germany has more factories than any other nation in western Europe.

This wall keeps people from leaving East Germany.

Great Britain has good harbors and a mild climate. It is located on islands off the west coast of Europe. Its full name is the United Kingdom of Great Britain and Northern Ireland. London is the capital of Great Britain.

The British have always been a nation of traders. British ships once sailed all over the world. Those ships brought back raw materials for British factories. The factories made clothes, machines, and other products. Those products were then shipped to other countries for sale. Raw materials came from the British colonies.

Since World War II, Great Britain has had bad times. The British Empire no longer exists. The former colonies now trade with other countries besides Great Britain. Also, many British factories are old. They are not as good as new factories in other countries.

The British people have always solved their problems in the past. Today, the British are trying to make factories more modern. This will help the workers to produce more goods. Great Britain no longer has great wealth. But Great Britain still has a lot of influence. Today, it is the leader of the Commonwealth of Nations. This is a group of former British colonies.

Fun Facts

Today, most cars have engines that run on gasoline. But many early cars ran on steam. In 1770, a French inventor made a steam tractor. Then, in the early 1800s, English inventors made horseless carriages that ran on steam. Hot coals were burned to make the steam. These coals often fell out on the road. Sometimes, they set the fields on fire. Steam cars also poured smoke into the air. And they made a lot of noise. To control them, the British government passed a law in 1865. The law set speed limits. Steam carriages could go only 6 kilometers (4 miles) per hour in the country. They could go only 3 kilometers (2 miles) per hour in town. The law also said that someone had to walk in front of each steam carriage to warn people. This person had to wave a red flag! As long as Britain had this law, it did not have many steam cars.

REVIEW

WATCH YOUR WORDS

1. West Germany and France are ___ nations.
   Asian   industrial   Communist
2. East Germany is a(n) ___ nation.
   Communist   Catholic   island
3. Vatican City is a ___.
   colony   capital   ministate
4. The United States and the Soviet Union were once ___.
   ministates   allies   kingdoms
5. West Germany and France have many ___.
   islands   ministates   industries

CHECK YOUR FACTS

6. Name the capitals of Great Britain, France, Italy, and West Germany.
7. Why was the Roman Empire important to Europe?
8. Which western European nation has the most factories?

9. Why did it hurt Great Britain to lose the British Empire?

USE YOUR CHART

10. Which nation in the chart has the most land?
11. Which nation in the chart has the most people?
12. What two nations are in both parts of the chart?
13. List three large nations that have few people.
14. List two small nations that have many people.

SHARPEN YOUR THINKING

15. What facts about Europe would you put in the *Guinness Book of World Records?*
16. Suppose you could live in Great Britain, France, Italy, or West Germany. Which would you choose? Would you know the language?

CHAPTER REVIEW

WATCH YOUR WORDS

1. Great Britain and Ireland are____.
   peninsulas islands continents

2. Most of Italy is a(n)____.
   island ministate peninsula

3. France is part of the____of Europe.
   mainland nation island

4. The Mediterranean is a(n)____.
   ocean lake sea

5. ____compete with one another.
   Rivals Allies Colonies

6. ____are on the same side.
   Rivals Allies Colonies

7. A tax on imports is____.
   free trade a tariff a deposit

8. No tax on imports is____.
   a deposit a tariff free trade

9. Which two words describe nations with many factories?
   illiterate industrial developed

10. Which two words are opposites?
    literate industrial illiterate

CHECK YOUR FACTS

11. What is the natural boundary between Europe and Asia?

12. Name four land regions of Europe.

13. What are the famous mountains in Switzerland called?

14. What is the North Atlantic Drift? How does it affect Europe's climate?

15. Name three raw materials that Europeans import.

16. Why are there many people and factories on the European plain?

17. Name three ways in which most Europeans are alike.

18. What are the world's largest and smallest nations?

19. Which nation of western Europe has the most people and factories?

20. Why aren't British factories as good as those in West Germany?

TRUE OR FALSE

21. Europe is larger than North America.

22. The Caspian Sea is the lowest part of Europe.

23. Most European nations grow all the food they need.

24. France exports food to other nations.

25. Europe's political boundaries have changed many times.

APPLY YOUR SKILLS

USE YOUR MAP SKILLS

26. Draw or trace an outline map of Europe. Color the peninsulas red and the islands green.

27. Label two oceans and five seas.

28. Label the Alps, the Pyrenees, the Caucasus, and the Ural Mountains.

29. Label Great Britain, France, West Germany, Italy, and the Soviet Union.

30. Mark a triangle in areas where both coal and iron ore are found.

SHARPEN YOUR THINKING

31. How is traveling across Europe different from traveling across the United States?

32 Europe has many mountains, islands, and peninsulas. Suppose the whole continent was a large, square plain. Would Europeans be any different?

33. Why did people say "The sun never sets on the British Empire"?

2 LIVING IN A COLD LAND

Lesson 1: A Nation on Two Continents

FIND THE WORDS

taiga   steppes   time zone

The Soviet Union is the largest nation on Earth. It spreads across two continents, Europe and Asia. It goes from the Black Sea and the Baltic Sea to the Pacific Ocean. Its full name is the Union of Soviet Socialist Republics. Maps often use just the initials, U.S.S.R. Many people also use the old name, Russia.

Land and Climate of the Soviet Union

Three-fourths of the Soviet Union is in Asia. But most of the people in the Soviet Union live in

Europe. The European part of the nation is west of the Ural Mountains. Much of this land is on the European plain. It is flat or gently rolling land, with some low hills. Here is where most Soviet farms and factories are found.

The Asian part of the nation is east of the Ural Mountains. Here is a huge area called Siberia. This area is very rich in natural resources. The Soviet government has tried to get people to settle there. But not many people want to move to Siberia. The climate there is cold much of the year.

The Soviet Union has five main climate areas. In the far north is the tundra. This is a very cold area north of the Arctic Circle.

Trees do not grow on the tundra. The soil under the surface stays frozen. Polar bears, seals, and reindeer live on the tundra. Here, there is much ice and snow.

South of the tundra is the **taiga** (TY guh). There are great forests in the taiga. Winters are long and cold. Yet it is not too cold for trees to grow. Wolves, bears, and elk live in the taiga. There are big cities in this region, too. Find Leningrad and Moscow on the climate map below.

South of the great forests of the taiga are grasslands. The grasslands in the Soviet Union are called the **steppes** (STEPS). A *steppe* is a grassy plain. Here, winters are not as long and cold as they are in

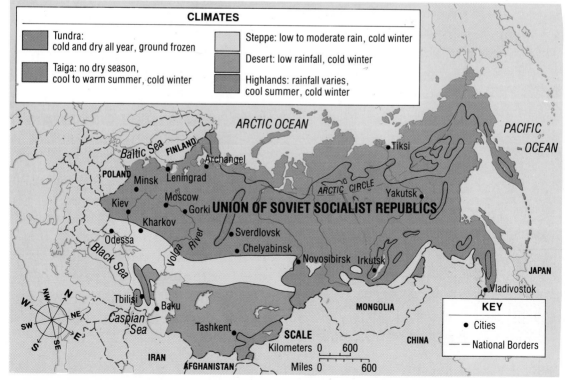

CLIMATES OF THE SOVIET UNION

CLIMATES	
Tundra: cold and dry all year, ground frozen	Steppe: low to moderate rain, cold winter
Taiga: no dry season, cool to warm summer, cold winter	Desert: low rainfall, cold winter
	Highlands: rainfall varies, cool summer, cold winter

KEY
• Cities
-- National Borders

the tundra and taiga. Summers are often dry. Sometimes, there are droughts on the steppes.

In the far south of the Soviet Union are deserts. Here, very little rain falls. But people have brought water from other places to irrigate parts of the land. Many people now work on irrigated farms in the deserts.

On the southern border of the Soviet Union are mountains. The highest mountains have snow on top all year round.

The Soviet Union is rich in natural resources. It has forests and farmlands. It has petroleum, coal, iron ore, and many other minerals. But these resources are scattered across the nation. Getting the resources to the people who use them is a problem. To solve this problem, the Soviet Union has built some of the longest railroads in the world.

The taiga is a subarctic climate region. Great evergreen forests grow there.

Traveling in Time and Space

You have looked at the climates of the Soviet Union from north to south. Here is another good way to see how large the Soviet Union is. Suppose you went all the way across this huge nation, from west to east. You would go about 10,940 kilometers (6,800 miles). And you would pass through 11 time zones!

One way to measure space is to think about time. People have divided Earth into time zones. Each **time zone** stands for 1 hour. There are 24 time zones on Earth. This is because Earth rotates on its axis once every 24 hours. Each time zone is 15 degrees wide in degrees of longitude.

Look at the map of the Soviet Union on page 261. Find the cities of Leningrad and Vladivostok (VLAD uh vos TOK). You can see that these cities are far apart. It is 2 P.M. in Leningrad. It is not long after lunch. The sun is still high in the sky. Many hours of daylight are left. At the same moment, it is 9 P.M. in Vladivostok. It is dark. People have already had dinner. Children are getting ready for bed.

Suppose you travel from west to east. The time gets 1 hour later when you enter a new time zone. Suppose you travel from east to west. Then, the time gets 1 hour earlier when you enter a new time zone.

WHERE WE ARE IN TIME AND PLACE

TIME ZONES IN THE SOVIET UNION

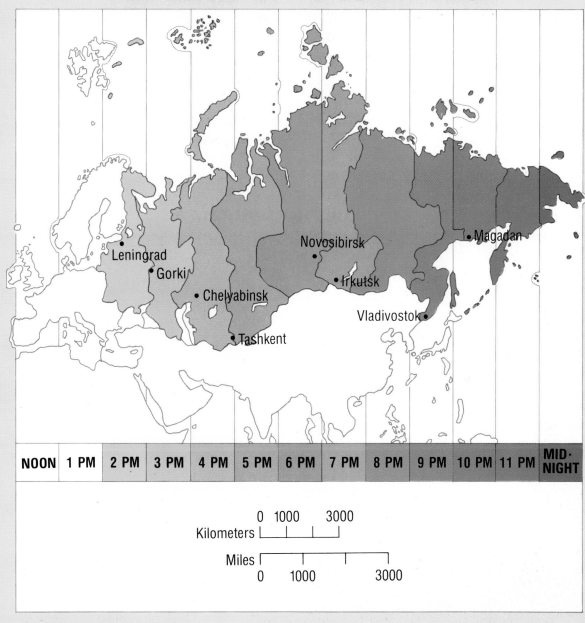

NOON	1 PM	2 PM	3 PM	4 PM	5 PM	6 PM	7 PM	8 PM	9 PM	10 PM	11 PM	MID-NIGHT

Kilometers
0 1000 3000

Miles
0 1000 3000

Now suppose you are catching a train in Leningrad. You plan to go by train all the way to Vladivostok. That way, you can see quite a lot of the Soviet Union. Use the transportation map below to trace your route.

Leningrad is a port on the Baltic Sea. The Baltic Sea is part of the Atlantic Ocean. Vladivostok is a port on the Pacific Ocean. In what direction will you travel from Leningrad to Vladivostok?

Leningrad is a very beautiful city. From Leningrad, you will go to Moscow (MOS kow). Moscow is the capital of the Soviet Union. It is also the largest city. After another day and night on the train, you will cross the Ural Mountains. Now you are in Asia! Next, you will arrive in the city of Chelyabinsk (chel YAH binsk). There, you will board the Trans-Siberian Railway to cross Siberia. This is the longest railroad in the world.

SOVIET UNION: TRANSPORTATION

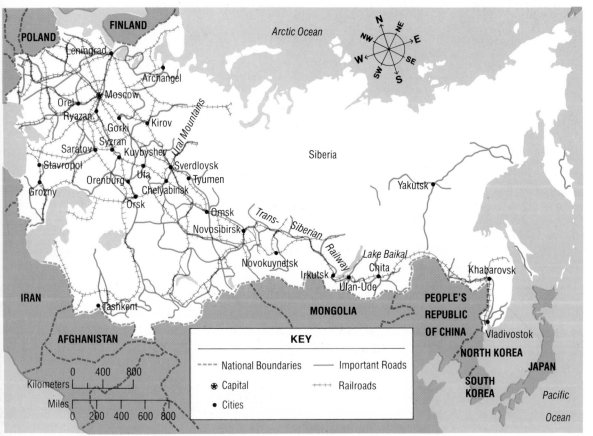

Leningrad was once called St. Petersburg. It has many beautiful canals. Leningrad is at 60° north latitude, 30° east longitude.

Near Chelyabinsk, a farmer carries hay in a wagon. Chelyabinsk is at 60° east longitude. Thus it is 30°—or two time zones—east of Leningrad. So the time in Chelyabinsk is 2 hours later than the time in Leningrad.

It will take you across much of Asia.

Now you will ride over hundreds of miles of steppes. Remember, steppes are grasslands. Then you will come to Novosibirsk (NOH voh si BIRSK). This is the largest city in Siberia. It has long, cold winters. Your next stop is Irkutsk (ir KOOTSK). Sometimes, the temperature there drops to 50 degrees below zero! Near Irkutsk is Lake Baikal (by KAWL). It is the deepest lake in the world.

Finally, you will reach Vladivostok. This city is the Soviet Union's window on the Pacific Ocean. It is west of Japan. From Vladivostok, ships sail to all parts of the world.

You have now traveled nearly 10,000 kilometers (6,000 miles). You will have to set your watch ahead 7 hours. But it has taken you much longer than that to travel over this great distance. Your train did not move as quickly as Earth turns!

Lake Baikal is the deepest lake in the world. Lake Baikal is at 110° east longitude. Thus it is 80°—or five time zones—east of Leningrad. The time at Lake Baikal is 5 hours later than Leningrad time.

REVIEW

WATCH YOUR WORDS

1. Grasslands in the Soviet Union are called the___.
   savanna   taiga   steppes

2. Great forests grow in the___.
   steppes   taiga   tundra

3. Polar bears live on the___.
   tundra   taiga   steppes

4. Farms in the desert are___.
   grassy   very cold   irrigated

5. You have to change your watch when you travel across___.
   boundaries   time zones   mountains

CHECK YOUR FACTS

Look at the Maps

6. In what climate area is Odessa? Kiev? Tiksi?

7. When it is 3 P.M. in Gorki, what time is it in Irkutsk?

8. Name the island nation to the east of Vladivostok.

Look at the Lesson

9. What are two other names for the Soviet Union?

10. Name three mineral resources found in the Soviet Union.

SHARPEN YOUR THINKING

11. Why do you think most Soviet people prefer Europe to Siberia?

12. The Soviet Union crosses 11 time zones. The United States crosses 7. What does this tell you?

Lesson 2: The Land of the Midnight Sun

FIND THE WORDS

twilight   midnight sun
headland
fjord   lichen   moss

In the far north of Europe is an area called Lapland. It is not a country. It stretches across four different nations. Lapland covers the northern parts of Norway, Sweden, and Finland. It also includes a peninsula of the Soviet Union. Most of Lapland is north of the Arctic Circle. People who live there are almost "on top of the world."

Remember, Earth is tilted on its axis. The sun is never directly overhead at the North Pole. The sun's rays hit Earth at a slant north of the Arctic Circle. That makes far northern regions cold. Winters are long and cold in Lapland. Summers are short and cool. The weather there is never warm.

LAPLAND

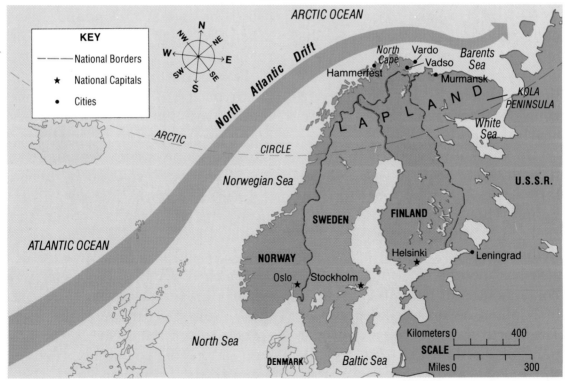

KEY
- - - - - National Borders
★ National Capitals
• Cities

N NW NE W E SW SE S

ARCTIC OCEAN

North Atlantic Drift

North Cape   Vardo
Hammerfest   Vadso   Barents Sea
Murmansk

KOLA PENINSULA

ARCTIC CIRCLE

L A P L A N D

White Sea

U.S.S.R.

Norwegian Sea

SWEDEN   FINLAND

ATLANTIC OCEAN

NORWAY   Helsinki   Leningrad
Oslo   Stockholm

North Sea

Kilometers 0   400
SCALE
Miles 0   300

DENMARK   Baltic Sea

This boat is going through a fjord in Norway. Norway stretches from 58° to 71° north latitude and from 5° to 30° east longitude.

Most parts of the United States have mid-latitude climates. In much of the United States, winter lasts about 3 months. But Lapland lies in the high-latitude climate zone. Winters in Lapland are nearly 9 months long!

Do you know what **twilight** is? It is the time after sunset and before dark. Twilight means "half light." The light is very faint at twilight. Lapland sometimes has twilight instead of night or day. It also has months of total darkness. For 2 months in the winter, people in Lapland never see the sun rise! The North Cape of Norway is the part of Lapland closest to the North Pole. At the North Cape in winter, there is only twilight at noon.

In the summer, the opposite is true. There are two months when the sun is always in the sky. It is light all day and all night. You can even see the sun at midnight! This part of Earth is called "the land of the **midnight sun.**" Look at the picture of the midnight sun on page 20.

In the west, Lapland is part of Europe's northern highlands. Norway is famous for its headlands and fjords. A **headland** is a high point of land that juts out into the water. A **fjord** (FYORD) is a long, narrow inlet with high cliffs on either side. Lapland also has many lakes and rivers. There are many fish to be caught in Lapland. Also, lakes are often used in place of roads.

Few trees grow in Lapland north of the Arctic Circle. Those that do are small and stunted because of the cold. In northeast Lapland is the tundra region. Most of the ground is covered by **lichen** (LY ken) and **moss.** Mosses and lichen are plants that cover the ground like a thick, soft rug. They are the reindeer's favorite foods!

South of the Arctic Circle is a subarctic climate zone. Here are great forests full of pine, fir, spruce, and birch trees. In the Soviet Union, do you remember the name of the forest zone?

The Lapps have to dress warmly. They live in a cold land, between about 66° and 71° north latitude.

The Lapps of Lapland

The people of Lapland are known as Lapps. They were given that name by the Swedish. *Lapp* means "nomad." These people call themselves the Samme, or Samelats. The Lapps look more like the Chinese than like other Europeans. Also, most Lapps are no more than 5 feet in height. The Lapps are not related to other groups of Europeans. Their ancestors probably came from central Asia thousands of years ago.

For hundreds of years, many Lapps were nomads, or wanderers. They hunted and fished for food. They trapped animals for furs. What was more important, they kept large herds of reindeer. The reindeer supplied them with most of the things they needed to live. They had reindeer meat, milk, and cheese to eat. They used reindeer skins to make tents, shoes, coats, and blankets. They used reindeer bones and antlers to make pots, bowls, knives, and other tools. They used other parts of the reindeer to make rope. They threw away very little of the reindeer they killed.

The Lapps were free to move their herds from place to place looking for food. In the winter, the herds went north. There, they would feed on the mosses and lichen. The Lapps lived near their herds in tents. When the Lapps moved on, they loaded their belongings on wooden sleighs. The sleighs were pulled by reindeer! In the summer, the herds went south to the forests. There, the young reindeer were born.

For centuries, the Lapps' way of life was much the same. The reindeer provided most of the things the Lapps needed to live. For other things, like medicines, the Lapps traded with people who lived farther south.

Lapland and Change

Today, Lapland is divided among four nations—Norway, Sweden, Finland, and the Soviet Union. Lapland also has some valuable resources, especially iron ore and trees. Each of these facts has helped change the way Lapps live.

The nations where the Lapps live now require Lapp children to go to school. School begins when

Some Lapps are still nomads. They live in tents and travel with their reindeer herds. Others work in forests, in mines, or on farms.

These Lapp children are enjoying a picnic.

Fun Facts

Dasher, Dancer, Prancer, Vixen, Comet, Cupid, Donner, Blitzen. Those eight reindeer—sometimes led by *Rudolph*—pull Santa's sleigh. They are make-believe reindeer. Real reindeer don't fly over the rooftops. But they do live near the North Pole. And, when they travel, they cover a lot of ground.

The reindeer of Europe and Asia are small, but strong. A reindeer can pull a sled weighing twice as much as the reindeer does. Even pulling that weight, it can go 64 kilometers (40 miles) a day. To find food, reindeer travel hundreds of miles. Their hooves allow them to get a good grip on the ice. Reindeer don't slip and slide around. Here is another interesting fact about reindeer. Female reindeer are the only female deer in the world that have antlers.

The Lapps have tamed their reindeer. But the reindeer native to North America have always been wild. They are called caribou. They don't pull sleds for anyone—even Santa Claus!

the children are about 7. Some of the children go to school for 4 years. Others go for 5 to 8 years if they pass an exam. Still others, if they pass another exam, can go to college. But many Lapp children do not live near schools. They may live too far from school to travel back and forth each day. So they have to live at boarding schools.

At the schools, the children study geography, history, reading, and math. They live, sleep, and eat at school, too. The Lapp children go home only on holidays or in the summer. Sometimes, when young people finish school, they no longer want to tend the herds. Some might get jobs in the mines. Others might work in the forests.

The forests in southern Lapland are very valuable. The trees are cut for lumber and for wood pulp. The lumber is used to build houses and other things made of wood. The pulp is used to make paper. In these forests, the Lapps can always find jobs. They live in wooden homes near their work.

There are large iron mines in Lapland also. The iron ore is taken from the ground and sent farther south. There, it is made into many different products. The Lapps can get jobs in the mines. When they do, they no longer tend herds of reindeer.

The governments that control Lapland no longer let the Lapps roam over all the land. This, too, is changing the Lapps' way of life. Some Lapps have settled along the rivers. There, they built wooden homes and started small farms. Many of these people still have herds of reindeer. But each year, fewer and fewer Lapps live as they did in the past.

REVIEW

WATCH YOUR WORDS

1. Near the North Pole on summer nights, you can see the____.
   savanna   rain forests
   midnight sun

2. Reindeer like to eat____and____.
   fish   mosses   cheese   lichen

3. A narrow inlet between steep cliffs is a____.
   fjord   headland   peninsula

4. A point of land that juts into the sea is a(n)____.
   fjord   island   headland

5. ____is after sunset but before dark.
   Sunrise   Twilight   Night

CHECK YOUR FACTS

6. Lapland is now part of what four nations?

7. Why are winters in Lapland long and cold?

8. Name five ways the Lapps used their reindeer.

9. Why do Lapp children go to boarding school?

10. Name two resources of Lapland. How are they used?

SHARPEN YOUR THINKING

11. Vadso and Vardo are ports on the Arctic Ocean. Even in winter, they are ice-free. Can you guess why?

12. Suppose that for 2 months every winter, you never saw the sun. How would your life be different?

CHAPTER REVIEW

WATCH YOUR WORDS

Match the word with the clue.

1. taiga	**A.**	grassy plains	
2. fjord	**B.**	cliff jutting into the sea	
3. headland	**C.**	cold region with no trees	
4. steppes	**E.**	narrow inlet between cliffs	
5. tundra	**F.**	region of subarctic forests	

CHECK YOUR FACTS

6. What is the largest nation on Earth?

7. Name four climate areas of the Soviet Union.

8. How many time zones are there on Earth?

9. How are Leningrad and Vladivostok alike? How are they different?

10. Where is Lapland? Who governs it?

11. What is the midnight sun?

12. Name some of the many things Lapps get from their reindeer.

TRUE OR FALSE

13. The climate is comfortable in Siberia.

14. North of the tundra is the taiga.

15. The Soviet Union has many natural resources.

16. Moscow is the capital of the Soviet Union.

17. Lapland is a nation.

18. Winters in Lapland are almost 9 months long.

19. In winter, Lapps can see the midnight sun.

20. Lapps work on farms, in forests, and in mines.

FIND THE TIME LINE

21. List these events in the right order.

—Governments said Lapp children had to go to school.
—The ancestors of the Lapps came to Lapland to live.
—Young Lapps finished school, and some found new jobs.
—Lapp families moved around Lapland with their reindeer herds.

USE YOUR MAPS

Look at the map on page 261.

22. Give the right direction (northeast, northwest, southeast, or southwest):

Leningrad is __a__ of Vladivostok. Novosibirsk is __b__ of Tashkent. Tashkent is __c__ of Irkutsk. Vladivostok is __d__ of Leningrad.

23. When it is 4 P.M. in Gorki, what time is it in Leningrad?

SHARPEN YOUR THINKING

24. Suppose Earth was not tilted on its axis. What would happen to "the land of the midnight sun"?

25. Suppose Earth had 12 time zones instead of 24. How wide would each time zone be?

26. Suppose you go west until you enter a new time zone. Will the time be earlier or later there?

27. Explain why the Lapps' way of life is changing.

28. How are the Lapps of Europe like the Mossi of Africa? How are they like the nomads of Africa?

UNIT REVIEW

WATCH YOUR WORDS

Use the words below to complete the unit summary. Use each term only once.

allies
free trade
industrial
islands
mainland

market
peninsulas
rivals
seas
tariffs

Not all of Europe is attached to the __1__. Some parts are __2__, surrounded by water. Europe also has many __3__, with water on three sides. Other parts of Europe have coasts on inland __4__.

Europe is a land of many nations. Some nations of western Europe used to be __5__. They competed with one another for power and land. Now, many of these nations are __6__. They work together to reach their goals. They are trading partners. In the Common Market, they practice __7__. That means they don't put __8__, or import taxes, on one another's goods.

Europe has many highly developed, __9__ nations. These nations have many factories. They manufacture many goods. The people who buy goods are the __10__.

CHECK YOUR FACTS

1. Name three nations of Europe that are on peninsulas.

2. Name one nation of Europe that is on islands.

3. Name three of Europe's seas.

4. Where is the European plain?

5. Name three groups of mountains in the Alpine system.

6. What mountains separate Europe from Asia?

7. Why is western Europe's climate mild?

8. What are two ways Europeans use coal?

9. List five languages that Europeans speak.

10. Why did the boundaries of Europe's nations change?

11. How is manufacturing different in Great Britain and West Germany?

12. What is a time zone?

13. Why are railroads important to the Soviet Union?

14. What are the seasons like in Lapland?

15. Name three kinds of work people do in Lapland.

USE YOUR MAP SKILLS

16. Draw or trace an outline map of Europe. Put these places on the map and label them:
    a. Great Britain, France, West Germany, Italy, and the Soviet Union
    b. the capitals of those five nations
    c. the Atlantic Ocean, Arctic Ocean, and Arctic Circle
    d. the Mediterranean Sea, Black Sea, and Caspian Sea
    e. the Pyrenees, Alps, Caucasus, and Ural Mountains
    f. Norway, Sweden, Finland, and Lapland

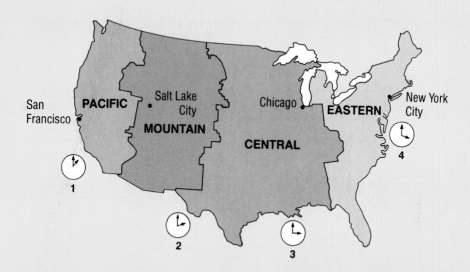

USE YOUR MAP

From Alaska to Maine, the United States crosses 6 time zones. This map shows 4. Use it to answer the questions below.

1. When it is noon in New York City, what time is it in San Francisco?

2. When it is 8 P.M. in San Francisco, what time is it in Chicago?

3. When it is 10 A.M. in Salt Lake City, what time is it in New York?

4. When the sun rises in New York, is it dark or light in San Francisco?

5. Why does the United States have different time zones?

SHARPEN YOUR THINKING

6. Why do more people live in Europe than in South America?

7. What things make Europe a more developed continent than Africa?

USE YOUR MAP SKILLS: SYNTHESIS

8. Make a map of an imaginary island nation in the Northern Hemisphere. Include a key, a scale, and a compass rose.

   a. *Put these things on your map:* northern forests, eastern mountains, a southern desert, a fertile plain, two rivers, three highways, a railroad, deposits of iron ore and coal

   b. *Answer these questions. Then show the answers on the map.*
      (1) Where would you put your capital city?
      (2) Where would you build a sawmill to cut wood?
      (3) Where would you put a steel mill?
      (4) Where would most of the people live?
      (5) Where would most farms and factories be found?

ASIA

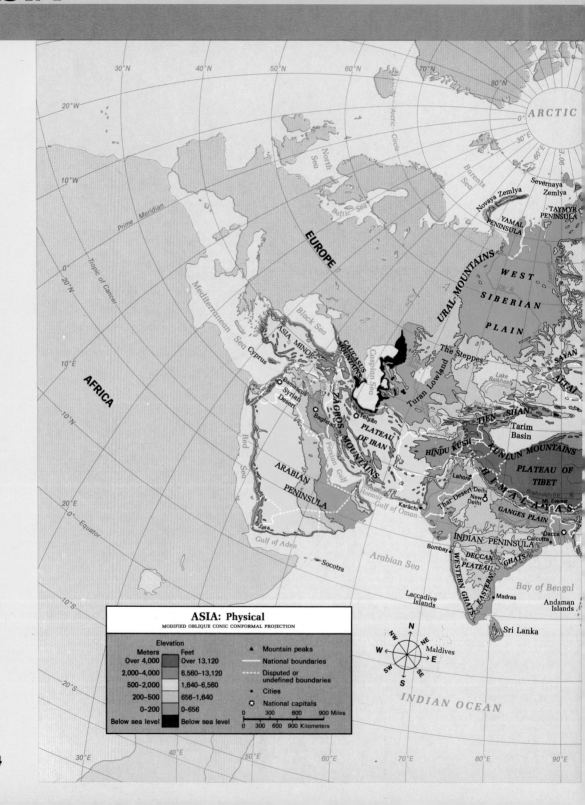

ASIA: Physical

MODIFIED OBLIQUE CONIC CONFORMAL PROJECTION

Elevation

Meters	Feet
Over 4,000	Over 13,120
2,000–4,000	6,560–13,120
500–2,000	1,640–6,560
200–500	656–1,640
0–200	0–656
Below sea level	Below sea level

▲ Mountain peaks
— National boundaries
- - - Disputed or undefined boundaries
• Cities
⊛ National capitals

0   300   600   900 Miles
0 300 600 900 Kilometers

OCEAN

80°N
70°N
60°N
50°N
40°N
30°N
160°W
Tropic of Cancer
170°W
20°N
180°
10°N
170°E
0° Equator
10°S 160°E
20°S
Tropic of Capricorn
30°S

150°E
120°E

New Siberian Islands

KOLYMA MOUNTAINS

CHERSKOGO RANGE

VERKHOYANSK RANGE

CENTRAL SIBERIAN PLATEAU

Lower Tunguska

Lake Baikal

MTS

MONGOLIAN PLATEAU

Gobi Desert

GREATER KHINGAN RANGE

MTS

CENTRAL RANGE

KAMCHATKA PENINSULA

Bering Sea

Aleutian Islands

International Dateline

Sea of Okhotsk

Kuril Islands

Sakhalin

Hokkaidō

Sea of Japan

Honshu

Mt. Fuji Tokyo

Osaka

Shikoku

Kyushu

KOREAN PENINSULA

Korea Strait

Peking
Tientsin
Seoul

Yellow Sea

NORTH CHINA PLAIN

Shanghai

Hwang Ho

East China Sea

Yangtze

BOHEA HILLS

Taiwan

Ryukyu Islands

Luzon Strait

Philippine Sea

PACIFIC OCEAN

Hanoi

Hainan

South China Sea

Manila Luzon

Mindoro

Samar

Panay

INDOCHINA PENINSULA

Rangoon

Bangkok

Ho Chi Minh City

Palawan

Negros

Mindanao

Gulf of Siam

Nicobar Islands

MALAY PENINSULA

Celebes Sea

Halmahera

MAOKE MOUNTAINS

New Guinea

Borneo

Celebes

Buru

Ceram

Aru Islands

Strait of Malacca

Banda Sea

Arafura Sea

Sumatra

Mentawai Islands

Java Sea

Sumbawa

Flores

Timor

Java

Lombok

Bali

Sumba

100°E
110°E
120°E
130°E
140°E
150°E

AUSTRALIA

CHAPTER 1 ASIA AND ITS PEOPLE

Lesson 1: Land and Climate

Asia has "the most" of many things. It is the largest continent on Earth. That means it has more land than any of the other six continents. It has Earth's highest mountains and lowest sea. It has the world's largest and highest plateau. Asia is also the continent with the most people. It has the nation with the most people, China. Three-fourths of the Soviet Union, the largest nation on Earth, is in Asia.

Look at Asia on a globe. Some of the islands of Asia are south of the equator. Some of the mainland is north of the Arctic Circle. So Asia covers a lot of the Northern Hemisphere. Measure Asia from south to north. It goes to 78° north latitude.

Asia also goes across most of the Eastern Hemisphere. It covers 165° of longitude. Asia crosses 11 of Earth's 24 time zones. You can see that Asia is huge!

Now look at the map of Asia on pages 274 and 275. The Arctic Ocean is to the north. To the west are the Mediterranean Sea and the Red Sea. The Indian Ocean is to the south. The Pacific Ocean is to the east. Northeast Asia almost touches North America.

Like Europe, Asia has many peninsulas and islands. One peninsula is in the west, between the Mediterranean Sea and the Black Sea. It is called Asia Minor. The Asian part of Turkey is there.

Three large peninsulas are in the south. The peninsula in the southwest is called Arabia. It is between the Red Sea and the Persian (PUR zhun) Gulf. Arabia is the largest peninsula on Earth. Much of this peninsula is desert land.

Find the peninsula in the middle. The southern part of India is on this peninsula. Notice the mountains in the northern part of India. These mountains are like a wall. They cut India off from the rest of Asia. This makes India seem like a separate part of the continent. So India is called a **subcontinent.**

The peninsula in the southeast is called Indochina (IN doh CHY nuh). Indochina was named for India and China. It is east of India and south of China. Indochina even has a small peninsula of its own! This is called the Malay (MAY lay) Peninsula. It stretches south almost to the equator.

Asia has another peninsula in the east. See if you can find it on the map. North Korea (kuh REE uh) and South Korea are there.

Mountains and deserts cross the center of Asia. The deserts stretch all the way from Arabia to China. Find the Gobi (GOH bee) Desert on the map. This desert is a huge area of rough, dry land.

The Arabian Desert is very hot and dry.

The Gobi Desert is in east-central Asia.

Fun Facts

Earth's largest continent:	Asia has three-tenths of the land on Earth.
Earth's highest mountain:	Mount Everest is 8,850 meters (29,028 feet) above sea level. Suppose you could put Pikes Peak in Colorado on top of Mount Rainier (ray NIR) in Washington. Mount Everest would still be higher!
Earth's lowest sea:	The Dead Sea is 400 meters (1,312 feet) below sea level. This is the lowest point on the surface of the Earth.
Earth's largest peninsula:	Arabia
Earth's largest and highest plateau:	The plateau of Tibet is 4,878 meters (16,000 feet) above sea level. It covers 200,000 square kilometers (77,000 square miles) of Earth's land.
The most people:	Almost 6 out of every 10 people on Earth live in Asia.
The nation with the most people:	China.

Mountains cut across Asia in many different directions. They separate northern Asia from southern Asia. On the map, you can trace these mountains with your finger. Follow them from the Black Sea northeast across the continent. Asia has more than 75 mountains that are higher than 6,098 meters (20,000 feet).

India's mountains are called the Himalayas (HIM uh LAY uhz). They are the highest mountain system on Earth. The highest mountain in the world is in the Himalayas. It is Mount Everest (EV ur ist). Mount Everest is on the border between Nepal and China. It is a towering 8,850 meters (29,028 feet) high.

Besides mountains, Asia has many high plateaus. Find Tibet in western China. The plateau of Tibet is called "the roof of the world." This plateau is the largest area of high land on Earth.

A continent as huge as Asia has many climates. You studied the climates of northern Asia when you studied the Soviet Union. Southwest Asia does not get much rain. People have to irrigate the dry land to grow crops.

South Asia and southeast Asia have a **monsoon climate.** In such a climate, there is a cool season, a hot season, and a rainy season. The islands of southeast Asia have tropical climates. Lowlands there are hot and wet all year.

Most of east Asia lies in the mid-latitude climate zone. In many ways, east Asia's climates are like those of the United States.

Mount Everest is the highest mountain in the world. It rises more than 5 miles above sea level. Mount Everest is between Nepal (nuh PAHL) and China. It is at 28° north latitude, 87° east longitude.

REVIEW

CHECK YOUR FACTS

1. Name five features in which Asia is first in the world.

2. Asia (does/does not) stretch from south of the equator past the Arctic Circle.

3. Name three peninsulas of Asia.

4. Name two desert areas in Asia.

5. What is the highest mountain system on Earth? What is the highest mountain?

6. What is the largest area of high land on Earth?

SHARPEN YOUR THINKING

What feature makes southern India a peninsula? What feature makes India a subcontinent?

Lesson 2: Resources of Asia

FIND THE WORDS

spice   OPEC

For many long years, Europeans searched for an ocean route to Asia. The Portuguese sailed all the way around Africa to reach India. Columbus thought he could reach China and Japan by sailing west. When he discovered America, he thought he had found the East Indies. India and the East Indies were famous for their spices.

Meanwhile, India had been trading with its neighbors for hundreds of years. India lay in the middle of important ocean trade routes. The first great empire in India was founded 1,800 years before Columbus set sail.

Many different spices grow in Asia. One group of islands in Indonesia was even called the Spice Islands. A **spice** is part of a plant that tastes hot, sharp, or sweet. Spices are used to flavor and season food. Europeans wanted Asian spices such as black pepper, ginger, nutmeg, and cloves. Spices made food seem better to eat. Also, people long ago did not have ice all year to keep food fresh. Spices covered the bad taste of food that had spoiled.

Europeans also prized Asian tea, cotton, and silk. Tea and cotton come from plants. Silk is made by moths, called silkworms, that spin cocoons of silk. Silk was China's secret for about 3,000 years. Everyone who saw and touched it wanted this soft, smooth cloth. Silk, cotton, and tea are still important to Asia. But now, Asia's petroleum is the resource other continents want most. The peninsula of Arabia has more petroleum than any other place on Earth! Today, petroleum is used to heat homes, to run engines, and to make electricity.

To most Asians, fertile soil is their continent's most important resource. Much of the land in Asia is very rugged or dry. But large areas of rich soil are found in Asia's river valleys. Enough rain usually falls there to grow good crops. These crops provide food for millions of people. Some rivers also have large, fertile deltas at their mouths. Much rice grows there. Rice is Asia's most important food crop. Wheat is also very important. Farmers in northern India and China grow wheat.

Look at the two resource charts on page 282. Each chart shows 10 of Asia's nations. It shows some major resources they have. They have other resources, too.

Much rice is grown on the fertile delta land of southern Vietnam.
The Mekong River delta is at 10° north latitude, 106° east
longitude. This is the coastal plain, as seen from an airplane.

First, look at the chart of living resources. Where would you find cotton, wheat, and rice? Did you know that most of the world's tea and rubber grow in Asia? Wood is cut from the forests. Fishing is important on peninsulas and islands.

Now look at the chart of non-living resources. You can see that many nations in southwest Asia have petroleum. Saudi Arabia, Iran, and Indonesia have a lot of petroleum. They export it, or sell it to other nations. Have you ever heard of **OPEC** (OH pek)? It is the Organization of Petroleum Exporting Countries. Half the OPEC countries are in southwest Asia,

around the Persian Gulf. Indonesia also belongs to OPEC.

On a continent as huge as Asia, many of Earth's resources are found. Asia has many more nations and resources than the ones shown on the charts. But Asia's resources are not distributed evenly across the continent. Also, not all resources are fully used. India is rich in natural resources. But many of these resources have not been developed. Indonesia has great mineral wealth. But it has little industry. It has fertile soil. But people in Indonesia do not grow enough food for their own needs. Nations are poor when

ASIA—LIVING RESOURCES: SUGAR AND SPICE...AND RICE!

	Rice	Wheat	Corn	Sugar sugar cane	Sugar sugar beets	Spice (pepper)	Tea	Cotton	Silk	Wood	Rubber
SAUDI ARABIA	✓	✓	✓								
TURKEY	✓	✓	✓		✓			✓			
IRAN	✓	✓	✓		✓		✓	✓	✓		
INDIA	✓	✓	✓	✓		✓	✓	✓	✓	✓	✓
MALAYSIA	✓					✓	✓			✓	✓
THAILAND	✓		✓	✓				✓		✓	✓
VIETNAM	✓		✓	✓			✓	✓		✓	✓
INDONESIA	✓		✓	✓		✓	✓			✓	✓
CHINA	✓	✓	✓	✓	✓		✓	✓	✓		
JAPAN	✓	✓			✓		✓		✓	✓	

ASIA—NONLIVING RESOURCES: MINERAL WEALTH

	Petroleum	Coal	Iron ore	Tin	Copper	Salt
SAUDI ARABIA	✓					
TURKEY	✓	✓	✓		✓	
IRAN	✓	✓	✓		✓	✓
INDIA		✓	✓		✓	✓
MALAYSIA	✓		✓	✓	✓	
THAILAND	✓		✓	✓		✓
VIETNAM		✓	✓	✓		
INDONESIA	✓	✓	✓	✓	✓	✓
CHINA	✓	✓	✓	✓	✓	✓
JAPAN		✓				

Saudi Arabia is one of the OPEC countries. It exports petroleum.

their people do not have the money, machines, and knowledge to use their resources.

Japan has very few natural resources. But Japan has much more industry than India and Indonesia. There are many more scientists and engineers in Japan. Even without a wealth of resources, Japan is a rich land.

REVIEW

WATCH YOUR WORDS

1. Black pepper is a_____.
   mineral   sugar   spice

2. The OPEC nations_____petroleum.
   import   export   lack

3. Rice and cotton are_____.
   living resources
   nonliving resources   foods

4. Coal and copper are_____.
   living resources
   nonliving resources   fuels

5. Wood and silkworms are_____.
   living resources
   nonliving resources   plants

CHECK YOUR FACTS
Look at the Charts

6. What is Asia's leading food crop?

7. What Asian nations have both cotton and silk?

8. Find a nation that has coal, iron ore, and tin.

9. Find a nation that has both pepper and salt.

10. What Asian nations have petroleum?

SHARPEN YOUR THINKING

Why do you think petroleum is worth more today than it was in the past? Why are spices worth less?

Lesson 3: People of Asia

FIND THE WORDS

B.C. A.D. **Orient Occident dialect**

Over half the people in the world live on the continent of Asia. So it is not surprising that there are many different groups of Asians. Look at the pictures of people in this unit. You can see what a wide variety of people Asia has.

All the world's major religions started in Asia. The Jewish, Christian, and Muslim religions began in southwest Asia. Look at the map of Israel and western Jordan on page 285. Find the area between the Jordan River and the Mediterranean Sea. This was the Promised Land in the Bible. Find the city of Jerusalem (juh ROO suh lum). Jerusalem is a holy city to Jews, Christians, and Muslims.

The calendar we use today starts with the birth of Jesus Christ. Christ was born in Bethlehem. The years before Christ was born we write as B.C. (before Christ). The years after Christ's birth we write as A.D. [*anno Domini* (AN oh DOM un NY), "in the year of the Lord"]. For dates A.D., we count forward from the birth of Christ. For dates B.C., we count

These school children live in Saudi Arabia. They are Asians.

back. When no letters are used with a date, it is A.D. The year 1000 means A.D. 1000.

The prophet Muhammad lived from A.D. 570 to 632. He lived to be 62. The religious teacher Buddha (BOO duh) lived from 563 to 483 B.C. He lived to be 80. Buddha lived more than 1,000 years before Muhammad. He lived 500 years before Christ. Muhammad lived 600 years after Christ. Do you see how A.D. and B.C. are used?

WHERE WE ARE IN TIME AND PLACE

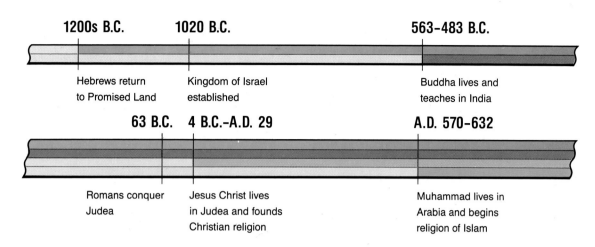

1200s B.C.
Hebrews return to Promised Land

1020 B.C.
Kingdom of Israel established

563–483 B.C.
Buddha lives and teaches in India

63 B.C.
Romans conquer Judea

4 B.C.–A.D. 29
Jesus Christ lives in Judea and founds Christian religion

A.D. 570–632
Muhammad lives in Arabia and begins religion of Islam

CRADLE OF RELIGIONS

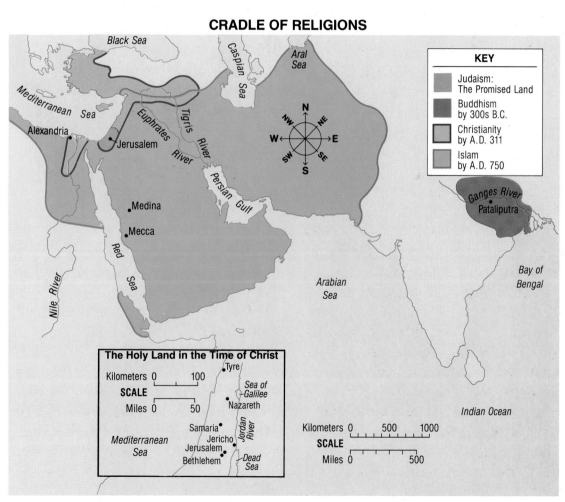

KEY

- Judaism: The Promised Land
- Buddhism by 300s B.C.
- Christianity by A.D. 311
- Islam by A.D. 750

Black Sea

Caspian Sea

Aral Sea

Mediterranean Sea

Alexandria

Jerusalem

Euphrates River

Tigris River

Persian Gulf

Medina

Mecca

Red Sea

Nile River

Arabian Sea

Ganges River

Pataliputra

Bay of Bengal

Indian Ocean

The Holy Land in the Time of Christ

Kilometers 0 — 100
SCALE
Miles 0 — 50

Tyre
Sea of Galilee
Nazareth
Samaria
Jericho
Jerusalem
Bethlehem
Jordan River
Dead Sea
Mediterranean Sea

Kilometers 0 500 1000
SCALE
Miles 0 500

Asian Cultures

Asia had many rich kingdoms and empires in the past. Have you heard of the king of Siam? Today, Siam is called Thailand. Have you heard of Persian carpets and Persian cats? Today, Persia is called Iran. Have you heard of the Land of the Rising Sun? That is another name for Japan.

The Great Wall of China has stood since 220 B.C. For how many years has it been standing? The Great Wall runs near 40° north latitude. It extends from 100° to 120° east longitude.

China

One of the oldest Asian cultures is that of China. Long ago, Europeans called Asia the Orient (OR ee unt). The **Orient** means "the east, toward the rising sun." They called western Europe and the Americas the Occident (OK suh dunt). The **Occident** means "the west, toward the setting sun." To Europeans, Asia was east. But Asians had a different point of view. Long ago, the Chinese named their country the Middle Kingdom. They named themselves "center-country people." To them, China was not east of Europe. It was at the center of the world.

The Chinese of long ago were expert at many arts. Some painted birds, flowers, horses, and other outdoor scenes. Others made fine vases or wove glossy silk cloth. Chinese craft workers made fine plates, cups, and bowls. People from Europe called these dishes "china." It was the Chinese who invented gunpowder. They used it to make firecrackers explode. They also made printing possible by inventing paper and type!

China was protected by mountains on the south and west. On the north, the Chinese built a wall to keep invaders out. They finished this wall around 220 B.C. The Great Wall of China still stands today. It is 2,400 kilometers (1,500 miles) long.

Today, the Chinese no longer call their land the Middle Kingdom. Now they call it "the Central Glorious People's United Country." In English, it is called the People's Republic of China. China has had a Communist government since 1949. Today, many people work in factories. But most of the people work together on large farms. There, they grow the nation's food.

People in China work very hard. They try to grow larger crops each year. But often, this is not possible. When drought and floods strike China, the government imports food. The government also provides schools and health care. Many Chinese people are learning to speak English now.

Still, Communist Party leaders make important decisions for the Chinese people. The government tells people where to live and what jobs to do. People are not free to choose for themselves.

Asians Today

Today, there are hundreds of different culture groups in Asia. Each of these groups has its own history, language, customs, and beliefs. Sometimes, many different culture groups live in one nation. In India alone, people speak more than 1,500 languages and dialects! A **dialect** (DY uh LEKT) is a different form of a language spoken in a special way.

The Chinese try to grow larger crops each year. Here, farm workers walk through an irrigation ditch. They have come to see a successful farm. China is one of the largest nations on Earth. It extends from 18° to 54° north latitude and from 74° to 135° east longitude.

You can see that Asians are very different from one another. Still, many Asians have much in common. About 80 out of every 100 of them are poor. Most are farm families who grow the food they eat. Many get less food than they need each day. Most Asians outside of China and Japan can expect to live only 50 years.

Asia has some of the world's largest cities. Even so, most Asians live in small villages. Life does not change quickly in Asian villages. In some places, people have farmed the same way for hundreds of years.

Most Asians live in small villages. Life there changes very slowly. This Asian village is near the Himalayas. These mighty mountains are the highest mountains on Earth. They stretch across Asia for about 2,410 kilometers (1,500 miles). The name *Himalayas* means "abode of snow."

REVIEW

WATCH YOUR WORDS

1. Europeans called Asia the——.
   Occident   Orient   Continent

2. Europeans called America the——.
   Continent   Orient   Occident

3. A different way of speaking a language is a——.
   culture   dialect   belief

4. Buddha was born in 563——.
   A.D.   A.M.   B.C.

5. Muhammad was born in 570——.
   A.D.   B.C.   P.M.

CHECK YOUR FACTS

6. List three religions that began in southwest Asia.

7. What are Siam, Persia, and the Middle Kingdom called today?

8. List two things that the Chinese invented.

9. What did the Chinese build to protect China on the north?

10. Do more Asians live in cities or in villages?

SHARPEN YOUR THINKING

Do you think your country is the middle of the world? Why, or why not?

Lesson 4: Nations of Asia

FIND THE WORDS

income   calorie

Asia has more nations than any other continent except Africa. Leaving out the Soviet Union, there are 39 Asian nations. Some, like China and India, are huge. Others are very small. The nation of Singapore is a city. Find Singapore on the map on page 291.

Now look at the chart on page 290. It gives you some facts about nine nations of Asia. The first five are nations with very many people. The last four are nations that are interesting for some other reason. The chart also includes the United States in the middle. That way, you can compare the United States with these Asian nations.

The first three columns tell you how large each nation is. Of the ten nations on Earth with the most people, seven are in Asia. Five of these Asian nations are in the chart. The other two are the Soviet Union and Pakistan. Also in the top ten are the United States, Brazil, and Nigeria.

The last three columns also give you some important facts. But you have to know how to read the figures. Column four tells you how many people in every 100 are farmers. Usually, the more farmers a nation has, the less developed it is. With fewer farmers, more people work in offices, factories, or stores. These people make goods or provide services for others. Look at the chart again. Find two highly developed nations in Asia.

Column five tells you the average income per person each year. This is what each person would get if all the nation's income were divided evenly. **Income** usually means money earned or received. In the chart, income also includes what people produce for their own use. Food can be income in this sense.

You can see that some nations have very low incomes. In nations with low incomes, most people are usually farmers. Notice the very high income in Saudi Arabia. Saudi Arabia used to be a poor nation. Now it sells petroleum to other nations. This has made Saudi Arabia very rich. The nation has built new highways, schools, and office buildings. It has also helped other Arab nations. Now, Saudi Arabia plans to build many new factories. It does not want to depend on petroleum alone.

The last column in the chart is very important. It tells how much food value each person gets on the

NINE ASIAN NATIONS

Nation	Area square miles	Area square kilometers	Number of people	Farmers per 100 people	Income per person per year	Daily food (in calories)
CHINA	3,630,747	9,403,600	1 billion	70	$ 440	2170
INDIA	1,237,061	3,203,975	738 million	70	$ 200	2070
INDONESIA	741,101	1,919,443	158 million	66	$ 300	1790
JAPAN	145,834	377,708	120 million	19	$ 8,500	3280
BANGLADESH	55,598	143,998	96 million	85	$ 106	1840
UNITED STATES	3,679,201	9,529,081	235 million	4	$11,280	3330
ISRAEL	7,848	20,325	4 million	10	$ 4,330	2960
SAUDI ARABIA	830,000	2,149,690	10 million	65	$13,750	2270
TAIWAN	13,900	36,002	19 million	42	$ 2,200	2620
TURKEY	300,948	779,452	48 million	67	$ 1,200	3250

Fun Facts ... about Japan

Japan is a very beautiful nation. It is covered with hills and mountains. It has many forests and lakes. The highest mountain in Japan is Mount Fuji (FOO jee). It is 3,776 meters (12,388 feet) above sea level.

The climate of Japan is much like the climate of the United States. In southern Japan, the summers are long and hot. The winters are mild and not cold. This is the kind of climate found in the southern United States. In northern Japan, the winters are cold and snowy. The summers are warm. This is the kind of climate found in the state of Maine. All of Japan gets enough rain to grow crops. This means that Japan has no deserts.

Japan's chief crop is rice. Two unusual farm products are mulberry trees and bamboo plants. The leaves of the mulberry tree are the favorite food of silkworms. The silkworms spin balls of silk threads, called cocoons. Factories make these threads into beautiful silk cloth and clothing. The bamboo plant is used in many ways. People eat the sprouts. They make baskets and furniture from the thick, hollow stems.

Fish are also an important resource to the Japanese. Find Japan on the map. Why do the Japanese eat fish?

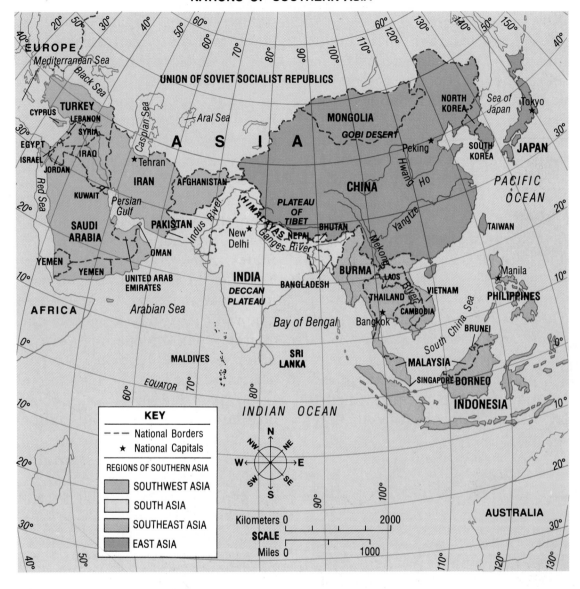

average each day. Every day, your body burns up energy. Food gives you that energy. A **calorie** is a unit of heat. It is used to measure the energy that food gives you. You need that food energy to stay healthy. On the average, 10-year-olds need about 2,400 calories a day. Young men need about 2,900 calories. Young women need about 2,100 calories.

Now look at the chart. The average person in the United States takes in 3,330 calories per day.

Many people may eat too much in the United States. They take in more calories than their bodies can burn. But in some Asian nations, people do not get enough food. Find two such nations in the chart. India is better off than Indonesia and Bangladesh. But one Indian in every four does not get enough calories to stay healthy.

Japan

Except for the Soviet Union, the most developed nation in Asia is Japan. This is true even though Japan does not have many natural resources. The Japanese people work well together. Since World War II, they have had good leaders and a democratic government. In industry, Japan ranks third in the world. Only the United States and the Soviet Union have more industry than Japan. They are giant nations. Japan covers only 377,708 square kilometers (145,834 square miles). It is smaller than the state of California. But Japan has five times as many people as California. Japan is one of the world's most crowded nations.

Japanese cars, TV sets, cameras, and other goods are sold all over the world. More Japanese goods are sold in the United States than in any other country. Yet the Japanese have to import most raw materials used in their factories. They buy large amounts of iron, coal, and petroleum from other nations. Japanese farmers are experts at growing large crops. But Japan does not have enough farmland. It is an island nation. It has fertile plains. But most of Japan is covered by mountains. There is not much level land. So the Japanese import some of their food. They buy wheat, vegetables, and fruit from the United States.

These children go to school in Tokyo, Japan. (36° north latitude, 140° east longitude)

Developing Nations

The nations of Taiwan, Singapore, and Israel are developing very fast. So are some of the OPEC nations, such as Saudi Arabia, Iraq, and Kuwait (koo WAYT). These OPEC nations are not fully developed. Still, they provide a better living for their people than most Asian nations do.

China and India

South of the Soviet Union, China and India are the largest nations in Asia. In fact, China is the fourth-largest nation in the world. It has by far the most people of any nation. One out of every four persons on Earth is Chinese! Now, China has more than a billion people.

China has rich natural resources. It has petroleum, coal, iron ore, and many other minerals. These minerals are all needed for industry. China now has more than 15 cities with over a million people. It is in these cities that China's factories are found. Still, most Chinese live and work on farms.

Only 40 years ago, India was a colony of Great Britain. Then, British India included what is now India, Pakistan, and Bangladesh. In 1947, British India became independent. It was divided into two nations. This division separated two different religious groups, Muslims and Hindus (HIN dooz). The part where Hindus lived became India. The two parts where Muslims lived became West and East Pakistan. In 1971, East Pakistan became a separate nation, Bangladesh.

Today, India has more people than any other nation except China. It is often called the world's largest democracy. That is

Tokyo (TOH kee OH) is the capital of Japan. Great numbers of people live in Tokyo. Japan is one of the world's top industrial nations.

because it has a government that is freely elected.

Indonesia

Indonesia is a little smaller than Saudi Arabia. But Indonesia has 15 times as many people. Indonesia is made up of thousands of islands. These islands stretch for over 5,000 kilometers (3,000 miles) along the equator. Some islands, such as Java and Bali, have many people. Others, such as Sumatra (soo MAH truh), have fewer people. Today, Indonesia is a poor nation. But it has many natural resources. Find it in the resource charts on page 282. Indonesia has a lot of fertile soil. It has petroleum, coal, iron ore, tin, and other minerals. So it will probably develop more in the future.

The Future

Most of the nations of Asia face the same problems. The number of Asians is growing every day. These people need food and jobs. All over Asia, people are working hard to improve their lives. Experts are teaching farmers better ways to grow food. Governments are working to provide more schools and better health care. Governments want businesses to build more factories. With more industry, resources can be better used. More Asians will have good jobs. Asian nations will have more valuable products to sell. They can earn more money from exports. Then they can use some of the money to import extra food. That way, poor Asian nations could become as well off as Japan!

REVIEW

WATCH YOUR WORDS

1. Money that people earn or receive is their____.
   expense   budget   income
2. People measure food energy in____.
   pounds   calories   fat

CHECK YOUR FACTS

Look at the Chart

3. What Asian nation is almost three times larger than India?
4. What Asian nation in the chart seems to be the poorest? Which three Asian nations seem to be the richest? (*Hint:* Look at the income column.)
5. What rich Asian nation has an unusually large number of farmers?
6. What four Asian nations have the most food for their people?

Look at the Lesson

7. After the Soviet Union, what is the most developed nation in Asia?
8. Which Asian nation has the most people? How many people does it have?
9. What three nations of today were part of India until 1947?
10. How are Asians working to improve their lives? Name three ways.

SHARPEN YOUR THINKING

Why are nations with many farmers less developed than nations with many city workers?

CHAPTER REVIEW

WATCH YOUR WORDS

1. The____means "the east."
   Occident   Orient   OPEC

2. India is called a(n)____of Asia.
   island   continent
   subcontinent

3. Regions that have a ____ have three seasons.
   monsoon climate   desert   tundra

4. Long ago, Europeans wanted Asia's ____.
   dialects   petroleum   spices

5. The letters ____ mean "before Christ's birth."
   A.D.   B.C.   D.C.

6. The letters ____ mean "after Christ's birth."
   A.D.   A.B.   B.C.

7. The____means "the west."
   pole   Orient   Occident

8. The money a person earns or is given is____.
   expense   savings   income

9. In India, people speak in many different____.
   nations   dialects   calories

10. The average American gets over 3000____per day.
    calories   spices   minutes

CHECK YOUR FACTS

11. What is the largest continent on Earth?

12. What nation of Earth has the most people?

13. What are Asia Minor, Arabia, and Indochina?

14. What do the letters of OPEC stand for?

15. Name three great religions that began in Asia.

16. What is East Pakistan called today?

APPLY YOUR SKILLS

USE YOUR CHARTS

Look at the chart on page 290.

17. What three Asian nations are richest in income?

18. In which two Asian nations do people get the most food?

19. In which two Asian nations do people get the least food?

Look at the charts on page 282.

20. Write *Saudi Arabia, Indonesia,* and *Japan* across the top of a piece of paper. Under each nation, list its living and nonliving resources from the chart.

21. Look at your answers to questions 17–19. Are the nations with the most natural resources the richest nations?

SHARPEN YOUR THINKING

22. Would you rather visit the desert of Arabia or the Himalayas? Why?

23. Which nation would you rather visit: Japan or China? Why?

24. Look at the resource charts. Which poor Asian nation would you choose to develop? Why?

WRITE ABOUT IT

25. Read more about one of the religions that began in Asia. Use a library book or an encyclopedia. Then write a one-page report.

CHAPTER 2 LIVING IN A MONSOON CLIMATE

Lesson 1: India Today

India is one of the largest nations in Asia. It has over three times as many people as the United States. But it has only one-third as much land. Thus India is a crowded country. It has over 738 million people. Only China has more people than India.

The Himalaya Mountains stretch across northern India. Three great rivers begin in the mountains. They are the Indus (IN duss), the Ganges (GAN jeez), and the Brahmaputra (BRAH muh POO truh). The Indus River flows through Pakistan. The Ganges and Brahmaputra flow through India and Bangladesh. All three rivers pass through lowlands on the way to the Indian Ocean. Many people live in the fertile valleys of these three great rivers.

296

Seasons in India

People in India divide the year into three seasons instead of four. They do this because they live in a monsoon climate. A **monsoon** is a wind that changes direction when the season changes. One season lasts from October to March. In India, these months are the coolest season of the year. But India's weather is still mostly warm, even then. Dry winds blow across India from the north and east. Almost no rain falls.

India's next season lasts from March through May. During these months, the weather turns hotter. The land becomes very dry. Most plants dry up at this time.

India's third season is the rainy season. It is called the **monsoon season,** and it begins in June. Wet winds blow across India from the south and west. They are called the summer monsoons. These winds bring heavy rains. The rains continue off and on from June through September. During the rainy season, farmers in India plant their crops.

Growing Food

India has thousands of small villages. Most of the people live in these villages. In fact, three out of every four Indians live in the countryside. They are farmers who grow the food they eat. More than half of these farmers are poor. Most farm families own or rent their farms. But many large families have very small pieces of land. Some families have no land at all. They work in exchange for food.

Fun Facts

All parts of India do not get the same amount of rain. The heaviest rains fall in the east. Cherrapunji (CHEHR uh POON jee) is north of the nation of Bangladesh. Every year, Cherrapunji gets about 500 inches of rain. One year, from 1860 to 1861, over 1,000 inches of rain fell there!

The picture at the right shows a city on the Ganges River during the monsoon season. Like Cherrapunji, this city is in northeast India. The streets are flooded. But the traffic keeps right on going.

Indira Gandhi

For 20 years, Indira Gandhi was the most powerful person in India. She was prime minister, or head of government, for most of this time. Jawaharlal Nehru, her father, had been India's first prime minster after independence.

Indira Gandhi faced serious problems. "Do you think it is easy to keep a country like India united?" she asked. Some people thought she took too much power. Yet most of India's voters saw her as a strong force for national unity.

On October 31, 1984, Indira Gandhi was killed by members of a minority

religious group. Her son, Rajiv Gandhi, was chosen as the new prime minister.

The government of India has been working to help farmers grow more food. First, the government wants farmers to use new rice and wheat seeds. These "miracle seeds" grow much more grain than regular seeds do. Farmers who use the new seeds can grow three or four crops a year. They can grow only one or two crops with regular seeds. But the rice from the new seeds does not taste as good. Also, the new seeds need fertilizers to grow well. Fertilizers are expensive. Poor farmers need credit to buy them. Someone with **credit** can buy goods without money by promising to pay later. To provide farmers with credit, local areas need banks.

Second, the government is building many canals for irrigation. **Irrigation** means irrigating, or bringing water to dry land. An **irrigation canal** is a ditch or pipe made by people. Water can flow through such a canal from one place to another. With irrigation, farmers can grow crops on dry lands. That means more of India's land can be used for farming.

Industry in India

India is one of the world's top 10 industrial nations. It is rich in natural resources. It has a lot of iron ore and coal. It manufactures steel, chemicals, machines, and consumer goods. It exports cotton cloth and tea. It has even sent a

India has a long, rich history. This building is the Taj Mahal (TAHZH muh HAHL). It is built of white marble set with jewels. The Taj Mahal is southeast of New Delhi, at 27° north latitude, 78° east longitude.

satellite into space. But India's businesses face many problems.

One problem is that India's businesses spend most of their money on machines. They do not provide enough jobs for India's people. Another problem is that the government has tried to control the businesses. This has slowed down business growth. A third problem is that India does not import or export many goods. Nations that import and export goods compete with other nations for business. Suppose two businesses try to get the same customer. Each business tries to do better than the other. Each tries to offer a better product or charge a lower price. This is **competition.**

People in India dug this irrigation canal. It carries water to fields where "miracle" rice seeds are grown.

There are other problems, too. India does not have enough electric power for its farms, factories, and mines. It does not have good transportation to move people and goods. Trains are slow. Ships have to wait in port for weeks to be unloaded. Trucks travel on narrow, crowded highways. Many villages have no roads.

Also, millions of Indians have no work at all. Millions more cannot find full-time jobs. Many people who have no land and no jobs leave their villages. They crowd into cities. There, they hope to find a way to make a living. But not many do. Most do not have enough education to get city jobs. With three harvests a year, there is more work on the farms.

Progress in India is not easy. Change is often slow. India is a very old land. People have lived there for thousands of years. Life in the villages has stayed much the same. Now, village people are being asked to give up familiar customs. It is hard for many people to change to new ways.

REVIEW

WATCH YOUR WORDS

1. A customer with ____ can buy now and pay later.
   competition   culture   credit

2. When businesses have ____ , they often try to do better.
   no competition   competition   machines

3. A(n) ____ brings water to dry land.
   irrigation canal   fertilizer   miracle seed

4. A(n) ____ adds special minerals to soil.
   miracle seed   fertilizer   irrigation canal

5. India's rains come in the ____.
   winter   fall   monsoon season

CHECK YOUR FACTS

Look at the Map (See page 291.)

6. What is the capital of India?

7. What bay is east of India?

8. What island nation is just southeast of India?

9. What river flows through northeast India?

10. What ocean is south of India?

Look at the Lesson

11. India has (more/fewer) people than the United States.

12. What is a monsoon?

13. How many seasons are there in India's monsoon climate?

14. How can India's farmers grow more food? Name two ways.

15. List two problems that India's businesses face.

SHARPEN YOUR THINKING

Why does competition often make people work harder?

Lesson 2: Life in a Village of India

FIND THE WORDS

extended family   landlord
seedbed   water buffalo   paddy

Each year, more people move to India's cities. Each year, more factories are built there. As you know, most Indians do not live in cities or work in factories. Most live in small villages and work on farms. Village life in India has not changed much for hundreds of years.

In the villages, most people live in extended families. An **extended family** is made up of grandparents, parents, and children. They all live together. Sometimes, the family also includes aunts, uncles, and cousins. All family members work for the good of the family.

In the villages of India, parents arrange their children's marriages. The young people do not choose whom they will marry. Each has to marry a suitable person of her or his own social class. When a young Indian woman marries, she leaves home. She goes to live with her husband's family. When a young Indian man marries, he stays at home. He brings his wife to live in his parents' house. The oldest mother in each house is the most respected family member.

In the villages, the houses are small. They may have only two or three rooms. Sometimes, a newly married couple will add on a room for themselves. Village homes are furnished very simply. People have cots for sleeping. They have pots, pans, and bowls for cooking and eating. Most homes have mats to cover the dirt floor. Most also have a place to store food. Family members spend most of their time outside.

Most village homes do not have electric power or running water.

This Indian woman has a mark on her forehead. It shows she belongs to a high social class.

Sometimes, a village has only one well. All the people get water for cooking and drinking from that same well. Sometimes, villagers also get drinking water from a nearby stream. But they might use the same stream for washing clothes. They might also use it for getting rid of wastes. Village people who do this are not healthy. Dirty water makes people sick. It carries disease.

In the villages, houses are built close together. That way, they do not take up too much land. Land is too valuable to be wasted. It has to be used for planting crops.

Just outside the villages are the fields. There, the crops are grown. Most families have to work in the fields. Some families own their own land. Many other families rent land from landlords. A **landlord** is a person who owns land and rents it to others. In the villages of India, the rent is not money. It is part of the crop the farmers grow. Other people neither own land nor rent it. They work by the day when they can find work to do.

Village people often help each other in many ways. Some may weave cloth. Others may make

In India, some farmers still use old ways of farming. Here, a camel turns a waterwheel. The water is used for irrigation.

pots and dishes. Still others may make tools or build things of wood. Village people trade their work and goods among themselves. That way, they get the things they need.

Growing Rice

This is the way many village people grow rice in India. First, they prepare a seedbed. A **seedbed** is a small piece of land with good soil. There, rice seeds can start to grow. Next, the people must get the rice fields ready. This is hard work. The ground must be broken up with a plow. That way, the soil below the surface is brought to the top. The rice will be planted in this loose, rich soil. Most villagers in India use a water buffalo to pull the plow. A **water buffalo** is a large, strong animal with wide horns.

Now the people have to wait for the winds to change. Soon the monsoon season will start. They watch for the first clouds to appear. At last, the rains begin! Then the women take the young rice plants out of the seedbed. They plant the rice in the flooded fields. Rice fields have to be kept under water.

In the months that follow, the rice crop grows. The weather stays hot and wet. The rice plants get heavy with seeds of grain. The people must keep the fields free of

Above: In many Asian villages, farmers use strong animals to pull their plows. This farmer is plowing rice paddies.
Below: Monsoon rains have flooded this paddy. Now Indian women can move young rice plants from the seedbed. They replant the rice in the fields. Soon, rice grains will grow.

weeds. They must also keep rats from eating the grain. You may have heard a rice field called a rice **paddy.** When rice seed is growing, it has a brown hull on it. A hull is an outer covering. The rice with the hull is also called paddy.

Around the end of August, the winds begin to shift again. The weather changes. Now there is less rain. The people can harvest and dry the rice. They tie the stalks into bundles. They will eat the grains of rice as food. They will burn the stalks as fuel. They may also use some stalks to repair their roofs. They put aside some of the rice grains, too. Those grains will be seed for next year's crop.

New Ways to Farm

The government of India is trying to help village people grow better crops. You read about these efforts earlier. In many villages, the government has given the farmers new rice seeds. These new seeds yield more grain. Experts have also shown the people how to use fertilizer. But often, the farmers have no money to buy fertilizer. They have no extra rice to sell. They need their whole crop to use as food. If they had credit, they could use the new methods to grow more rice.

All over south Asia, governments are trying to turn more land into farmland. The main way to do this is to irrigate dry land. In a monsoon climate, water can be stored during the rainy season. Then, during the dry season, it can be used to wet the land. This is one kind of irrigation. Another kind is bringing water to lands that are dry all year. In the next lesson, you will learn about an irrigation project in India.

REVIEW

WATCH YOUR WORDS

1. Rice seeds are first planted in a
   ___.
   field   stream   seedbed
2. Indian farmers often use ___ to pull their plows.
   electric power   water buffaloes   paddies
3. Village people in India live in ___.
   extended families   large houses   fields

CHECK YOUR FACTS

4. Name four relatives who may belong to an extended family.

5. How do Indian farmers who rent land pay their landlords?
6. Where do village people get their water? Why do some people get sick?
7. List five steps in growing rice.
8. When do the farmers plant rice in the fields?
9. Name two kinds of irrigation.

SHARPEN YOUR THINKING

Do most people in the United States live in extended families? Why, or why not?

Lesson 3: An Irrigation Project in India

FIND THE WORDS

feeder canal

There is an area of dry land in northwestern India. It is known as the Great Indian Desert. This desert also stretches into eastern Pakistan. Find it on the map of India on page 306. The Great Indian Desert is a land of sand dunes, bushes, and grasses. There are no trees. Little rain falls in the desert, even during the monsoon season. But much of the land in the desert is fertile. It simply needs water for plants to grow.

Parts of this desert have been irrigated for hundreds of years. Canals from the Indus River bring water to large areas. In the late 1800s, the British added to this irrigation system. They built new dams to hold water back. They also built new canals to send the water across the land.

Part of the Great Indian Desert lies in Rajasthan (RAH juh STAHN). Rajasthan is the second-largest state in India. In 1948, the government of the state decided to build a big irrigation project. The state got the help of the national government of India. The plan was to create 10,000 square kilometers (about 4,000 square miles) of new farmland. That is an area a little smaller than our state of Connecticut. The land would be sold to farmers who had no land. The state would lend poor farmers money to buy the farms.

There were three rules for the people who bought farms. First, they could own no other land.

Irrigation canals like this one in India can bring water to the desert.

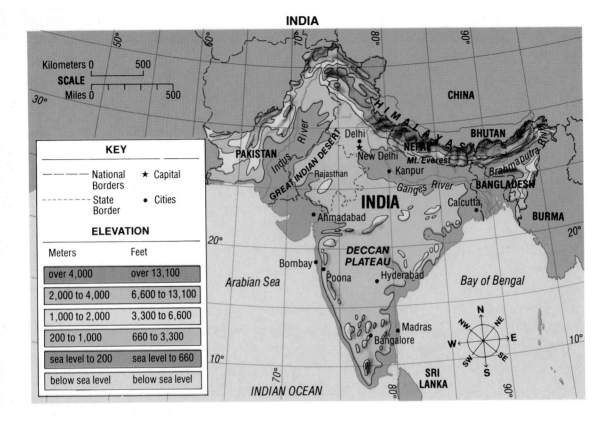

INDIA

KEY

— — — National Borders
★ Capital
— - — State Border
• Cities

ELEVATION

Meters	Feet
over 4,000	over 13,100
2,000 to 4,000	6,600 to 13,100
1,000 to 2,000	3,300 to 6,600
200 to 1,000	660 to 3,300
sea level to 200	sea level to 660
below sea level	below sea level

Second, they had to know how to farm. Third, they had to have been born in Rajasthan. Thousands of people got farms in this way. Years later, between 1974 and 1980, the irrigation system was improved. More canals were built. The people lined the canals with tiles. That way, the water flowed more freely. More desert land was made into farms. Here is a story about one family that was helped by this project.

Sita (SEE tah) and Ranjit (RUN jeet) both grew up in Rajasthan. Both had several sisters and brothers. Both lived on farms and helped their parents with the work. When Sita and Ranjit were old enough, their parents arranged for them to marry. Sita left her parents and went to live in Ranjit's parents' house. After a while, the family built on an extra room for Sita and Ranjit. They had already added a room for Ranjit's brother Janak (JAN uk) and Rima (REE mah), his wife.

As time passed, Ranjit and Sita saw that life was getting harder for the family. The family fields didn't get any larger. But these fields had to feed more and more people each year. Sita and Ranjit

Sita and Rima get water from a well in their village.

had three children. Janak and Rima had four. And now the youngest brother, Pandit (PUN deet), was going to get married. Ranjit's two sisters had married and moved away. But with all the new families, the farm could not produce enough food for everyone.

Then Ranjit and Sita heard of the Rajasthan Canal project. They both knew that life would be better if they had their own land. So Ranjit made the long trip to apply for a loan to buy a farm. He had to make several trips before he was successful. Finally, he was told that he could get a loan. He was told where to find the farm that he could buy.

When Sita and Ranjit left home with their children, they were afraid. They did not know what the future would hold.

At last, they arrived at their farm. There, they saw there was much work to be done. Water had to be brought to their fields. To do this, they had to help build small canals, called **feeder canals.** These feeder canals were connected to the large canals. The large canals brought the water from the Indus River. Ranjit and Sita also had to build a house for themselves in the village. They saw that many other families were also starting new farms. All the farm families had the same work to do.

Ranjit and Sita did not have to wait for the monsoon season to plant their crops. They only waited until the weather was warm. Now, they could control the amount of water that flowed to their fields.

Several years passed by. Life became better for Sita and Ranjit and their children. They grew more than enough food for themselves. They had food left over to sell. With the money they earned, they made payments on their loan. They bought sheep to supply them with wool. They also bought things for their home.

Then Sita and Ranjit asked Rima and Janak to come and join them. The farm could support the two families. Two families were also needed to do all the work. Now, both families live on the irrigated farm.

All over India, the government is building irrigation projects. The government leaders want India to raise more food. They want to make India a modern nation. They want to help the people help themselves. To do this, they must make changes where the people live. And most people in India live on farms.

REVIEW

CHECK YOUR FACTS

1. Where is the Great Indian Desert?
2. From what great river does the water come to irrigate this desert?
3. What were the three rules for people who bought new farms?
4. In what state of India do Sita and Ranjit live?
5. How did Sita and Ranjit bring water from the large canals to their fields?

SHARPEN YOUR THINKING

What things did the government of India do to help Sita and Ranjit? What things did they do to help themselves?

CHAPTER REVIEW

WATCH YOUR WORDS

1. Farmers in India plant their crops during the ___.
   cool season   dry season
   monsoon season

2. With ___ , people can grow food in the desert.
   paddies   irrigation   seedbeds

3. Farmers with ___ do not have to wait for rain.
   landlords   competition
   irrigation canals

4. A rice field is called a ___.
   paddy   feeder canal   monsoon

5. Often, rival businesses try to get the same customers. This is ___.
   credit   competition   income

6. Poor farmers need ___ to buy land and fertilizer.
   credit   competition   landlords

7. A(n) ___ owns land and rents it out to others.
   extended family   paddy   landlord

8. Sita, Rima, Ranjit, and Janak belong to a(n) ___.
   dialect   extended family   landlord

9. A ___ is a wind that changes direction with the season.
   paddy   dialect   monsoon

10. ___ bring water to family fields.
    OPECs   Feeder canals   Paddies

CHECK YOUR FACTS

11. Which nation has more people, India or the United States?

12. Name two rivers that start in the Himalaya Mountains.

13. When is the monsoon season in India? Describe the weather.

14. How are India's new rice and wheat seeds better than regular seeds?

15. What is an irrigation canal?

16. How can India turn more land into farmland?

17. How do village people grow rice without irrigation? List each step.

APPLY YOUR SKILLS

USE YOUR MAPS

Look at the map of India on page 306.

18. Give the right cardinal direction.
    India is _a_ of Pakistan. Pakistan is _b_ of Bangladesh. The Himalaya Mountains are _c_ of Delhi.

19. Give the right direction (northeast, northwest, southeast, or southwest):
    The Great Indian Desert is in the _a_ of India. Calcutta is _b_ of Delhi. Madras is _c_ of Calcutta. Bombay is _d_ of Madras.

20. What is the capital of India?

SHARPEN YOUR THINKING

21. What things are helping India's farmers grow more food?

22. What things tell you that India is not a fully developed nation?

23. Suppose India had twice as many people 100 years from now. What might happen?

24. How is India's climate different from the climate where you live?

25. Why is good transportation important to businesses?

UNIT REVIEW

WATCH YOUR WORDS

Use the words below to complete the unit summary. Use each term only once.

A.D.
B.C.
extended family
feeder canals
irrigation canals

monsoons
monsoon season
Occident
OPEC
Orient

paddy
peninsulas
seedbed
spices
subcontinent

Asia is the largest continent on Earth. It has __1__ such as Asia Minor, Indochina, and Arabia. It even has a(n) __2__, India. Europeans called Asia the __3__, which means "the east." They called western Europe and the Americas the __4__, which means "the west." In the past, Europeans wanted Asia's __5__ to flavor their food. Today, many industrial nations buy Asia's petroleum. Some Asian nations that export petroleum belong to __6__.

Many religions started in Asia. Our calendar begins with the birth of Jesus Christ. Buddha lived before Christ. He was born around 563 __7__. Muhammad lived after Christ. He was born around __8__ 570.

Most people in India are farmers. In the past, they had to wait for the __9__ to plant crops. During that time of year, winds called __10__ bring heavy rains. Now, many __11__ have been built in India. They bring water to dry lands. Small __12__ bring water from the large canals to family fields. To grow rice, farmers first plant seeds in a(n) __13__. Later, they move the rice plants to a field called a rice __14__. Everyone in the __15__ helps with the work.

CHECK YOUR FACTS

1. Which continent of Earth has the most people?

2. Which nation of Earth has the most people?

3. What is the highest mountain in the world? What mountains form the highest mountain system?

4. What is the lowest sea in the world?

5. What is Earth's largest and highest plateau?

6. What peninsula of Asia has the most petroleum?

7. Name two of Asia's most important food crops.

8. What are these countries called today: Siam, Persia, the Land of the Rising Sun, the Middle Kingdom?

9. Where did the Chinese build the Great Wall of China? Why did they build it there?

10. Which is the most developed nation: China, Israel, or Japan?

TRUE OR FALSE

11. India has more people than China.

12. Most of India's people live in cities.

13. Most of India's people work on farms.

14. India is one of the world's top 10 industrial nations.

15. India has good transportation.

USE YOUR MAP SKILLS

16. Give the "address" of Japan in latitude and longitude.

SKILL DEVELOPMENT

USE YOUR MAP SKILLS

1. Draw or trace an outline map of Asia. Color the peninsulas red and the islands green.
2. Label the Mediterranean Sea, the Red Sea, the Black Sea, the Caspian Sea, and the Persian Gulf.
3. Label the Indian Ocean, the Pacific Ocean, and the Arctic Ocean.
4. Label the Indus and Ganges rivers, the Himalayas, and the Gobi Desert.

WRITE ABOUT IT

5. Which Asian nation would you most like to visit? Pretend that your answer could win you a free trip. Then write your reasons.

FIND THE TIME LINE

6. List these events in the right order.

   —The rice is harvested.
   —Rice seeds are planted in a seedbed.
   —The rice fields are flooded.
   —The rice plants get heavy with grain.
   —Seeds are saved for the next rice crop.
   —Rice fields are plowed.
   —Rice plants are planted in the fields.
   —The monsoon rains begin.

USE YOUR CHARTS

7. Look at the chart of nine Asian nations on page 290.
   a. Which one of these nations has the most income per person?
   b. Which two of these nations have the most daily food?

8. Look at the resource charts on page 282.
   a. What nation has 10 of the living resources?
   b. What nation has the fewest living resources?
   c. Which two nations have all six minerals shown?
   d. Which two nations have only one major mineral?

USE YOUR CHART SKILLS

9. Copy the chart below on a separate sheet of paper. Then fill in the blanks. Get the missing facts from the charts on pages 282 and 290.

Nations	Living resources	Nonliving resources	Number of people	Income per person
CHINA	8		1 billion	
INDIA		4	million	$200
INDONESIA	7		158 million	
JAPAN		1	million	$8,500
SAUDI ARABIA	3		10 million	

10. Answer these questions based on your chart.
    a. Which nation in this chart has the fewest people?
    b. Which nation has the most income per person?
    c. Which nation is second in income per person?
    d. Which three nations have the most resources?

311

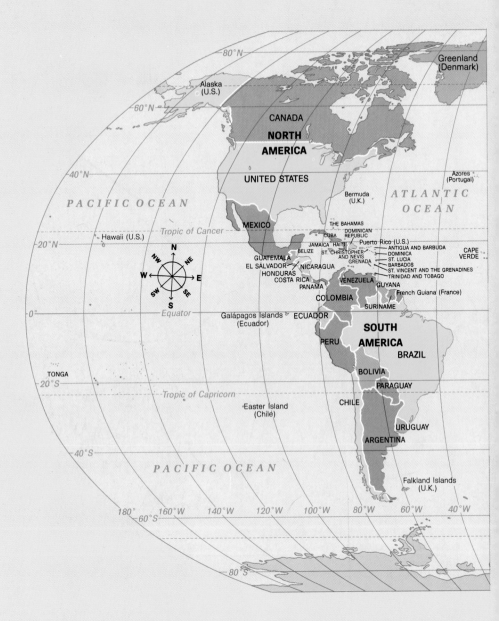

80°N

Greenland
(Denmark)

Alaska
(U.S.)

60°N

CANADA

**NORTH
AMERICA**

40°N

UNITED STATES

Azores
(Portugal)

PACIFIC OCEAN

Bermuda
(U.K.)

*ATLANTIC
OCEAN*

Tropic of Cancer

THE BAHAMAS

20°N

Hawaii (U.S.)

MEXICO

CUBA

DOMINICAN
REPUBLIC
Puerto Rico (U.S.)

JAMAICA HAITI

ANTIGUA AND BARBUDA

GUATEMALA
BELIZE
ST. CHRISTOPHER
AND NEVIS
DOMINICA
ST. LUCIA
GRENADA
BARBADOS
ST. VINCENT AND THE GRENADINES
TRINIDAD AND TOBAGO

CAPE
VERDE

EL SALVADOR
NICARAGUA
HONDURAS
COSTA RICA
PANAMA

VENEZUELA

GUYANA

COLOMBIA

SURINAME

French Guiana (France)

0°

Equator

Galápagos Islands
(Ecuador)

ECUADOR

**SOUTH
AMERICA**

PERU

BRAZIL

BOLIVIA

20°S

TONGA

Tropic of Capricorn

PARAGUAY

CHILE

Easter Island
(Chile)

URUGUAY

40°S

ARGENTINA

PACIFIC OCEAN

Falkland Islands
(U.K.)

180° 160°W 140°W 120°W 100°W 80°W 60°W 40°W

60°S

80°S

N
NW NE
W   E
SW SE
S

THE WORLD: Political
ROBINSON PROJECTION

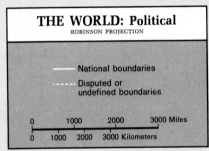

—— National boundaries

- - - Disputed or
undefined boundaries

0   1000   2000   3000 Miles

0 1000 2000 3000 Kilometers

Alb.	— Albania	Mon.	— Monaco
And.	— Andorra	Neth.	— Netherlands
Aust.	— Austria	P.D.R. of	— People's Democratic
Bel.	— Belgium	Yemen	Republic of Yemen
Czech.	— Czechoslovakia	Switz.	— Switzerland
E. Ger.	— E. Germany	W. Ger.	— West Germany
Hung.	— Hungary	Yugo.	— Yugoslavia
Isr.	— Israel		
Leb.	— Lebanon		
Liech.	— Liechtenstein		
Lux.	— Luxembourg		

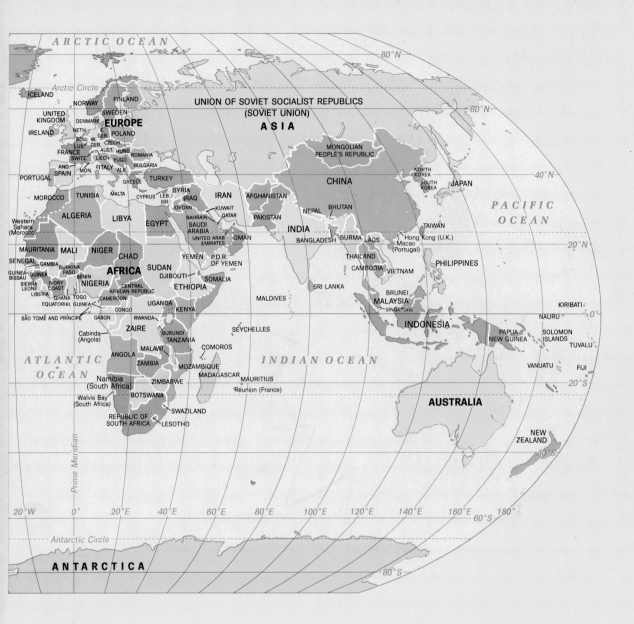

ARCTIC OCEAN

Arctic Circle

ICELAND

NORWAY   FINLAND

UNITED   SWEDEN
KINGDOM   DENMARK   **EUROPE**

IRELAND   NETH.
           BEL.   W. CZECH
FRANCE   LUX. GER. POLAND
      SWITZ. AUST. HUNG.
         LIECH. YUGO. ROMANIA
PORTUGAL   ITALY ALB. BULGARIA
         MON.
      SPAIN   GREECE TURKEY
AND.

MOROCCO   TUNISIA   MALTA   CYPRUS LEB. SYRIA
                              ISR. IRAQ
ALGERIA   LIBYA   EGYPT   JORDAN

Western   BAHRAIN
Sahara   SAUDI   QATAR
(Morocco)   ARABIA
                        UNITED ARAB   OMAN
MAURITANIA   MALI   NIGER   EMIRATES
                          YEMEN   P.D.R.
SENEGAL GAMBIA BURKINA CHAD **AFRICA** OF YEMEN
GUINEA- GUINEA FASO BENIN SUDAN
BISSAU   IVORY NIGERIA DJIBOUTI
SIERRA   COAST   CENTRAL SOMALIA
LEONE   GHANA TOGO CAMEROON AFRICAN REPUBLIC ETHIOPIA
LIBERIA EQUATORIAL GUINEA
SÃO TOMÉ AND PRÍNCIPE GABON CONGO   UGANDA   KENYA
                      RWANDA
Cabinda   ZAIRE   BURUNDI
(Angola)   TANZANIA
            ANGOLA   MALAWI   COMOROS
ATLANTIC   ZAMBIA   MOZAMBIQUE
OCEAN   Namibia   ZIMBABWE   MADAGASCAR
          (South Africa)
Walvis Bay   BOTSWANA
(South Africa)   SWAZILAND
      REPUBLIC OF   LESOTHO
      SOUTH AFRICA

UNION OF SOVIET SOCIALIST REPUBLICS
(SOVIET UNION)

A S I A

MONGOLIAN
PEOPLE'S REPUBLIC   NORTH
                                 KOREA
CHINA   SOUTH   JAPAN
                                 KOREA

AFGHANISTAN
         PAKISTAN   TAIWAN
IRAN   NEPAL BHUTAN
                 INDIA   Hong Kong (U.K.)
         BANGLADESH BURMA Macao
                      LAOS (Portugal)
                  THAILAND
                  CAMBODIA VIETNAM PHILIPPINES

         SRI LANKA
                              BRUNEI
      MALDIVES   MALAYSIA
                              SINGAPORE
                              INDONESIA

      SEYCHELLES

INDIAN OCEAN

MAURITIUS
Réunion (France)

PACIFIC
OCEAN

KIRIBATI
         NAURU
PAPUA   SOLOMON
NEW GUINEA   ISLANDS
              TUVALU
VANUATU   FIJI

AUSTRALIA

NEW
ZEALAND

Prime Meridian

20°W   0°   20°E   40°E   60°E   80°E   100°E   120°E   140°E   160°E   180°

Antarctic Circle

A N T A R C T I C A

80°N
60°N
40°N
20°N
0°
20°S
40°S
60°S
80°S

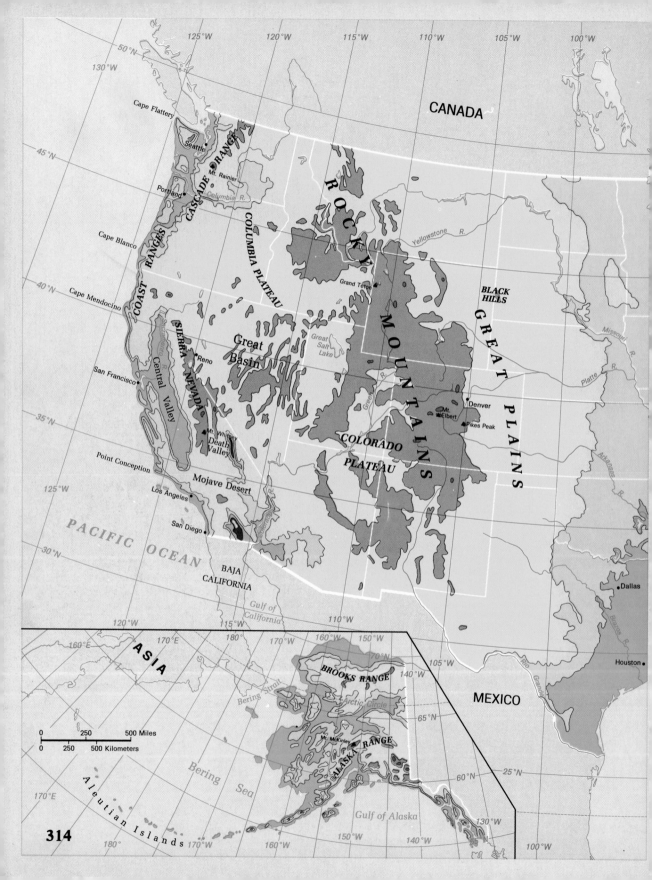

CANADA

Cape Flattery

Seattle •
CASCADE RANGE

Portland •
Mt. Rainier

Columbia R.

COLUMBIA PLATEAU

Cape Blanco

COAST RANGES

Cape Mendocino

SIERRA NEVADA

Reno •

San Francisco •

Central Valley

Mt. Whitney
Death Valley

Point Conception

Los Angeles •

San Diego •

Mojave Desert

BAJA CALIFORNIA

Gulf of California

PACIFIC OCEAN

Great Basin

Great Salt Lake

Grand Teton

ROCKY MOUNTAINS

Green R.

COLORADO PLATEAU

BLACK HILLS

Yellowstone R.

GREAT PLAINS

Mt. Elbert
Denver •
Pikes Peak

Colorado R.

Missouri R.

Platte R.

Arkansas R.

Dallas •

Houston •

Rio Grande

Brazos R.

MEXICO

ASIA

BROOKS RANGE

Bering Strait

Arctic Circle

70°N

65°N

60°N

Mt. McKinley
ALASKA RANGE

Bering Sea

Gulf of Alaska

Aleutian Islands

0   250   500 Miles
0   250   500 Kilometers

25°N

314

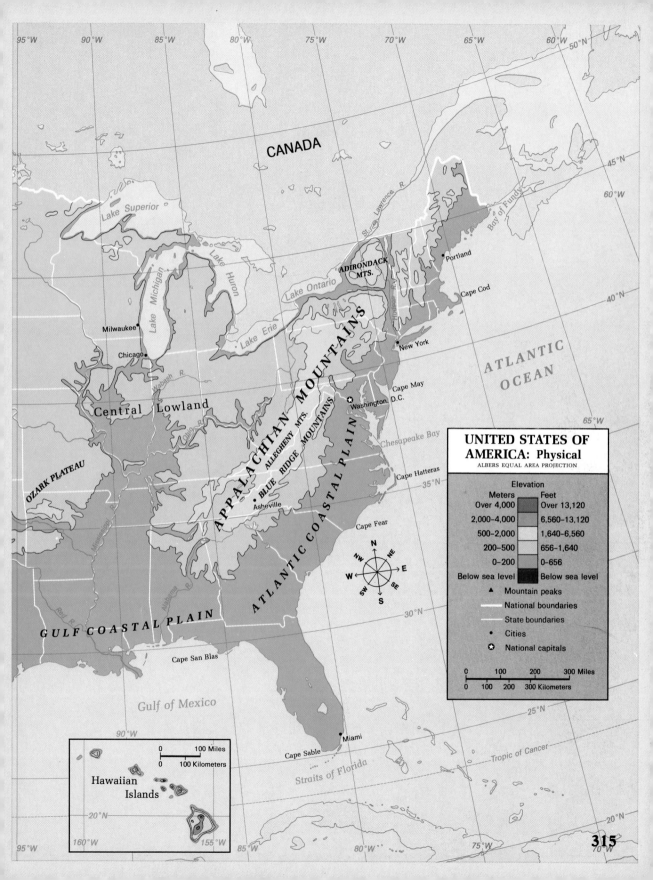

CANADA

Lake Superior

Lake Michigan

Lake Huron

ADIRONDACK MTS.

- Portland

Cape Cod

Lake Ontario

Milwaukee

Lake Erie

Chicago

New York

Central Lowland

Cape May

Washington, D.C.

Chesapeake Bay

OZARK PLATEAU

A P P A L A C H I A N   M O U N T A I N S

ALLEGHENY MTS.

BLUE RIDGE MOUNTAINS

Cape Hatteras

Asheville

ATLANTIC OCEAN

ATLANTIC COASTAL PLAIN

Cape Fear

N
NW   NE
W   E
SW   SE
S

GULF COASTAL PLAIN

Cape San Blas

Gulf of Mexico

Miami

Cape Sable

Straits of Florida

Tropic of Cancer

UNITED STATES OF AMERICA: Physical

ALBERS EQUAL AREA PROJECTION

Elevation

Meters		Feet
Over 4,000		Over 13,120
2,000–4,000		6,560–13,120
500–2,000		1,640–6,560
200–500		656–1,640
0–200		0–656
Below sea level		Below sea level

▲ Mountain peaks
National boundaries
State boundaries
• Cities
✪ National capitals

0	100	200	300 Miles
0	100	200	300 Kilometers

Hawaiian Islands

0	100 Miles
0	100 Kilometers

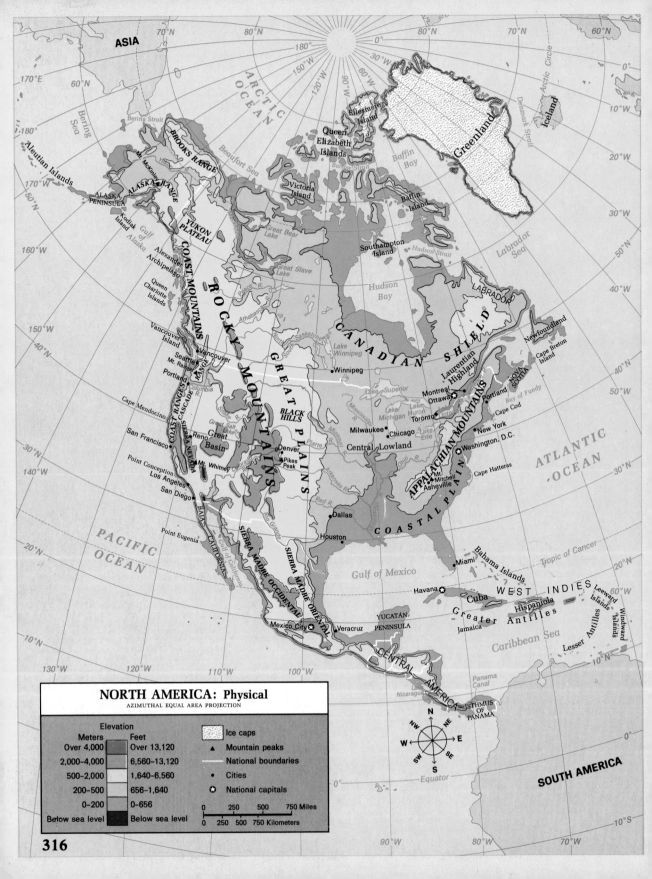

NORTH AMERICA: Physical

AZIMUTHAL EQUAL AREA PROJECTION

Elevation

Meters	Feet
Over 4,000	Over 13,120
2,000-4,000	6,560-13,120
500-2,000	1,640-6,560
200-500	656-1,640
0-200	0-656
Below sea level	Below sea level

Ice caps

▲ Mountain peaks

National boundaries

• Cities

✪ National capitals

0   250   500   750 Miles

0   250   500   750 Kilometers

316

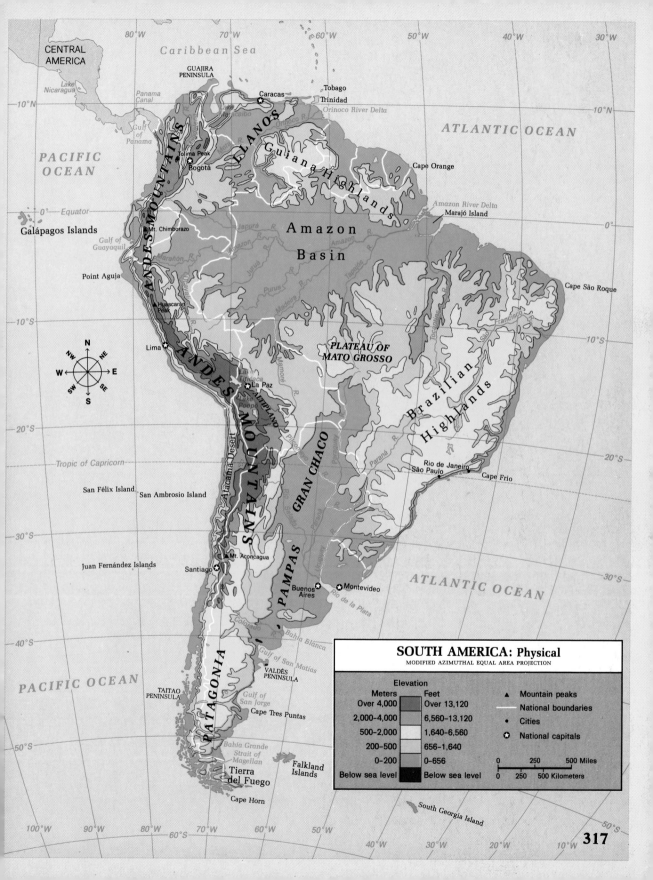

SOUTH AMERICA: Physical
MODIFIED AZIMUTHAL EQUAL AREA PROJECTION

Caribbean Sea

CENTRAL
AMERICA

Lake
Nicaragua

GUAJIRA
PENINSULA

Tobago
Trinidad

Caracas

Orinoco River Delta

PACIFIC
OCEAN

Panama
Canal

Gulf
of
Panama

Lake
Maracaibo

LLANOS

Orinoco

Meta

Guiana Highlands

ATLANTIC OCEAN

Cape Orange

Tolima Peak

Bogotá

Amazon River Delta
Marajó Island

Galápagos Islands

Equator

Mt. Chimborazo

Japurá

Amazon

Amazon
Basin

Gulf of
Guayaquil

Marañón

Negro

Cape São Roque

Point Aguja

Purus

Juruá

Madeira

Tapajós

Huascarán
Peak

Lima

ANDES MOUNTAINS

PLATEAU OF
MATO GROSSO

São Francisco

Tocantins

Lake
Titicaca

La Paz

ALTIPLANO

Lake
Poopó

Mamoré

Brazilian
Highlands

Atacama Desert

GRAN CHACO

Pilcomayo

Paraguay

Tropic of Capricorn

San Félix Island

San Ambrosio Island

Paraná

Rio de Janeiro
São Paulo

Cape Frio

Juan Fernández Islands

Mt. Aconcagua

Paraná

Uruguay

Santiago

PAMPAS

Buenos
Aires

Montevideo

Colorado

Río de la Plata

ATLANTIC OCEAN

PACIFIC OCEAN

PATAGONIA

Bahía Blanca

Gulf of San Matías

VALDÉS
PENINSULA

TAITAO
PENINSULA

Gulf of
San Jorge

Cape Tres Puntas

Bahía Grande
Strait of
Magellan

Falkland
Islands

Tierra
del Fuego

Cape Horn

South Georgia Island

Elevation

Meters	Feet
Over 4,000	Over 13,120
2,000–4,000	6,560–13,120
500–2,000	1,640–6,560
200–500	656–1,640
0–200	0–656
Below sea level	Below sea level

▲ Mountain peaks
— National boundaries
• Cities
✪ National capitals

0   250   500 Miles
0   250   500 Kilometers

317

ARCTIC OCEAN

Barents Sea

North Cape

KOLA
PENINSULA

White
Sea

Iceland
Mt. Hekla

Arctic Circle

Norwegian
Sea

LAPLAND

KJÖLEN MTS.

SCANDINAVIAN PENINSULA

Torne

Lake
Onega

Vestfjorden

Glomma

Gulf of Bothnia

Lake
Ladoga

ATLANTIC
OCEAN

Faeroe Is.

Shetland Is.

Oslo

Helsinki

Leningrad

Gulf of Finland

Outer Hebrides

Orkney Is.

Vättern
Lake

Stockholm

Vänern
Lake

British Isles

Gotland

Baltic
Sea

North Sea

Dublin

Irish Sea

PENNINE
CHAIN

JUTLAND

Dnepr Lowland

St. George's
Channel

Amsterdam

Berlin

NORTH EUROPEAN PLAIN

London

Thames

Warsaw

Brussels

Ruhr

Elbe

Oder

Vistula

English Channel

ARDENNES

Bonn

Seine

BRITTANY
PENINSULA

Paris

Prague

CARPATHIAN MTS.

Loire

JURA MTS.

Lake
Constance

Danube R.

Vienna

Bay
of Biscay

CENTRAL
MASSIF

ALPS

Budapest

Hungarian
Basin

Garonne

Mt. Blanc

Milan

TRANSYLVANIAN
ALPS

PYRENEES
MTS.

PLAIN OF LOMBARDY

Venice

Belgrade

Bucharest

Duero R.

MESETA

Madrid

Tajo R.

IBERIAN
PENINSULA

Ebro R.

DINARIC ALPS

Adriatic Sea

BALKAN MTS.

Lisbon

Corsica

Rome

APENNINE PENINSULA

APENNINES

Sofia

BALKAN
PENINSULA

Istanbul

Sardinia

PINDUS MTS.

Mt. Olympus

Balearic Is.

Naples

Mt. Vesuvius

Tyrrhenian
Sea

Aegean
Sea

Strait of Gibraltar

Athens

Ionian
Sea

Sicily

AFRICA

Malta

Crete

Mediterranean Sea

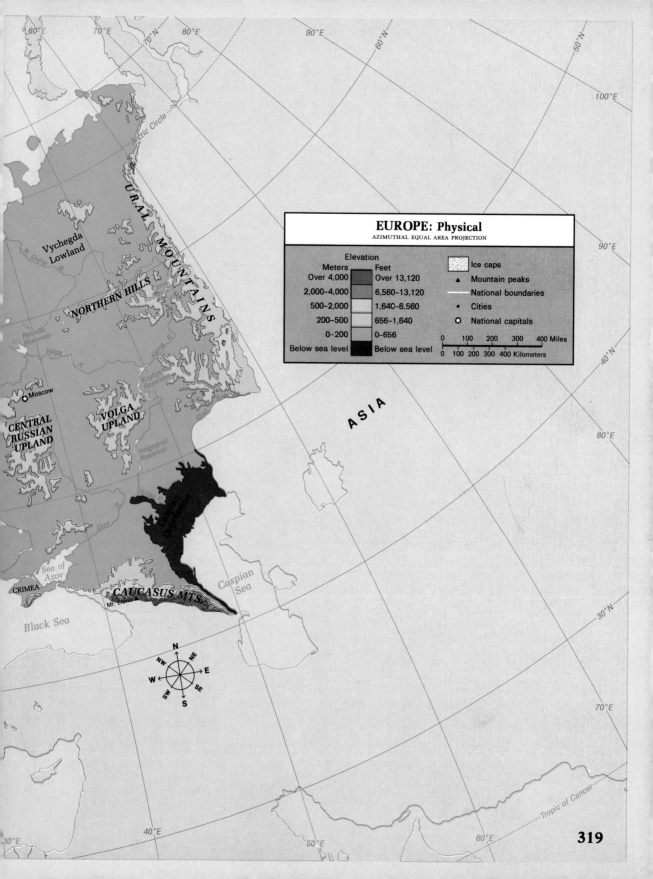

EUROPE: Physical
AZIMUTHAL EQUAL AREA PROJECTION

Elevation

Meters	Feet
Over 4,000	Over 13,120
2,000–4,000	6,560–13,120
500–2,000	1,640–6,560
200–500	656–1,640
0–200	0–656
Below sea level	Below sea level

Ice caps
▲ Mountain peaks
— National boundaries
• Cities
✪ National capitals

0   100   200   300   400 Miles
0 100 200 300 400 Kilometers

URAL MOUNTAINS

Vychegda Lowland

N. Dvina R.

NORTHERN HILLS

Rybinsk Reservoir

Vema Reservoir

Kama R.

Volga R.

Kuybyshev Reservoir

✪ Moscow

CENTRAL RUSSIAN UPLAND

VOLGA UPLAND

Volgograd Reservoir

Ural R.

Volga R.

Caspian Depression

Don R.

Sea of Azov

CRIMEA

CAUCASUS MTS.

Mt. Elbrus ▲

Black Sea

Caspian Sea

ASIA

N
NW   NE
W   E
SW   SE
S

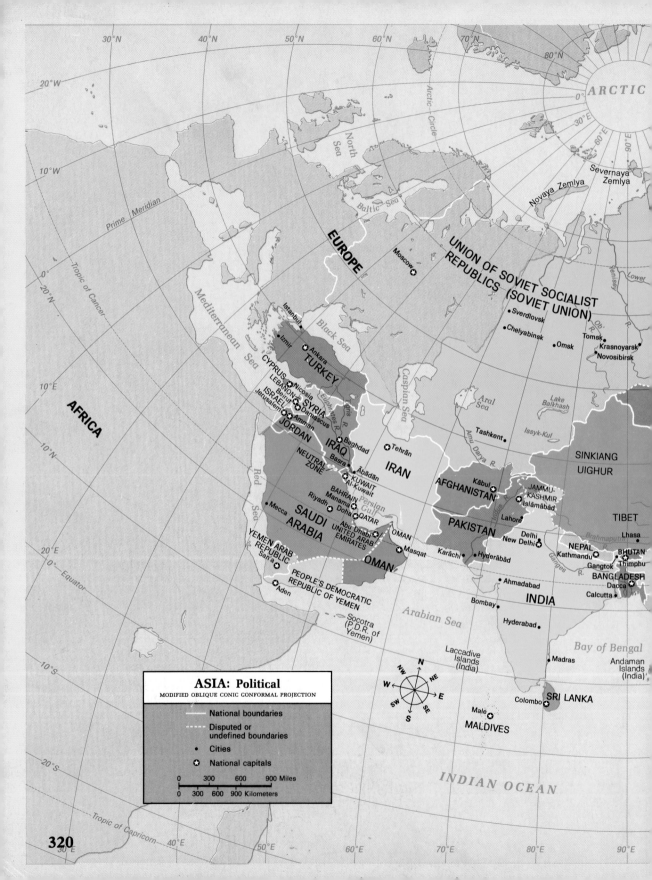

ARCTIC

20°W

30°N   40°N   50°N   60°N   70°N   80°N

0°

30°E

10°W

North
Sea

60°E

Novaya Zemlya

Severnaya
Zemlya

0°

Prime Meridian

10°N

Arctic Circle

Baltic Sea

EUROPE

Moscow

UNION OF SOVIET SOCIALIST
REPUBLICS (SOVIET UNION)

Lower

Yenisey

Ob

20°N

Tropic of Cancer

0°

Sverdlovsk

Chelyabinsk

Tomsk

Krasnoyarsk

Omsk

Novosibirsk

Ob. R.

Mediterranean Sea

AFRICA

10°E

Black Sea

Istanbul

Izmir   Ankara

CYPRUS   Nicosia

TURKEY

LEBANON   Beirut

SYRIA   Damascus

ISRAEL

Jerusalem   Amman

JORDAN

Euphrates R.

Tigris R.

Baghdad

IRAQ

Caspian Sea

Tehrân

Aral
Sea

Lake
Balkhash

Tashkent

Issyk-Kul

Amu Darya R.

SINKIANG
UIGHUR

10°N

Red Sea

NEUTRAL
ZONE

Basra

Âbâdân

IRAN

AFGHANISTAN   Kâbul

JAMMU-
KASHMIR

Islâmâbâd

TIBET

20°E

0°   Equator

Mecca

KUWAIT
Al-Kuwait

BAHRAIN
Riyadh   Manama
Doha

QATAR

SAUDI
ARABIA

Abu Dhabi
UNITED ARAB
EMIRATES

Persian Gulf

OMAN

Masqat

PAKISTAN

Lahore

Delhi
New Delhi

Karâchi   Hyderâbâd

NEPAL

Kathmandu

Gangtok

BHUTAN
Thimphu

Brahmaputra

Lhasa

Ganges

YEMEN ARAB
REPUBLIC   San'a

Aden

PEOPLE'S DEMOCRATIC
REPUBLIC OF YEMEN

OMAN

Ahmadabad

Bombay

INDIA

BANGLADESH
Dacca

Calcutta

10°S

Socotra
(P.D.R. of
Yemen)

Arabian Sea

Hyderabad

Bay of Bengal

Laccadive
Islands
(India)

Madras

Andaman
Islands
(India)

ASIA: Political

MODIFIED OBLIQUE CONIC CONFORMAL PROJECTION

National boundaries

Disputed or
undefined boundaries

• Cities

✪ National capitals

N
NW   NE
W   E
SW   SE
S

Colombo   SRI LANKA

Male

MALDIVES

20°S

Tropic of Capricorn

30°E

40°E

50°E

60°E

70°E

80°E

90°E

0   300   600   900 Miles

0   300   600   900 Kilometers

INDIAN OCEAN

320

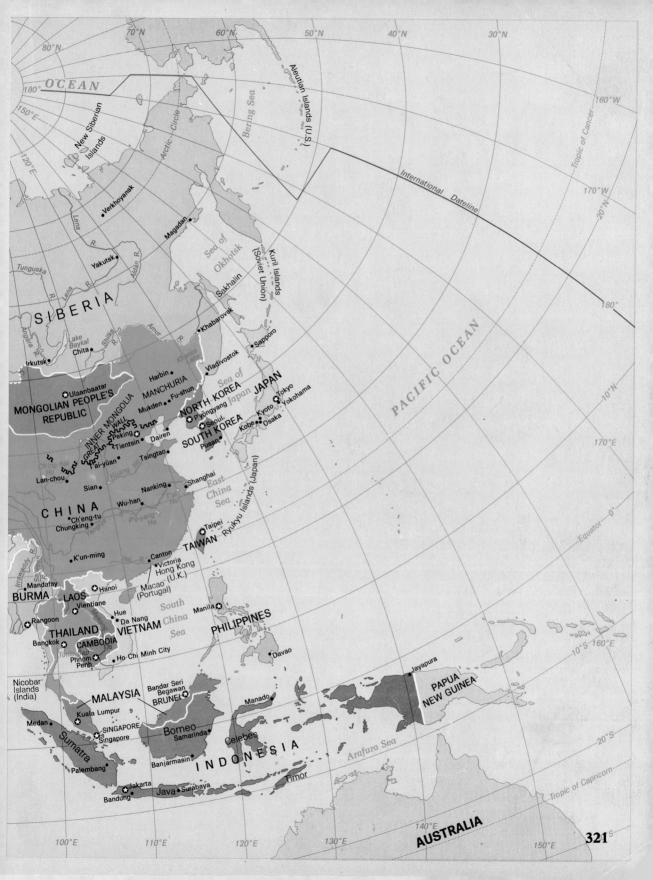

OCEAN

New Siberian
Islands

Arctic Circle

Verkhoyansk

Magadan

Bering Sea

Aleutian Islands (U.S.)

International Dateline

Tropic of Cancer

160°W

170°W

20°N

180°

Sea of
Okhotsk

Yakutsk

Tunguska R.

Lena R.

Aldan R.

SIBERIA

Angara R.

Lake
Baykal

Chita

Irkutsk

Ulaanbaatar

MONGOLIAN PEOPLE'S
REPUBLIC

INNER MONGOLIA

GREAT WALL

T'ai-yüan

Ch'ing-hai
Hu

Lan-chou

K'un-ming

CHINA

Sian

Ch'eng-tu

Chungking

Wu-han

Yangtze

Huang Ho

Nanking

Shanghai

Shilka R.

Amur R.

Khanka
Lake

Harbin

MANCHURIA

Mukden

Fu-shun

Peking

Tientsin

Dairen

Tsingtao

Khabarovsk

Vladivostok

Sapporo

NORTH KOREA

P'yongyang

Seoul

SOUTH KOREA

Pusan

Sea of
Japan

JAPAN

Kobe

Kyoto

Osaka

Tokyo

Yokohama

PACIFIC OCEAN

10°N

170°E

Ryukyu Islands (Japan)

East
China
Sea

T'ai
Hu

P'o-yang
Hu

Taipei

TAIWAN

Canton

Victoria
Hong Kong
(U.K.)

Macao
(Portugal)

South
China
Sea

Hai R.

Sea of
Japan

Kuril Islands
(Soviet Union)

Sakhalin

180°

Equator

0°

Irrawaddy R.

Mandalay

BURMA

Rangoon

LAOS

Hanoi

Vientiane

THAILAND

Bangkok

CAMBODIA

Phnom
Penh

Tonle
Sap

Hue

Da Nang

VIETNAM

Ho Chi Minh City

Manila

PHILIPPINES

Davao

10°S

160°E

Nicobar
Islands
(India)

Medan

Sumatra

Palembang

MALAYSIA

Kuala Lumpur

SINGAPORE

Singapore

Bandar Seri
Begawan

BRUNEI

Borneo

Samarinda

Banjarmasin

Manado

Celebes

INDONESIA

Jakarta

Bandung

Java

Surabaya

Timor

Arafura Sea

Jayapura

PAPUA
NEW GUINEA

20°S

140°E

AUSTRALIA

130°E

120°E

110°E

100°E

150°E

Tropic of Capricorn

321

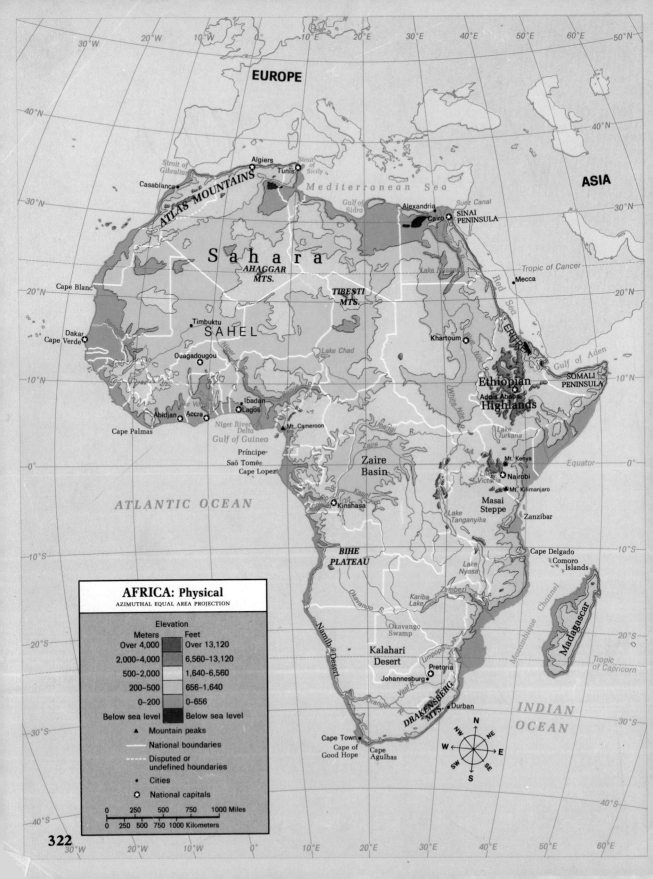

AFRICA: Physical

AZIMUTHAL EQUAL AREA PROJECTION

Elevation

Meters	Feet
Over 4,000	Over 13,120
2,000–4,000	6,560–13,120
500–2,000	1,640–6,560
200–500	656–1,640
0–200	0–656
Below sea level	Below sea level

▲ Mountain peaks

—— National boundaries

----- Disputed or
undefined boundaries

• Cities

✪ National capitals

| 0 | 250 | 500 | 750 | 1000 Miles |
| 0 | 250 | 500 | 750 | 1000 Kilometers |

EUROPE

ASIA

Strait of Gibraltar

Algiers ✪
Tunis ✪
Casablanca •

ATLAS MOUNTAINS

Mediterranean Sea

Strait of Sicily

Gulf of Sidra

Alexandria •
Cairo ✪ SINAI PENINSULA

Suez Canal

Tropic of Cancer

Mecca •

S a h a r a

AHAGGAR MTS.

Lake Nasser

Red Sea

TIBESTI MTS.

Cape Blanc

Dakar ✪
Cape Verde

SAHEL
Timbuktu •

Khartoum •

ERITREA

Gulf of Aden

SOMALI PENINSULA

Ouagadougou ✪

Niger

Lake Chad

Blue Nile

Ethiopian Highlands
Addis Ababa ✪

Abidjan ✪
Accra ✪
Ibadan •
Lagos ✪

Lake Volta

Cape Palmas

Mt. Cameroon ▲
Niger River Delta
Gulf of Guinea

Ubangi R.

White Nile

Lake Turkana

Príncipe
São Tomé
Cape Lopez

Zaire R.

Zaire Basin

Mt. Kenya ▲
Lake Victoria
Nairobi ✪
Mt. Kilimanjaro ▲

Zanzibar

Equator

ATLANTIC OCEAN

Kinshasa ✪

Kasai R.

Masai Steppe

Lake Tanganyika

BIHE PLATEAU

Lake Nyasa

Cape Delgado
Comoro Islands

Okavango R.

Zambezi

Kariba Lake

Mozambique Channel

Madagascar

Namib Desert

Okavango Swamp

Kalahari Desert

Limpopo R.

Pretoria ✪
Johannesburg •

Tropic of Capricorn

Vaal R.

DRAKENSBERG MTS.

Orange R.

Durban •

INDIAN OCEAN

Cape Town ✪
Cape of Good Hope
Cape Agulhas

N
NW NE
W   E
SW SE
S

322

STATES OF THE UNITED STATES

	Population/Admitted to the Union	Capital	Area Sq. mi.—Sq. km.		State Flag	State Bird	State Flower
Alabama (AL) Yellowhammer State	3,990,000 **1819**	Montgomery	51,609	133,667		Yellowhammer	Camellia
Alaska (AK) Last Frontier	500,000 **1959**	Juneau	586,400	1,518,776		Willow Ptarmigan	Forget-me-not
Arizona (AZ) Grand Canyon State	3,053,000 **1912**	Phoenix	113,909	295,024		Cactus Wren	Saguaro (Giant Cactus)
Arkansas (AR) Land of Opportunity	2,349,000 **1836**	Little Rock	53,104	137,539		Mockingbird	Apple Blossom
California (CA) Golden State	25,622,000 **1850**	Sacramento	158,693	411,014		California Valley Quail	Golden Poppy
Colorado (CO) Centennial State	3,178,000 **1876**	Denver	104,247	270,000		Lark Bunting	Rocky Mountain Columbine
Connecticut (CT) Constitution State	3,154,000 **1788**	Hartford	5,009	12,973		Robin	Mountain Laurel
Delaware (DE) First State	613,000 **1787**	Dover	2,057	5,328		Blue Hen Chicken	Peach Blossom

	Population/ Admitted to the Union	Capital	Area Sq. mi.—Sq. km.		State Flag	State Bird	State Flower
Florida (FL) Sunshine State	10,976,000 **1845**	Tallahassee	58,560	151,670		Mockingbird	Orange Blossom
Georgia (GA) Empire State of the South	5,837,000 **1788**	Atlanta	58,876	152,489		Brown Thrasher	Cherokee Rose
Hawaii (HI) Aloha State	1,039,000 **1959**	Honolulu	6,450	16,706		Nene or Hawaiian Goose	Hibiscus
Idaho (ID) Gem State	1,001,000 **1890**	Boise	83,557	216,413		Mountain Bluebird	Syringa (Mock Orange)
Illinois (IL) Land of Lincoln	11,511,000 **1818**	Springfield	56,400	146,076		Cardinal	Native Violet
Indiana (IN) Hoosier State	5,498,000 **1816**	Indianapolis	36,291	93,994		Cardinal	Peony
Iowa (IA) Hawkeye State	2,910,000 **1846**	Des Moines	56,290	145,791		Eastern Goldfinch	Wild Rose

STATES OF THE UNITED STATES

	Population/ Admitted to the Union	Capital	Area Sq. mi.—Sq. km.		State Flag	State Bird	State Flower
Kansas (KS) Sunflower State	2,438,000 **1861**	Topeka	82,264	213,064		Western Meadowlark	Sunflower
Kentucky (KY) Bluegrass State	3,723,000 **1792**	Frankfort	40,395	104,623		Kentucky Cardinal	Goldenrod
Louisiana (LA) Pelican State	4,462,000 **1812**	Baton Rouge	48,523	125,675		Brown Pelican	Magnolia
Maine (ME) Pine Tree State	1,156,000 **1820**	Augusta	33,215	86,027		Chickadee	White Pine Cone and Tassel
Maryland (MD) Old Line State	4,349,000 **1788**	Annapolis	10,577	27,394		Baltimore Oriole	Black-eyed Susan
Massachusetts (MA) Bay State	5,798,000 **1788**	Boston	8,257	21,386		Chickadee	Arbutus
Michigan (MI) Wolverine State	9,075,000 **1837**	Lansing	58,216	150,779		Robin	Apple Blossom

325

STATES OF THE UNITED STATES

	Population/ Admitted to the Union	Capital	Area Sq. mi.—Sq. km.		State Flag	State Bird	State Flower
Minnesota Gopher	4,162,000 **1858**	St. Paul	84,068	217,736		Common Loon	Pink and White Lady's Slipper
Mississippi (MS) Magnolia State	2,598,000 **1817**	Jackson	47,716	123,584		Mockingbird	Magnolia
Missouri (MO) Show Me State	5,008,000 **1821**	Jefferson City	69,686	180,487		Bluebird	Hawthorn
Montana (MT) Treasure State	824,000 **1889**	Helena	147,138	381,087		Western Meadowlark	Bitterroot
Nebraska (NE) Cornhusker State	1,606,000 **1867**	Lincoln	77,227	200,018		Western Meadowlark	Goldenrod
Nevada (NV) Silver State	911,000 **1864**	Carson City	110,540	286,299		Mountain Bluebird	Sagebrush
New Hampshire (NH) Granite State	977,000 **1788**	Concord	9,304	24,097		Purple Finch	Purple Lilac

326

STATES OF THE UNITED STATES

	Population/ Admitted to the Union	Capital	Area Sq. mi.—Sq. km.		State Flag	State Bird	State Flower
New Jersey (NJ) Garden State	7,515,000 **1787**	Trenton	7,836	20,295		Eastern Goldfinch	Purple Violet
New Mexico (NM) Land of Enchantment	1,424,000 **1912**	Santa Fe	121,666	315,115		Roadrunner	Yucca Flower
New York (NY) Empire State	17,735,000 **1788**	Albany	49,576	128,402		Bluebird	Rose
North Carolina (NC) Tar Heel State	6,165,000 **1789**	Raleigh	52,586	136,198		Cardinal	Flowering Dogwood
North Dakota (ND) Flickertail State	686,000 **1889**	Bismarck	70,665	183,022		Western Meadowlark	Wild Prairie Rose
Ohio (OH) Buckeye State	10,752,000 **1803**	Columbus	41,222	106,765		Cardinal	Scarlet Carnation
Oklahoma (OK) Sooner State	3,298,000 **1907**	Oklahoma City	69,919	181,090		Scissor-tailed Flycatcher	Mistletoe

STATES OF THE UNITED STATES	Population/ Admitted to the Union	Capital	Area Sq. mi.—Sq. km.		State Flag	State Bird	State Flower
Oregon (OR) Beaver State	2,674,000 **1859**	Salem	96,981	251,181		Western Meadowlark	Oregon Grape
Pennsylvania (PA) Keystone State	11,901,000 **1787**	Harrisburg	45,333	117,412		Ruffed Grouse	Mountain Laurel
Rhode Island (RI) Ocean State	962,000 **1790**	Providence	1,214	3,144		Rhode Island Red	Violet
South Carolina (SC) Palmetto State	3,300,000 **1788**	Columbia	31,055	80,432		Carolina Wren	Carolina Jessamine
South Dakota (SD) Sunshine State	706,000 **1889**	Pierre	77,047	199,552		Ring-necked Pheasant	American Pasqueflower
Tennessee (TN) Volunteer State	4,717,000 **1796**	Nashville	42,244	109,412		Mockingbird	Iris
Texas (TX) Lone Star State	15,989,000 **1845**	Austin	267,336	692,397		Mockingbird	Bluebonnet

328

STATES OF THE UNITED STATES

	Population/ Admitted to the Union	Capital	Area Sq. mi.—Sq. km.		State Flag	State Bird	State Flower
Utah (UT) Beehive State	1,652,000 **1896**	Salt Lake City	84,916	219,932		Sea Gull	Sego Lily
Vermont (VT) Green Mountain State	530,000 **1791**	Montpelier	9,609	24,887		Hermit Thrush	Red Clover
Virginia (VA) Old Dominion	5,636,000 **1788**	Richmond	40,815	105,711		Cardinal	Dogwood
Washington (WA) Evergreen State	4,302,000 **1889**	Olympia	68,192	176,617		Willow Goldfinch	Coast Rhododendron
West Virginia (WV) Mountain State	1,952,000 **1863**	Charleston	24,282	62,890		Cardinal	Rhododendron
Wisconsin (WI) Badger State	4,766,000 **1848**	Madison	56,154	145,439		Robin	Wood Violet
Wyoming (WY) Equality State	511,000 **1890**	Cheyenne	97,914	253,597		Meadowlark	Indian Paintbrush

MAJOR NATIONS OF THE WORLD

Continent/ Nation	Area sq mi	sq km	Population	Capital City and Population
AFRICA Algeria	919,595	2,381,741	21,351,000	Algiers 2,442,000
Angola	481,353	1,246,700	7,770,000	Luanda 700,000
Benin	43,484	112,622	3,910,000	Porto-Novo 208,000
Botswana	231,805	600,372	1,038,000	Gaborone 79,000
Burkina Faso (Upper Volta)	105,869	274,200	6,733,000	Ouagadougou 375,000
Cameroon	183,569	475,442	9,506,000	Yaoundé 436,000
Central African Republic	240,535	622,984	2,585,000	Bangui 387,000
Chad	495,755	1,284,000	5,116,000	N'Djamena 303,000
Congo	132,047	342,000	1,745,000	Brazzaville 422,000
Egypt	386,643	1,001,400	47,000,000	Cairo 5,074,000
Ethiopia	472,434	1,223,600	31,998,000	Addis Ababa 1,412,000
Gabon	103,347	267,667	958,000	Libreville 350,000
Ghana	92,100	238,537	13,804,000	Accra 1,045,000
Guinea	94,926	245,857	5,579,000	Conakry 763,000
Ivory Coast	123,847	320,763	9,178,000	Abidjan 1,850,000
Kenya	224,961	582,646	19,362,000	Nairobi 1,100,000
Liberia	43,000	111,369	2,180,000	Monrovia 425,000
Libya	679,362	1,759,540	3,684,000	Tripoli 980,000
Madagascar	226,658	587,041	9,645,000	Antananarivo 600,000

MAJOR NATIONS OF THE WORLD

Continent/ Nation	Area sq mi		Population	Capital City and Population
	sq mi	sq km		
Malawi	45,747	118,484	6,829,000	Lilongwe 186,000
Mali	478,766	1,240,000	7,562,000	Bamako 404,000
Morocco	172,414	446,550	23,565,000	Rabat 893,000
Mozambique	302,329	783,030	13,413,000	Maputo 355,000
Namibia	318,261	824,292	1,083,000	Windhoek 61,000
Niger	489,191	1,267,000	6,284,000	Niamey 399,000
Nigeria	356,669	923,768	88,148,000	Lagos 1,061,000
Senegal	75,955	196,722	6,541,000	Dakar 979,000
Sierra Leone	27,925	72,325	3,805,000	Freetown 316,000
Somalia	246,200	637,657	6,393,000	Mogadishu 600,000
South Africa	434,674	1,125,800	31,698,000	Pretoria* 528,000
Sudan	967,500	2,505,813	21,103,000	Khartoum 476,000
Tanzania	364,900	945,087	21,202,000	Dar es Salaam** 757,000
Tunisia	63,170	163,610	7,202,000	Tunis 557,000
Uganda	91,134	236,036	14,268,000	Kampala 332,000
Zaire	905,567	2,345,409	32,158,000	Kinshasa 2,444,000
Zambia	290,586	752,614	6,554,000	Lusaka 538,000
Zimbabwe (Rhodesia)	150,804	390,580	8,325,000	Salisbury 656,000
ASIA Afghanistan	250,000	647,497	14,448,000	Kabul 913,000

*(second capital) Cape Town 214,000
**(emerging capital) Dodoma 46,000

Continent/ Nation	Area sq mi	sq km	Population	Capital City and Population
Bangladesh	55,598	143,998	99,585,000	Dacca 3,440,000
Burma	261,228	676,577	36,196,000	Rangoon 2,459,000
China	3,630,747	9,403,600	1,034,097,000	Peking 9,500,000
India	1,237,061	3,203,975	746,388,000	New Delhi 324,000
Indonesia	741,101	1,919,443	169,442,000	Jakarta 6,503,000
Iran	636,296	1,648,000	43,280,000	Tehrán 5,734,000
Iraq	167,925	434,924	15,000,000	Baghdad 2,184,000
Israel	7,848	20,325	4,024,000	Jerusalem 429,000
Japan	145,834	377,708	119,896,000	Tokyo 8,170,000
Jordan	35,135	91,000	2,689,000	Amman 777,500
Kampuchea (Cambodia)	69,898	181,035	6,300,000	Phnom Penh 500,000
Korea (North)	46,540	120,538	19,630,000	Pyŏngyang 1,280,000
Korea (South)	38,025	98,484	41,999,000	Seoul 9,501,000
Laos	91,429	236,800	3,732,000	Vientiane 174,000
Lebanon	4,015	10,400	2,601,000	Beirut 702,000
Malaysia	128,430	332,632	15,330,000	Kuala Lumpur 938,000
Mongolia	604,250	1,565,000	1,860,000	Ulaanbaatar 480,000
Nepal	56,135	145,391	16,578,000	Kathmandu 235,000
Pakistan	319,867	828,453	96,628,000	Islāmābād 201,000
Philippines	115,831	300,000	55,528,000	Manila 1,630,000

MAJOR NATIONS OF THE WORLD

Continent/ Nation	Area sq mi	sq km	Population	Capital City and Population
Saudi Arabia	830,000	2,149,690	10,794,000	Riyadh 667,000
Sri Lanka	24,962	64,652	15,925,000	Colombo 588,000
Syria	71,498	185,180	10,075,000	Damascus 1,112,000
Taiwan	13,900	36,002	19,117,000	Taipei 2,450,000
Thailand	198,115	513,115	51,725,000	Bangkok 5,175,000
Turkey	300,948	779,452	50,207,000	Ankara 1,878,000
United Arab Emirates	32,278	83,600	1,523,000	Abu Dhabi 537,000
Vietnam	127,242	329,556	59,030,000	Hanoi 2,000,000
Yemen	75,290	195,000	4,890,000	San'a 278,000
Yemen, People's Democratic Republic of	128,560	332,968	2,147,000	Aden 264,000
AUSTRALIA AND NEW ZEALAND Australia	2,967,909	7,686,850	15,462,000	Canberra 240,000
New Zealand	103,883	269,057	3,238,000	Wellington 343,000
EUROPE Austria	32,377	83,855	7,579,000	Vienna 1,502,000
Belgium	11,781	30,513	9,872,000	Brussels 980,000
Bulgaria	42,823	110,912	8,969,000	Sofia 1,173,000
Czechoslovakia	49,378	127,889	15,466,000	Prague 1,186,000
Denmark	16,633	43,080	5,112,000	Copenhagen 479,000
Finland	130,558	338,145	4,873,000	Helsinki 484,000
France	211,208	547,026	54,872,000	Paris 2,189,000
Germany (East)	41,768	108,179	16,718,000	Berlin (East) 1,197,000

Continent/ Nation	Area sq mi	sq km	Population	Capital City and Population
Germany (West)	96,016	248,678	61,387,000	Bonn 292,000
Greece	50,944	131,944	9,884,000	Athens 3,016,000
Hungary	35,921	93,036	10,681,000	Budapest 2,072,000
Iceland	39,769	103,000	239,000	Reykjavík 89,000
Ireland	27,136	70,283	3,575,000	Dublin 915,000
Italy	116,319	301,266	56,998,000	Rome 2,827,000
Netherlands	15,892	41,160	14,437,000	Amsterdam 676,000
Norway	149,158	386,317	4,145,000	Oslo 447,000
Poland	120,728	312,683	36,887,000	Warsaw 1,641,000
Portugal	35,516	91,985	10,045,000	Lisbon 808,000
Romania	91,699	237,500	22,683,000	Bucharest 2,228,000
Soviet Union (U.S.S.R.)	8,600,383	22,274,900	272,500,000	Moscow 8,642,000
Spain	194,882	504,741	38,435,000	Madrid 3,188,000
Sweden	173,780	450,089	8,335,000	Stockholm 653,000
Switzerland	15,943	41,293	6,500,000	Bern 141,000
United Kingdom	94,249	244,102	56,023,000	London 6,756,000
Yugoslavia	98,766	255,804	22,997,000	Belgrade 1,470,000
NORTH AMERICA AND THE CARIBBEAN Belize	8,866	22,963	158,000	Belmopan 3,000
Canada	3,831,033	9,992,330	25,142,000	Ottawa 718,000
Costa Rica	19,730	51,100	2,693,000	San José 241,000

MAJOR NATIONS OF THE WORLD

Continent/ Nation	Area sq mi	sq km	Population	Capital City and Population
Cuba	44,218	114,524	9,995,000	Havana 1,951,000
Dominican Republic	18,704	48,442	6,416,000	Santo Domingo 1,313,000
El Salvador	8,124	21,041	5,100,000	San Salvador 440,000
Guatemala	42,042	108,889	7,956,000	Guatemala 1,300,000
Haiti	10,714	27,750	5,803,000	Port-au-Prince 763,000
Honduras	43,277	112,088	4,424,000	Tegucigalpa 534,000
Mexico	761,604	1,972,547	77,659,000	Mexico City 9,683,000
Nicaragua	50,193	130,000	2,914,000	Managua 615,000
Panama	29,762	77,082	2,101,000	Panama 386,000
United States	3,679,201	9,529,081	236,413,000	Washington, DC 638,000
SOUTH AMERICA Argentina	1,068,301	2,776,889	30,097,000	Buenos Aires 2,908,000
Bolivia	424,164	1,098,581	6,037,000	Sucre* 80,000
Brazil	3,265,075	8,456,508	134,380,000	Brasília 410,999
Chile	292,135	756,626	11,655,000	Santiago 4,132,000
Colombia	439,737	1,138,914	28,248,000	Bogotá 3,968,000
Ecuador	109,483	283,561	9,091,000	Quito 1,110,000
Paraguay	157,048	406,752	3,623,000	Asunción 708,000
Peru	496,224	1,285,216	19,157,000	Lima 4,746,000
Uruguay	68,037	176,215	2,926,000	Montevideo 1,237,000
Venezuela	352,144	912,050	18,552,000	Caracas 2,944,000

*(second capital) La Paz 881,000

CHART AND GRAPH APPENDIX

CHILDREN OF THE WORLD
(under the age of 15)

TABLE

Continent	Number of Children (in millions)	Percent of Children
Africa	211	14
Asia	1,009	65
Australia	7	1
Europe	108	7
North America	97	6
South America	108	7

PIE GRAPH

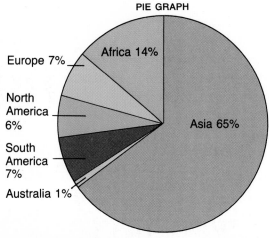

BAR GRAPH

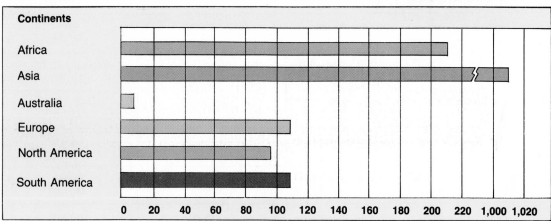

(Millions of children under age 15)

The same facts are shown here in different ways. The table and graphs present facts about children. A *table* lists facts. You can use a table to make graphs. A *graph* shows pictures of facts.

The table above shows that Africa has 211 million (211,000,000) children. It also shows percentages. What percent of the world's children does Africa have?

A *pie graph* shows how the parts fit into the whole. It gives percentages rather than total numbers. When you add up the percentages, they total 100. What percent of the world's children live in North America?

A *bar graph* helps you compare things quickly. It can use numbers or percentages. This graph shows millions of children. What two continents have the same number of children? What two continents have the most children? There is a break in the bar for Asia. This shows that all the numbers would not fit on the graph.

CHILDREN OF THE WORLD
(under the age of 15)

PICTOGRAPH

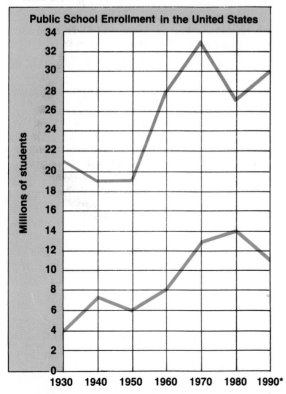

= 20 million children

Africa	🧒🧒🧒🧒🧒🧒🧒🧒🧒🧒🧒
Asia	🧒🧒
Australia	🧒
Europe	🧒🧒🧒🧒🧒🧒
North America	🧒🧒🧒🧒🧒
South America	🧒🧒🧒🧒🧒🧒

LINE GRAPH

Public School Enrollment in the United States

Millions of students (vertical axis: 0 to 34)

Years (horizontal axis): 1930 1940 1950 1960 1970 1980 1990*

—— Elementary students—Grades K–8
—— Secondary students—Grades 9–12   *projected

A *pictograph* is a chart that uses picture symbols. What number does each symbol in this pictograph stand for? The pictograph shows that *about* 10 million children live in Australia. You can find the actual number in the table. What is that number?

A *line graph* shows change over time. The one here gives changes for two groups. Name the groups. The numbers across the bottom identify the years. The numbers on the side represent millions of students. The most students ever in elementary school at once was 33 million (33,000,000). In what year were they enrolled?

337

GAZETTEER

Africa second-largest continent of Earth, in the Eastern Hemisphere (21, 190–231)
Alabama Southern state of the United States, on the Gulf of Mexico (109)
Alaska Pacific state of the United States, in northwestern North America (34, 131)
Alps major mountain system of south central Europe (237–238)
Amazon (AM uh ZON) **River** second-longest river of Earth, in northern South America south of the equator (150, 166)
Andes (AN deez) **Mountains** longest mountain system of Earth, extending down the west coast of South America (148, 166)
Antarctica (ANT AHRK tuh kuh) southernmost continent of Earth (21, 27)
Appalachian (AP uh LAY chun) **Mountains,** or **Appalachians** major mountain system of eastern North America, stretching from Canada to Alabama (75)
Arabia (uh RAY bee uh) Earth's largest peninsula, in southwestern Asia (277)
Arctic (AHRK tik) **Ocean** ocean surrounding the North Pole (21)
Argentina (AHR jun TEE nuh) nation in southern South America (163, 164)
Arizona (AR uh ZOH nuh) Mountain state in the southwestern United States (126)
Arkansas (AHR kan SAW) Southern state of the central United States (109, 112)
Asia (AY zhuh) largest continent of Earth, in the Eastern Hemisphere (274–311)
Asia Minor peninsula of southwestern Asia, south of the Black Sea (277)
Atacama (AH tuh KAH muh) **Desert** desert in northern Chile (148, 167)
Atlantic Ocean ocean separating North and South America from Europe and Africa (21)
Australia continent in the Eastern Hemisphere, southeast of Asia (21)

Balkan Peninsula peninsula of Europe east of Italy (238)
Baltimore port city in north central Maryland; 39°N, 77°W (384)
Bangladesh nation in southern Asia, mostly surrounded by India (39, 290)

Belize (buh LEEZ) nation in Central America, south of Mexico (92)
Bering Sea part of the Pacific Ocean between Alaska and Asia (93)
Berlin city divided into East Berlin, capital of East Germany, and West Berlin, part of West Germany; 53°N, 13°E (254)
Black Sea sea between Europe and Asia Minor (258)
Bolivia (buh LIV ee uh) nation in west central South America (24, 164, 169–185)
Bonn (BON) capital of West Germany; 51°N, 7°E (254)
Boston capital of Massachusetts, a port on the Atlantic; 42°N, 71°W (103)
Brazil (bruh ZIL) largest nation in South America (162, 164)
Burkina Faso (bour KEE nah FAH soh) nation in western Africa (215–229)

Cairo (KY roh) capital of Egypt; largest city in Africa; 30°N, 31°E (194, 203)
California Pacific state of the southwestern United States (21, 131–138)
Canada nation in northern North America (26, 86–89)
Caribbean Sea (KAR uh BEE un) part of the Atlantic Ocean between Central America and South America (74)
Caspian (KAS pee un) **Sea** inland body of water between Europe and Asia (236)
Caucasus Mountains mountains between Europe and southwestern Asia (238)
Central America narrow part of North America south of Mexico (91–92)
Central Lowland plains region of North America between the Appalachians and the Great Plains (75–76, 120)
Chicago city in northeastern Illinois, on Lake Michigan; 42°N, 88°W (122, 123)
Chile (CHIL ee) nation in southwestern South America (162, 164)
China nation in eastern Asia (286–293)
Colorado (KOL uh RAH doh) Mountain state of the western United States (126)
Connecticut (kuh NET uh kut) New England state of the United States (99)
Costa Rica (KOS tuh REE kah) nation in Central America (92)
Cuba island nation south of Florida (32)

Dacca (DAK uh) capital of Bangladesh; 24°N, 90°E (39)
Delaware Middle Atlantic state of the United States, on the East Coast (105)

Detroit (dih TROIT) city and port in southeastern Michigan; 42°N, 83°W (123)

District of Columbia district in the eastern United States where the nation's capital is located; 39°N, 77°W (98)

East Germany nation in central Europe: the German Democratic Republic (254)

Ecuador (EK wuh DOR) nation in northwestern South America (38, 164)

Egypt (EE jipt) nation in northeastern Africa, on the Mediterranean (199–201)

Elbrus (EL broos), **Mount** highest mountain in Europe; 43°N, 42°E (238)

El Salvador nation in Central America (92)

England country on an island west of Europe, part of Great Britain (38)

Ethiopia (EE thee OH pee uh) nation in eastern Africa (210)

Europe (YOOR up) continent in the Eastern Hemisphere, west of Asia (21, 232–273)

Everest, Mount highest mountain on Earth, in Asia; 28°N, 87°E (278–279)

Finland nation in northern Europe (265)

Florida Southern state of the United States, on the East Coast (51, 110)

France nation in western Europe (252)

Georgia Southern state of the United States, on the East Coast (110, 116)

Germany See EAST GERMANY; WEST GERMANY

Ghana nation in western Africa (207, 215)

Gobi (GOH bee) **Desert** desert in east central Asia (277)

Grand Canyon gorge in northwestern Arizona; 36°N, 112°–114°W (127)

Great Britain (BRIT n) island nation west of Europe, including England, Scotland, and Wales; see UNITED KINGDOM (255)

Great Indian Desert desert in northwestern India and eastern Pakistan (305)

Great Lakes five large lakes (Superior, Michigan, Huron, Erie, and Ontario) between the United States and Canada (77)

Great Plains plateau region of North America east of the Rockies (50, 75, 120)

Great Salt Lake large salty lake in northern Utah; 41°N, 113°W (77)

Greece nation in southern Europe (238)

Guatemala (GWAH tuh MAH luh) nation in Central America south of Mexico (92)

Hawaii (huh WAH ee) Pacific state of the United States, on Pacific islands (96)

Himalaya (HIM uh LAY uh) **Mountains,** or **Himalayas** highest mountain system of Earth, in south central Asia (148, 296)

Honduras (hon DOO rus) nation in Central America (92)

Hudson Bay large body of water in northern Canada (86)

Idaho (EYE duh hoh) Mountain state of the western United States (126)

Illinois (IL uh NOI) Midwestern state of the United States, on Lake Michigan (119)

India nation in southern Asia (293–309)

Indiana Midwestern state of the United States, on Lake Michigan (119)

Indian Ocean ocean between Africa and Australia (199, 277)

Indochina peninsula in southeastern Asia (277)

Indonesia nation on islands south of eastern Asia (281–282, 290–294)

Iowa (EYE uh wuh) Midwestern state of the United States (119)

Iran nation in southwestern Asia (282)

Israel (IZ ree ul) nation in southwestern Asia, on the Mediterranean (284, 290)

Italy nation in southern Europe (252)

Japan (juh PAN) nation east of Asia, on islands in the Pacific Ocean (290, 292)

Jordan nation in southwestern Asia (284)

Kalahari (KAH luh HAH ree) **Desert** desert in southern Africa (196)

Kansas (KAN zus) Midwestern state of the United States (50, 119)

Kentucky Southern state of the east central United States (109)

Kenya nation in eastern Africa (196)

Kilimanjaro, Mount highest mountain in Africa; 3°S, 37°E (197)

La Paz (lah PAHZ) second capital of Bolivia; 17°S, 68°W (170)

Lapland region in northwestern Europe, north of the Arctic Circle (265–271)

Leningrad city in the northwestern part of the Soviet Union, a port on the Baltic Sea; 60°N, 30°E (260–262)

London capital of England and of the United Kingdom; 52°N, 0° longitude (39)

Louisiana (loo EE zee AN uh) Southern state of the United States, on the Gulf of Mexico (109, 110)

Maine New England state of the United States, on the East Coast (99)

Malay (MAY lay) **Peninsula** peninsula in southeastern Asia (277)

Mali nation in western Africa (215)

Maryland Middle Atlantic state of the United States, on the East Coast (104)

Massachusetts (MAS uh CHOO sits) New England state of the United States (99)

McKinley, Mount highest mountain in North America, in Alaska; 63°N, 151°W (75)

Mediterranean (MED uh tuh RAY nee un) **Sea** sea between Europe and Africa (194, 236)

Mexico nation in southern North America, south of the United States (24)

Mexico City capital of Mexico; 19°N, 99°W (44)

Mexico, Gulf of part of the Atlantic Ocean east of Mexico (74)

Michigan (MISH ih gun) Midwestern state of the United States (119)

Minnesota (MIN uh SOH tuh) Midwestern state of the United States (76)

Mississippi (MIS ih SIP ee) Southern state of the United States (112, 116)

Mississippi River longest river in the United States, flowing from northern Minnesota to the Gulf of Mexico (76, 112)

Missouri (mih ZOOR ee *or* mih ZOOR uh) Midwestern state of the United States (119)

Missouri River second-longest river in the United States, flowing from Montana into the Mississippi River (76)

Montana Mountain state of the northwestern United States (76, 127)

Moscow (MOS kou) capital of the Soviet Union; 56°N, 38°E (259)

Nebraska (nuh BRAS kuh) Midwestern state of the United States (119)

Nepal (nuh PAHL) nation in Asia between India and China (278)

Nevada (nuh VAD uh *or* nuh VAH duh) Mountain state of the United States (126)

New England six northeastern states of the United States (99)

New Hampshire New England state of the United States, on the East Coast (99)

New Jersey Middle Atlantic state of the United States, on the East Coast (105)

New Mexico Mountain state of the southwestern United States (126)

New Orleans (OR lee unz, OR lins, *or* or LEENZ) port city in southeastern Louisiana; 30°N, 90°W (38, 116)

New York Middle Atlantic state of the United States, on the East Coast (105)

New York City port city in southeastern New York state; 41°N, 74°W (105–107)

Nicaragua (NIK uh RAH gwah) nation in Central America (92)

Nigeria (ny JIR ee uh) nation in western Africa (205, 210)

Nile (NYL) **River** longest river of Earth, in eastern Africa, flowing from the equator to the Mediterranean Sea (193, 204)

North America continent of the Western Hemisphere, bounded by the Atlantic, Pacific, and Arctic oceans (21, 70–143)

North Carolina Southern state of the United States, on the East Coast (109)

North Dakota (duh KOH tuh) Midwestern state of the northern United States (119)

North Korea (kuh REE uh) nation in eastern Asia (277)

North Sea part of the Atlantic Ocean east of Great Britain (235, 243)

Norway nation in northern Europe (235)

Ohio (oh HY oh) Midwestern state of the United States, on Lake Erie (119)

Ohio River river in the eastern United States, flowing into the Mississippi (123)

Oklahoma (OH kluh HOH muh) Southern state in the central United States (81)

Ontario province in eastern Canada (86)

Oregon (OR uh gun) Pacific state of the northwestern United States (131)

Ottawa (OT uh wuh) capital of Canada; 45°N, 76°W (86)

Pacific Ocean ocean separating North and South America from Asia and Australia (21)

Pakistan nation in southern Asia (293)

Panama southernmost nation in Central America (72, 92)

Paraguay (PAR uh GWY) nation in central South America (164)

Paris capital of France; 49°N, 2°E (254)

Pennsylvania (PEN sul VAYN yuh) Middle Atlantic state of the United States (104)

Persian (PUR zhun) **Gulf** body of water between Arabia and Iran (277)

Peru (puh ROO) nation in western South America (156, 164)

Philadelphia (FIL uh DEL fee uh) port city in Pennsylvania; 40°N, 75°W (105–108)

Portugal (POR chuh gul) nation in southwestern Europe (21, 190, 235)

Puerto Rico (PWEHR toh REE koh) commonwealth on islands south of Florida, part of the United States (92, 98)

Quebec 1 province in eastern Canada (86, 89) **2** city in southeastern Canada

Quito (KEE toh) capital of Ecuador; 0° latitude, 79°W (38)

Red Sea sea between Arabia and Africa (196, 277)

Rhode (ROHD) **Island** New England state of the United States (99)

Rio de Janeiro (REE oh dih juh NAR oh) port city in Brazil; 23°S, 43°W (165)

Rio Grande (REE oh GRAND) river in the southwestern United States, dividing the United States from Mexico (27)

Rocky Mountains, or **Rockies** major mountain system of western North America, stretching from Alaska to New Mexico (47)

Rome capital of Italy; 42°N, 13°E (254)

Sahara (suh HAR uh) largest desert on Earth, in northern Africa (62, 193, 204)

Saudi Arabia nation in southwestern Asia on the Arabian Peninsula (281–283, 290)

Sierra Madres (see EHR uh MAH drays) major mountain system of Mexico (90)

Sierra (see EHR uh) **Nevada** mountain range in eastern California (75)

Siberia (sy BIR ee uh) region of the Soviet Union, in Asia (259)

South Africa southernmost nation in Africa (24, 210)

South America a continent of the Western Hemisphere (21, 144–187)

South Carolina Southern state of the United States, on the East Coast (109)

South Dakota (duh KOH tuh) Midwestern state of the United States (119)

South Korea nation of eastern Asia (277)

Soviet Union largest nation on Earth, in eastern Europe and northern Asia (258)

Spain nation in southwest Europe (235)

Sucre (SOO kray) legal capital of Bolivia; 19°S, 65°W (170)

Sudan (soo DAN) nation in northeastern Africa south of Egypt (210)

Sweden nation in northern Europe (265)

Tennessee (TEN uh SEE) Southern state of the east central United States (109)

Texas Southern state of the central United States, on the Gulf of Mexico (27)

Timbuktu town in Mali; 17°N, 3°W (202)

Titicaca, Lake lake between Peru and Bolivia; 16°S, 69°W (166, 170)

Tokyo capital of Japan; 36°N, 140°E (292)

Turkey nation in western Asia and southeastern Europe (282, 290)

United Kingdom of Great Britain and Northern Ireland nation on islands west of Europe (255)

United States nation in North America, bounded by the Atlantic, Pacific, and Arctic oceans (21)

Ural Mountains mountain system that divides Europe and Asia (235)

Uruguay (YUR uh GWY) nation in southeastern South America (164)

Utah (YOO taw *or* YOO tah) Mountain state of the western United States (126)

Venezuela (VEN uh ZWAY luh) nation in northern South America (156, 164)

Vermont (vur MONT) New England state of the United States (51)

Victoria, Lake lake in eastern Africa, source of the Nile River (193)

Vietnam (vee ET NAHM) nation of southeastern Asia (252, 282)

Virginia Southern state of the United States, on the East Coast (21, 109)

Vladivostok (VLAD uh vos TOK) city in the Soviet Union, a port on the Pacific; 43°N, 132°E (260–263)

Washington Pacific state of the northwestern United States (135)

Washington, DC capital of the United States; 39°N, 77°W (34)

West Germany nation in central Europe: the German Federal Republic (253–254)

West Virginia Middle Atlantic state of the United States (105)

Whitney, Mount mountain in eastern California; 37°N, 118°W (75)

Wisconsin Midwestern state of the United States, on the Great Lakes (119)

Wyoming (wy OH ming) Mountain state of the northwestern United States (126)

Yucatán (YOO kuh TAN) **Peninsula** southeastern peninsula of Mexico (90)

Zaire (zah IR) nation in Africa (210)

GLOSSARY

A.D. *anno Domini* (AN oh DOM un NY), "in the year of the Lord," used with dates after the birth of Jesus Christ (284)

adapt to change when conditions around you change (179)

ally (AL EYE) a person or nation that works with you, not against you (254)

alpaca a sheeplike animal of South America with long, soft wool (156)

altiplano (AHL tee PLAH noh) the Spanish word for a plateau (149)

ancestor a member of one's family who lived long ago (160)

Antarctic (ant AHRK tik) the climate area closest to the South Pole (55)

Antarctic Circle the line of latitude that is about 66° south of the equator (55)

Arctic (AHRK tik) the climate area closest to the North Pole (55)

Arctic Circle the line of latitude that is about 66° north of the equator (55)

artifact (AHR tuh FAKT) any object that people make (65)

assembly a group of people who meet to make laws (217)

atmosphere (AT muh SFIR) the air that surrounds Earth (51)

axis (AK sis) an imaginary line through the center of Earth, from pole to pole, around which Earth turns (18)

baobab (BAY oh bab) an African tree with branches that look like roots. (219)

bay a part of the ocean that is partly surrounded by land (99)

B.C. "before Christ," used with dates before the birth of Jesus Christ (284)

barge a long, flat boat (112)

barren unable to support growing things (193)

behavior what people do (65)

belief what people think is true or right (65)

boundary a line that divides one place from another (26)

breadbasket a region where a lot of grain is grown (121)

cacao (kuh KAY oh) a kind of tree that produces seeds used to make chocolate and cocoa (154)

calorie a unit of heat. It is used to measure the energy food gives you. (291)

campesino (KAM puh SEE noh) Spanish word meaning "small farmer" (178)

canal a waterway that people build across land. A ship canal connects one body of water with another. An irrigation canal brings water to dry land. (74, 298, 307)

canyon a deep, narrow valley with steep sides (127)

capital a city where the government of a state or nation meets (97)

capitol a building where a group of representatives meets to make laws (97)

cardinal directions the four most important directions: north, south, east, and west (32)

centimeter (SEN tuh MEE tur) a unit of measurement equal to ¹⁄₁₀₀ of a meter or ²⁄₅ of an inch (31)

civics the study of the rules and rights of people in a nation (182)

civil war a war between different groups in the same nation (213)

climate the average weather a place has over a long period of time (51)

coast land next to an ocean (74)

coastline a natural boundary next to an ocean (169)

colony an area of land ruled by a foreign country (97)

commercial farming farming in which crops are grown to be sold (207)

commonwealth a place that is governed by its people (98)

Communist being a nation where the government owns and runs all the businesses (254)

compass a map drawing of arrows that point north, south, east, and west (32)

competition rivalry between businesses that want to get the same customers (299)

342

compound a group of houses built close together (223)

Congress the legislature of the United States (97)

conquer to defeat in battle (158)

conquistador (kohn kees tah DOR) a Spanish conqueror (158)

conservation (KON sur VAY shun) the wise use of natural resources such as water, forests, soil, and fuels (84)

conserve to use resources wisely (84)

continent (KON tuh nunt) one of the seven large masses of land on Earth (21)

courtyard in a house or group of houses, a roofless area with walls around it (223)

credit the ability to buy goods without money by promising to pay later (298)

criollos (kree OHL yohs) Spanish settlers who were born in South America, not in Spain (177)

culture a people's way of living, including their behavior, beliefs, language, and artifacts (65)

culture group a group of people who have a common language, beliefs, and way of living (212)

customary (KUSS tuh MER ee) **system** the system of measurement that measures in inches, feet, yards, and miles (31)

dairy a farm where milk and cream are produced. Milk and other foods made from it are called dairy products. (80)

dam a wall that blocks river water (128)

degree (symbol: °) one of the 360 parts (360°) into which a circle is divided (37)

delta an area of rich soil at the mouth of a river (112)

deposit a mass of a mineral found in the ground (241)

descendant someone's child, grandchild, great-grandchild, or the like (160)

desert a very dry place where few plants can grow (62)

developed having more factories and businesses than farms (243)

dialect a different form of a language spoken in a special way (287)

distance the space between one place and another (30)

drought (DROWT) a long period of time with little or no rain (222)

dry season a period when the weather in the savanna is hot and dry (194)

earthquake a violent shaking and trembling of the ground (137)

elevation (EL uh VAY shun) the height of land above sea level (41)

empire a group of lands or nations under one government (158)

equator (ih KWAY tur) an imaginary line around the middle of the Earth (23)

export (EK sport) a product that one country sells to another (156)

extended family a family made up of grandparents, parents, and children, all living together (301)

famine (FAM in) a serious shortage of food that lasts a long time (222)

federal district a special area where the capital of a nation is located (98)

feeder canal a small canal connected to a larger irrigation canal (307)

fertile soil soil which contains the minerals that plants need (58)

fertilizer minerals added to the soil to help crops grow (205)

finished goods products that have been manufactured or made ready for use (208)

fjord (FYORD) a long, narrow inlet with high cliffs on either side (266)

foothills hills near the bottom of a mountain (75)

free trade trade between nations in which there are no taxes on imports (249)

geyser (GY zur) a hot spring that shoots water and steam into the air (127)

globe a round model of Earth (21)

governor the chief leader of a state (97)

grid a pattern of squares on a map (35)

gulf part of an ocean with land curving part way around it (74)

hacienda (HAH see EN duh) the Spanish word for a ranch or plantation (174)

harbor a protected place on a coast where ships can anchor (105)

hardwood a tree that loses its leaves, such as an oak or maple (102)

harvest to gather in crops (222)

headland a high point of land that juts out into a body of water (266)

hemisphere (HEM uh SFIR) one of four half circles that Earth can be divided into: the Northern, Southern, Eastern, or Western Hemisphere (23)

herding keeping animals together while they find grass to eat (202)

high-altitude high above sea level (170)

high-latitude climate a cool or cold climate found near the North Pole or the South Pole (54, 55)

hill an area of high land lower than a mountain (47)

illiterate not knowing how to read or to write (225)

import (IM port) a product that one country buys from another (156)

income money earned or received (289)

Indo-European of the language family to which most languages spoken in Europe belong (247)

industrial (in DUSS tree ul) manufacturing many goods (252)

industry (IN duss tree) a branch of manufacturing and trade (252)

inland beyond the coast, toward the middle of a country (190, 192)

intermediate (IN tur MEE dee it) **directions** northeast, northwest, southeast, and southwest (34)

irrigate to bring water to (dry land), as by using pipes or canals (128, 298)

Islam a religion founded in the 7th century by the prophet Muhammad (199)

island a piece of land completely surrounded by water (235)

isthmus (ISS muss) a narrow strip of land that connects two larger masses of land (74)

jungle in the tropics, a very thick growth of plants and trees (150)

key a list explaining the symbols and colors used on a map (26)

kilometer (KIL uh MEE tur *or* kih LOM uh tur) a unit of measurement equal to 1,000 meters or ⅗ of a mile (31)

lake a large body of water surrounded by land (77)

landforms the shapes of land on Earth. Mountains, hills, plains, and plateaus are landforms. (46)

landlocked surrounded by land (215)

landlord a person who owns land or a house and rents it to others (302)

language the words people use to speak or write (65)

legislature (LEJ iss LAY chur) a group of representatives that meets to make laws for a state or nation (97, 217)

lichen (LY ken) a crustlike plant that grows on rocks and tree trunks (266)

lines of latitude (LAT uh TOOD) the lines on a map or globe that run east and west. They measure distance north and south of the equator. (37)

lines of longitude (LON juh TOOD) the lines on a map or globe that run north and south. They measure distance east and west of the prime meridian. (37)

literate able to read and write (248)

living resources plants and animals (57)

llama a wooly animal of South America that looks like a camel without a hump (156)

llanos (YAH nohs) an area of treeless plains in northern South America (152)

lock a part of a ship canal with gates on either side (74)

mainland the chief land mass of a continent (235)

map a flat drawing of Earth or a part of Earth (25)

market a place where goods can be sold; also, the people who buy the goods (244)

memorize to learn by saying things over and over until you know them (182)

meridian (muh RID ee un) a line of longitude (39)

meter a unit of measurement equal to about 3 feet, 3 inches (41)

metric (MEH trik) **system** the system of measurement that measures in centimeters, meters, and kilometers (31)

middle class a class of people made up of those who are neither rich nor poor (165)

mid-latitude climate a climate area in which the weather changes from season to season (51, 54)

midnight sun the sun seen at midnight during the summer in the Arctic and Antarctic (266)

ministate a tiny nation (250)

mission a religious settlement (132)

monsoon a wind that changes direction when the season changes (297)

monsoon climate a climate with three seasons: the cool season, the hot season, and the rainy season (278)

monsoon season the rainy season in India and southern Asia (297)

moon a smaller world that moves around a planet (16)

moss a small green plant that covers the tundra like a thick, soft rug (266)

mountain the highest form of land on Earth (46)

mountain range a group or row of mountains (46)

mouth the place where a river flows into the ocean (194)

Muslim (MUZ lum) someone who believes in the religion called Islam (199)

nation a land where people live under one government (26)

natural boundary a natural dividing line between places, such as a river (27)

natural gas a mixture of gases found in the ground, used as a fuel (105)

natural resource anything found on Earth that people can use (57)

nonliving resources land, water, and minerals (58)

nomad (NOH mad) a person who travels from place to place looking for grass and water for animals to eat (202)

North Pole the place that is farthest north on Earth (18)

oasis a place in a desert where there is water (62, 193)

Occident (OK suh dunt) **1** the west **2** western Europe and the Americas (286)

ocean one of the four very large bodies of salt water on Earth (21)

official language the language used by a nation's government and schools (228)

OPEC Organization of Petroleum Exporting Countries (281)

orbit (OR bit) a special flight path around a star or planet (17)

Orient (OR ee unt) **1** the east **2** Asia (286)

pack animal an animal that carries a load on its back (180)

paddy a rice field (303)

pampas a region of grassy plains in Argentina and Uruguay (152)

parallel (PAR uh LEL) a line of latitude (38, 39)

peninsula (puh NIN suh luh) a piece of land almost surrounded by water (90, 235)

petroleum (puh TROH lee um) a thick, dark liquid found in the ground and used as a fuel; oil (81)

pharaoh (FER oh) a king of ancient Egypt (199)

physical map a map that shows the height or shape of land (44)

physical-political map a map that shows both physical features and political boundaries (44)

plain a big, open area of flat land (47)

planet a world that moves around a star (15)

plantation a large farm where crops are grown (174)

plateau (pla TOH) an area of high, flat land (47)

political boundary a line that divides one city, state, or nation from another (27)

political map a map that shows political boundaries (44)

pollution (puh LOO shun) dirt or wastes in the air or water (85)

population (POP yuh LAY shun) the number of people who live in a place (60)

population map a map that shows how many people live in a place (60)

port a town on the water where ships can load and unload goods (107)

poultry (POHL tree) birds such as chickens and turkeys (80)

prairie a large area of flat or rolling grassland with few trees (76)

preserve to keep (something) by not letting it be destroyed (85)

prime meridian (PRYM muh RID ee un) the imaginary line at which longitude starts. It passes through Greenwich, England. (39)

profit the extra money left from a sale after expenses are paid (226)

progress (PROG ress) an improvement of conditions (167)

province a part of Canada that is like a state in the United States (86)

pyramid (PIR uh mid) a stone structure with sides shaped like triangles, used as a tomb or place of worship (93, 199)

rainy season a period when the weather in the savanna is hot and wet (194)

ranch a large farm where animals are raised (174)

rapids rocky places in a river that make the water flow very fast (190)

raw material a product found in nature that can be improved by manufacturing (208)

refine to make a resource pure by separating it into parts (115)

region an area with the same kind of landforms or climate (66)

resource anything people can use (57)

revolve (rih VOLV) to move in a special path around something else (17)

rival a person who tries to get the same thing as someone else (248)

rotate (ROH tayt) to turn around an axis (18)

savanna (suh VAN uh) a tropical grassland (54)

scale a diagram that shows what a map distance equals in real distance (29)

sea a body of water smaller than an ocean. It can be a part of an ocean. (235)

sea level the surface of the ocean (41)

seaport a town on the coast where ships can load and unload (169)

season a part of the year in which the weather in a place is much the same (18)

seaway a water route to and from the ocean (88)

seedbed small piece of land with good soil where seeds can start to grow (303)

sierra (see EHR uh) a range of steep, jagged mountains (75)

silt rich soil carried by a river (193)

softwood a tree with cones and needles, such as a pine, fir, or spruce (102)

solar system (SOH lur SIS tum) the sun and its family of planets and moons (16)

sorghum (SOR gum) a grain plant that is used to make syrup (219)

source the place where a river starts (193)

South Pole the place that is farthest south on Earth (18)

spice a part of a plant used to flavor and season food (280)

star a great mass of burning gas that gives off light and heat (15)

state one of the 50 parts that make up the United States. Each state has its own land, people, and government. (97)

steppes (STEPS) grassy plains (259)

subarctic (sub AHRK tik) just south of the Arctic Circle (55)

subcontinent part of a continent that seems separate from the rest. The mountains that cut India off from the rest of Asia make India a subcontinent. (277)

subsistence farming farming in which people grow just enough food for their own needs (202)

sun the star around which the planet Earth moves (15)

swamp low, wet land largely covered with water (113)

symbol a mark or picture on a map that stands for a real thing (26)

taiga (TY guh) a subarctic climate area where there are great forests (259)

tariff (TAIR if) a tax on imports (249)

territory a part of a country that has not yet become a state or a province (86, 98)

tilted (TILL tid) at a slant (18)

time zone one of 24 areas on Earth within which all places have the same clock time. Each time zone is 15 degrees wide in degrees of longitude. (260)

tropical climate a warm or hot climate found near the equator (51)

tropical rain forest a lowland area near the equator where heavy rains make thick forests grow (54)

tundra (TUN druh) the climate area just south of the Arctic, where soil beneath the surface stays frozen all year (55)

twilight the time after sunset and before dark; "half light" (266)

unemployed without a job (226, 227)

unity a feeling of oneness; the sense of belonging to a larger whole (212)

uplands an area of hills and plateaus (237)

valley the low, flat land between hills or mountains (47)

volcano an opening in the earth through which hot melted rock, ashes, smoke, and gases can shoot (134)

warrior (WOR ee ur) a fighter (217)

water buffalo a large, strong animal with wide horns (303)

wilderness wild land (110)

INDEX

CREDITS

12–13, 43, 48–49, 70–71, 73, 88, 147, 163, 191, 211, 232–233, 251, 274–275, 312–322:
Maps by R. R. Donnelley Cartographic Services. **22, 23, 25, 26, 30, 33, 35, 37, 39, 42, 52–
53, 54, 60–61, 78, 82, 83, 87, 101, 104, 109, 111, 121, 126, 132, 155, 164, 171, 175, 192,
201, 206, 235, 239, 242, 245, 248, 259, 265, 285, 291, 306:** Maps by David Lindroth, Inc.
323–337: Charts by Boultinghouse & Boultinghouse, Inc. Other charts by Function Thru
Form, Inc. **20:** Russ Kinne/Photo Researchers, Inc. **21:** Robert Capece/McGraw-Hill. **24:**
Loren McIntyre/Woodfin Camp. **29:** The Bettmann Archive. **38:** (L) Art Resource; (R) Paolo
Koch/Photo Researchers, Inc. **46:** M. Serralier/Photo Researchers, Inc. **47:** (B) Peter Arnold,
Inc.; (T) Peter Menzel/Stock, Boston. **50:** Michael Collier/Stock, Boston. **54:** (L) Carl
Purcell. **54–55:** (L) Victor Englebert; (R) Stephen J. Kraseman/Photo Researchers, Inc. **58:**
(B) Dan McCoy/Rainbow; (T) Jacques Jangoux/Peter Arnold, Inc. **61:** Bernard Wolff/Photo
Researchers, Inc. **62:** Dan McCoy/Rainbow. **64:** Eve Arnold/Magnum Photos. **65:** Kal
Muller/Woodfin Camp. **66:** Marc & Evelyne Bernheim/Woodfin Camp. **72:** Jim Goodwin/
Photo Researchers, Inc. **74:** Baron Wolman/Woodfin Camp. **76:** Sigmund Samuel/
Canadiana Gallery. **77:** Paolo Koch/Photo Researchers, Inc. **81:** Porterfield-Chickering/
Photo Researchers, Inc. **84:** Kent & Donna Dannen/Photo Researchers, Inc. **89:** Erich

Hartmann/Magnum Photos. **90:** Russ Kinne/Photo Researchers, Inc. **91:** Porterfield-Chickering/Photo Researchers, Inc. **92:** Marc Bernheim/Woodfin Camp. **93:** George Holton/Photo Researchers, Inc. **96:** Paolo Koch/Photo Researchers, Inc. **102:** William Strode/Woodfin Camp. **105:** Hank Morgan/Rainbow. **107:** Leif Skoogfors/Woodfin Camp. **113:** Gary Cralle/The Image Bank. **114:** Farrell Grehan/Photo Researchers, Inc. **115:** H. Gloaguen/Photo Resarchers, Inc. **119:** The Granger Collection. **122:** Jim Anderson/Woodfin Camp. **123:** David Barnes/Photo Researchers, Inc. **127:** William Carter/Photo Researchers, Inc. **128:** William Hubbell/Woodfin Camp. **133:** George Holton/Photo Researchers, Inc. **135:** Roger Werth/Longview Daily News/Woodfin Camp. **136:** Ira Block/Woodfin Camp. **137:** Baron Wolman/Woodfin Camp. **144–145:** Hans Silvester/Photo Researchers, Inc. **146:** Peter Menzel/Stock, Boston. **148:** Hotel Portillo. **149:** Jacques Jangoux/Peter Arnold, Inc. **150:** Loren McIntyre/Woodfin Camp. **152:** (M) Loren McIntyre/Woodfin Camp; (T) Rene Buri/Magnum Photos. **154:** Reflejo/Woodfin Camp. **156:** George Holton/Photo Researchers, Inc. **159:** (BL) Sergio Larrain/Magnum Photos; (BR) Malcolm Kirk/Peter Arnold, Inc.; (ML) Jacques Jangoux/Peter Arnold, Inc.; (MR) Victor Englebert; (TL) Jacques Jangoux/Peter Arnold, Inc.; (TR) Jacques Jangoux/Peter Arnold, Inc. **160:** (L) American Museum of Natural History; (R) Jacques Jangoux/Peter Arnold, Inc. **165:** (L) Barbara Kirk/Peter Arnold, Inc.; (R) Carl Frank/Photo Researchers, Inc. **166:** (B) Peter Frey/The Image Bank; (TR) Shostal Associates. **169:** Christina Dittmann/Rainbow. **170:** Georg Gerster/Photo Researchers, Inc. **172:** DPI. **173:** George Holton/Photo Researchers, Inc. **174:** American Museum of Natural History. **176:** George Holton/Photo Researchers, Inc. **177:** (L) Jerry Cooke/Photo Researchers, Inc.; (R) Yoram Lehman/Peter Arnold, Inc. **179:** Jacques Jangoux/Peter Arnold, Inc. **180:** (BL) Victor Englebert; (BR) Bernard P. Wolff/Photo Researchers, Inc.; (T) Ingebord Lippmann/Magnum Photos. **181:** Jacques Jangoux/Peter Arnold, Inc. **182:** (L) Bernard P. Wolff/Photo Researchers, Inc.; (R) Carl Frank/Photo Researchers, Inc. **183:** Jerry Frank/DPI. **184:** Victor Englebert. **188–189:** Ben Hawley/McGraw-Hill. **190:** Marc & Evelyne Bernheim/Woodfin Camp. **192:** (L) Carl Purcell. **192–193:** Thomas Nebbia/Woodfin Camp. **194:** Russ Kinne/Photo Researchers, Inc. **196:** Phil Carol/Monkmeyer Press Photos. **198:** Kal Muller/Woodfin Camp. **199:** Klaus D. Francke/Peter Arnold, Inc. **200:** (L) William Mares/Woodfin Camp; (R) John G. Ross/Photo Researchers, Inc. **202:** Marc & Evelyne Bernheim/Woodfin Camp. **203:** (L) Bruce Brander/Photo Researchers, Inc.; (R) Carl Purcell. **205:** Bruno Barbey/Magnum Photos. **207:** William Mares/Monkmeyer Press Photos. **208:** William H. Hodge/Peter Arnold, Inc. **212:** Dennis Falck. **215:** Ben Hawley/McGraw-Hill. **217:** (L) Ben Hawley/McGraw-Hill; (R) Florita Botts/Nancy Palmer Agency. **218:** Ben Hawley/McGraw-Hill. **220:** Dennis Falck. **221:** (B) Ben Hawley/McGraw-Hill; (TR) Valerie Christian; (TL) Ben Hawley/McGraw-Hill. **222:** Georg Gerster/Photo Researchers, Inc. **223:** Ben Hawley/McGraw-Hill. **224:** Ben Hawley/McGraw-Hill. **225:** Ben Hawley/McGraw-Hill. **226:** I. Lippman/Peter Arnold, Inc. **227:** Ben Hawley/McGraw-Hill. **234:** FPG. **236:** G. Ronn/C. Ostman. **237:** Georg Gerster/Photo Researchers, Inc. **241:** Klaus D. Francke/Nancy Palmer Agency. **243:** (T) Klaus D. Francke/Nancy Palmer Agency; (B) Jean Mougin/Vivan/Woodfin Camp. **246:** Paul Fusco/Magnum Photos. **247:** (BM) Harvey Lloyd/The Stock Market; (BR) Camilla Smith/Rainbow; (TR) Francis Lapping, DPI. **254:** (T) Susan McCartney/Photo Researchers, Inc.; (B) A. L. Goldman/Photo Researchers, Inc. **255:** (L) Jan Lukas/Photo Researchers, Inc.; (R) Monkmeyer Press Photo. **258:** George Holton/Photo Researchers, Inc. **260:** Sovfoto. **263:** (L) Klaus Francke/Peter Arnold, Inc.; (R) Howard Sochureck/Woodfin Camp. **264:** Sovfoto. **266:** M. Desjardins/Photo Researchers, Inc. **267:** Tom Pix/Peter Arnold, Inc. **268:** (L) George Holton/Photo Researchers, Inc.; (R) Marvin F. Newman/Woodfin Camp. **269:** Sovfoto. **276:** Craig Aurness/Woodfin Camp. **277:** (L) Klaus D. Francke/Peter Arnold, Inc.; (R) Warren Slater/Monkmeyer Press Photo. **279:** Bill O'Connor/Peter Arnold, Inc. **281:** Andrew Rakoczy/FPG. **283:** Anthony Howarth/Woodfin Camp. **284:** Jason Laure/Woodfin Camp. **286:** Susan Harris/Alpha Photos. **287:** Joel Norwood/Katherine Young Agency. **288:** Leslie Holzer/Katherine Young Agency. **292:** Jason Laure/Woodfin Camp. **293:** Bob Davis/Woodfin Camp. **296:** Roland & Sabina Michaud/Woodfin Camp. **297:** Paolo Koch/Photo Researchers, Inc. **298:** Jehangir Gazdar/Woodfin Camp. **299:** (B) Jacques Jangoux/Peter Arnold, Inc.; (T) Malcolm S. Kirk/Peter Arnold, Inc. **301:** William Carter/Photo Researchers, Inc. **302:** Marc & Evelyne Bernheim/Woodfin Camp. **303:** Victor Englebert. **305:** Marc & Evelyne Bernheim/Woodfin Camp. **307:** Jacques Jangoux/Peter Arnold, Inc.